Convergences:
Inventories of the Present

Edward W. Said, General Editor

Chopin
at the
Boundaries

Sex, History, and Musical Genre

ʃ

Jeffrey Kallberg

Harvard University Press

Cambridge, Massachusetts

London, England

1996

4/26/96   45.00

Library of Congress Cataloging-in-Publication Data
Kallberg, Jeffrey, 1954–
    Chopin at the boundaries : sex, history, and musical genre /
Jeffrey Kallberg.
        p.   cm.
    Includes bibliographical references (p.   ) and index.
    ISBN 0-674-12790-0 (alk. paper)
    1. Chopin, Frédéric, 1810–1849—Criticism and interpretation.
2. Music—19th century—History and criticism.   3. Music and
society.   I. Title.
    ML410.C54K16   1996
    786.2'092—dc20   95-42776

7692

To my mother, Elaine A. Patchett

Contents

Preface

Chopin unsettles us. At once exalted and shadowy, he cuts a curious figure in contemporary culture. Ethereal composer and enervated *enfant mâle* (or so the popular biographical image of him would have us believe), he parries attempts to reconcile the music with the man. A Pole who wrote most of his works among Frenchmen, his music exudes exoticism at the same time as it partakes of the European common-practice tradition. Champion of the miniature at a time when many around him gravitated toward ever grander musical colossi, he confounds our abilities to hear his contemporaries and him on equal footing. A male composer who wrote in "feminine" genres like the nocturne for domestic settings like the salon, he confuses our sense of the boundaries of gender. Central to our repertory, Chopin nevertheless remains a marginalized figure.

Now Chopin hardly qualifies as a composer in need of special pleading. But (to mention just one realm where we might observe the phenomenon) a glance toward the world of concert pianists lays bare the uncommon level of anxiety that he arouses. We might note first those great pianists who mostly avoid performing Chopin (Rudolf Serkin, Glenn Gould, and Alfred Brendel come immediately to mind). Is there any other composer of similar stature who is shunned by a group of pianists of such renown? We can hardly imagine a pianist attaining fame while sidestepping, say, Beethoven; certainly great Chopin interpreters like Artur Rubenstein, Dinu Lipatti, and Maurizio Pollini (who might seem somehow to balance culturally those who slight Chopin) have felt it necessary to explore other pianistic terrain as well. What is it specifically about Chopin that allows him to be shunned by concert artists of the highest order?

Some explanation may come from two pianists who, though they perform Chopin, were or are troubled by the experience. Speaking recently to the *New York Times,* Murray Perahia and Hélène Grimaud expressed different kinds of apprehension over being too closely associated with Chopin in the minds of the listening public. Perahia mentioned his misgivings while describing how a forced hiatus from the concert stage resulting from an injured thumb had occasioned a rethinking of his art (*New York Times,* 3 April 1994, Arts and Leisure section, p. 25). The lyrical style that he had cultivated early in his career seemed best displayed in smaller-scale works (among his most notable recordings from that time were refined performances of Chopin, Mozart, and Schumann). But at some point before his injury, Perahia grew disenchanted with being so particularly affiliated with the miniature, and he set out to broaden his repertory and style into more grandiose, overtly virtuosic realms. He remarked: "One instinctively doesn't want to be thought of as a miniaturist. I considered it pejorative. Now I don't. But at that time I felt dissatisfied. I was looking for something bigger. I was looking to gain a more heroic style, more epic. I made the mistake of thinking it could be gained through loudness. I had to learn my lesson, that I wasn't being true to myself."

How did he find his "true" self again in the world of miniatures? Among other explanations, the pianist cited his newly found absorption in the theories of Heinrich Schenker, an Austrian contemporary of Freud. Schenker's theories of deep structure particularly affected Perahia's thinking about Chopin: "Schenker is a framework that I keep in the back of my mind, although with Chopin it's more in the foreground [Perahia's specific reference is to a forthcoming performance of the Ballade in F Minor]. I feel I become more free, not less, when I'm aware of these structures because I get away from the pedantry of measure-by-measure and into something much bigger." In other words, Perahia's *rapprochement* with the musical miniature, as Michael Kimmelman pointed out in the conclusion to his article, came by reconceiving, through Schenker, the nature of this repertory. If the miniature now comes encumbered with the large-scale structure whose heft he originally sought in a repertory that was "something bigger," then the "miniaturist" too can display a depth of attainment akin to those pianists who specialize in more "heroic" pieces. Perahia diminished his anxiety about Chopin (and other miniaturists) through a transfusion of Schenkerian deep structure.

A few weeks later, Hélène Grimaud directly spelled out in the *Times* the gendered terms of her anxiety about Chopin (*New York Times,*

29 May 1994, Arts and Leisure section, pp. 22, 36). Grimaud (whose discographical focus on Rachmaninoff and Brahms the author of the interview, John Rockwell, termed "odd not only for a French pianist but also for a female one") mentioned that she had moved away from playing Chopin and Debussy, "feeling she was typecast there in her teens." She described her resistance to Chopin as part of a rebellion against performing in ways that might be "expected" of a female pianist: "At the conservatory I was always told that Chopin was my thing. Maybe I was not ready, physically, to play Brahms, but I haven't changed that much since." Instead of focusing on Chopin (and Debussy), Grimaud would rather "play like a man": "People always say to me now that I play like a man. I never felt feminine at all . . . I'm not gay, but I always thought I should have been a man."

By what "instinct" could Perahia rebel against being labeled a miniaturist? Why did formalist theory provide a salve to his conscience? Why should Grimaud's worries about being perceived as "feminine" devolve precisely onto Chopin? To understand the complexly unsettling status of Chopin in our culture, we cannot just examine present experience, for the anxieties that I have detailed have a long history when applied to Chopin. But if we situate him and his music historically within his native Polish and adopted French cultures, we can begin to fathom the powerful effects these historical constructions can and do have today. This book suggests some of the pathways that historical inquiries into Chopin might pursue.

The seven essays that I have gathered here hardly sprang to life under a single, unifying methodological umbrella. The matter is really the other way around: reflecting on and writing these essays resulted in the foundational convictions that I currently hold. In collecting these essays, then, I have made no attempt to disguise the evolution in my thinking on such matters as the role of close formal analysis in historical investigations of Chopin. But I can nevertheless point to some consistent principles in the motivation behind these various studies. Through an exploration of some of the historical contexts of Chopin's music and the social constructions of meaning that were applied to it, I wanted in each of the essays to reduce the sense of distortion that has governed attempts to understand the composer's works. And not conversely, I also tried to expose and partially recover aspects of Chopin's style perceived in his day to be marginal or foreign, but which today's listeners have transformed or repressed.

Historically oriented and socially grounded, the seven chapters of this book play continuously and variously on the tensions between past and present that figure into our understandings of Chopin and his music. The chapters fall naturally into three groups. The essays of the first part combat the misconception that Chopin's piano works were conceived and understood as primarily autonomous forms of music, free of any extra-musical significance. In Chapter 1 I examine how the Nocturne in G Minor, op. 15, no. 3, became freighted, through the conduit of genre, with ideological significance; in Chapter 2 I explore what it meant—culturally, historically, and musically— that commentators in the nineteenth century persistently couched their reactions to the piano nocturne in feminine imagery; and in the third chapter I investigate how sexual meanings figured into the understanding of Chopin through processes of linguistic deflection and deferral around images from the worlds of art, literature, and medicine. The second part of the book tackles the presentist assumptions that govern contemporary critical assumptions about Chopin's creative process and style. In these two essays I attempt to shed light on some of the social constructions that ought to enter into our understanding of the ways Chopin composed and the purposes he might have had in mind when he did. Chapter 4 focuses on a group of pieces Chopin wrote at the end of his creative life, and Chapter 5 on the Preludes, op. 28. Finally, the essays of the last part expose the ineluctably social nature of the musical work in the nineteenth century, in order to demonstrate that what determined its status as a "work" was not only the creative act by the composer but also its engagement through the institutions of publishing with a variety of publics. In Chapter 6 I examine in detail the complicated international negotiations required for Chopin to bring his music before the public eye, while in the final chapter I demonstrate how the musical variants that resulted from the editions published through these negotiations constitute a fundamental aspect of the work of art as conceived by both Chopin and his audiences.

Over the years, I have benefited from countless insightful suggestions from friends and colleagues. I want first warmly to thank Philip Gossett and Gary Tomlinson, who not only read and improved most of the chapters in this book, but in many ways inspired them through their own exemplary scholarship. Charles Rosen, reading an earlier draft of the book, enhanced the final version by offering me a number of critically and musically discerning suggestions. I am grateful to Edward W. Said for showing interest in my work, and for encouraging me to publish it in his laudable series. Without Jean-Jacques Eigeldinger's superb research on Chopin and his friendly willingness to share ideas, my own labors would have been immeasurably more complicated. To Bonnie J. Blackburn, Marcia Citron, Carol J. Clover, Krzysztof Grabowski, Douglas Johnson, Joseph Kerman, Robert L. Marshall, Wojciech Nowik, John Rink, Jim Samson, Ruth A. Solie, Susan T. Sommer, Leo Treitler, Alan Tyson, Robert Winter, and Deborah Wong, I offer my appreciation for their comments on individual chapters. And for their highly professional and caring efforts on behalf of this book, Lindsay Waters, Alison Kent, and Mary Ellen Geer of Harvard University Press have earned my unending praise.

No less important to me are those institutions who supported my work in various ways. For providing time free of all constraints but the scholarly, I am thankful for fellowships from the John Simon Guggenheim Memorial Foundation and the National Endowment for the Humanities. The University of Pennsylvania has generously furnished me with scholarly leaves and funded travel to collections abroad; most recently, through a grant from their Research Fund, they have helped defray costs associated with the publication of this book. And I want to offer special thanks to the staff of two of these collections who have particularly assisted—and, indeed, enabled—my work on Chopin for many years: the Towarzystwo imienia Fryderyka Chopin, Warsaw, and the Département de la Musique of the Bibliothèque Nationale, Paris.

Many friends have seen me through the stages of writing these essays (whether they knew it or not). I have happy memories of the support provided at various times by Gloria Apt, Lawrence F. Bernstein, Victoria Cooper, Joseph Farrell, Jacob Lateiner, Jennifer Marik, Eugene Narmour, Rip Rense, Ralph Rosen, Mike Rugg, Norman E. Smith, Margaret and Karol Sołtan, Gary Tomlinson (again), and Eugene K. Wolf. I find myself most grateful for what made this book truly possible: the daily love and care of Charlotta Thunander. And I offer special thanks to Erik Hans Kallberg, whose birth lent the latter stages of the production of this book an air of wonder and grace.

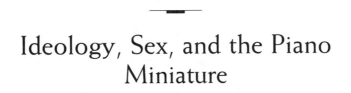

I

Ideology, Sex, and the Piano Miniature

‖ 1 ‖

The Rhetoric of Genre:
Chopin's Nocturne in G Minor

Every limit is a beginning as well as an ending.
George Eliot, *Middlemarch,* "Finale"

Idiosyncrasies abound in Chopin's Nocturne in G Minor, op. 15, no. 3. Robert Schumann, one of Chopin's most acute early listeners, responded aphoristically to it: "Florestan once rather paradoxically uttered: 'In the *Leonora* Overture of Beethoven there was more future than in his symphonies,' which would more correctly be applied to the most recent Chopin Notturno in G Minor."[1] "Future" is an enigmatic critical category, one that could reflect numerous aspects of the piece. But in making this vague distinction, Schumann must have reacted at least in part to the many differences between this Nocturne and other members of its genre.

Unorthodox gestures stand out on every page of the Nocturne. Many of the stylistic devices popularly thought to typify the genre do not appear in op. 15, no. 3. The melodies are bare-boned and static, strikingly different from the floridly ornamented tunes of earlier nocturnes. The accompaniment nowhere deploys the widely-spanned broken chords that we think of as a hallmark of the genre. The rhythmic stress falls persistently on the second beat of the measure, unlike the downbeat accents found in most nocturnes. The large-scale tonal plan moves by semitones, not by subdominant-related keys. Most strikingly, there is no return at the end to the opening theme.

Thus the Nocturne in G Minor seems almost to defy its type. If so, how can ideas of musical genre help us understand the piece? Genre and idiosyncrasy might seem to be antithetical: the one apparently emphasizes norms, the other singularity. And individuality of just the sort found in the Nocturne in G Minor has led some to dismiss genre as a conceptual category that is of little use in criticism. Nevertheless it was Chopin who called the piece a Nocturne. Unless the title was arbitrary or cynical, the concept of genre must have meant something to Chopin and his audience—and so must Chopin's gesture in labeling this piece.

Our challenge is to recover this meaning, to discover what Chopin hoped to communicate through genre in the Nocturne. By invoking "communication" rather than "classification," this statement already presumes a rather different understanding of the concept of genre than what we commonly encounter in musical studies.[2] Hence, before I turn to the work itself, I want first to explore some of the assumptions about genre that govern my interpretation of the Nocturne.

The Rhetoric of Genre

> But in reality genre is much less of a pigeonhole
> than a pigeon.
>
> —Alastair Fowler, *Kinds of Literature*[3]

While often construed as a concept inherent in musical compositions themselves, genre is better perceived as a social phenomenon shared by composers and listeners alike. The distinction is basic. The literature abounds with efforts to define particular genres according to the music itself. Usually, such studies purport to answer questions like "What is a sonata?" or "What is a motet?" by providing either a history of the use of the term, or a description of the apparent contents of the class. That is, they seek to define the genre according to those characteristics shared by all of its members, mistakenly assuming that shared characteristics inevitably form part of any definition.[4] The result often is a category so attenuated as to be virtually useless or one so broad as to embrace entire epochs.

But, as Wittgenstein and others have argued, shared characteristics are only partially relevant to definitions.[5] They provide factual information about a term; they classify it. But they do not explain its meaning. The meaning of a term instead is connected to the willingness of a particular community to use that word and not another; meaning sheds light on the characteristic uses of a particular term as opposed to others that are available. This is why definitions that consider only the term itself are of limited value: they fail to consider the community that employs the word. A proper definition, then, will investigate the responses to various uses of the word. Meaning, in short, must emerge from the context of the term.

Hence the need for studies of genre to look away from the immanent characteristics of the music: without a broader focus, the meanings of genres will continue to elude us.[6] Shared characteristics will doubtless still figure in most definitions, but they should more importantly treat the appropriate responses to the term, "appropriateness" being largely determined by the conventions associated with the genre.[7] Research into the effects of genre should involve the reconstruction of contexts and traditions, and the perceptions of composers and their audiences, both historical and modern.

This formulation properly locates genre as a communicative concept, one that actively informs the experience of a musical work. It is this experience that we want to recapture for Chopin's Nocturne in G Minor.

Genre exerts a persuasive force. It guides the responses of listeners—this is why I refer in my title to the "rhetoric" of genre.[8] The choice of genre by a composer and its identification by the listener establish the framework for the communication of meaning. The genre institutes what E. D. Hirsch has termed a "code of social behavior" and Hans Robert Jauss a "horizon of expectation" (a term derived from Husserl's phenomenology of perception), a frame that consequently affects the decisions made by the composer in writing the work and the listener in hearing the work.[9] A kind of "generic contract" develops between composer and listener: the composer agrees to use some of the conventions, patterns, and gestures of a genre, and the listener consents to interpret some aspects of the piece in a way conditioned by this genre.[10] The contract may be signaled to the listener in a number of ways: title, meter, tempo, and characteristic opening gestures are some of the common means.[11] The contract may include notions of what cannot appear in a genre as well; such constraints can tell us a great deal about what is permissible in a genre.[12]

Generic contracts, like their legal counterparts, may be broken; indeed, frustrated expectations often play a key role in the communicative process. Departures from perceived norms or expectations in genre have been a persistent stumbling block for many critics. The notion persists that genres represent fixed and prescriptive types, that their value is limited because no composer of any achievement would remain bound by inhibitory rules. Prescriptions and norms have been fundamental to generic theory for centuries, and still are today, but it does not follow that they must restrict composers. On the contrary, the rejection of the prescriptions of a genre by a composer can be seen as a major force in the promotion of change.

Thus Claudio Guillén has styled genres "an invitation to form," and suggested that genre as a category looks backward and forward at the same time.[13] The "form" embodies tradition and experience; it offers an ordered mental space in which to work. The "invitation" involves creating the form all over again, in the process reconstituting and altering it in some way. The way in which the invitation is accepted can reveal much about a composer's attitude toward the past, whether respectful and conservative or contrary and reformative. A composer can choose to write in a certain genre in order to challenge its attributes instead of to demonstrate an allegiance to them.

Contracts may be breached by listeners as well. Willfully or not, listeners sometimes read different implications into a generic title than those the composer intended. This commonly happens when a gap separates the listener from the time in which the genre was current. Explanations of the works of J. S. Bach in the early nineteenth century, for example, cloaked Bach's genres in modern garb. In 1813, a reviewer of the English Suite in D Minor urged his readers to ignore the antiquated title "Sarabande" and instead simply to think of the movement as an "Andante."[14] Associations with an old dance form were to be denied; instead readers were to perceive the "feeling" of the movement. Even more common is the misreading of a genre with a long life span: later listeners interpret earlier exemplars according to the current precepts. Musicology has taken the uncovering of such "mistaken" readings as one of its paradigmatic tasks (an example is the effort to recover the context of the symphony in the eighteenth century).[15] Less common, but potentially significant to the historian, is the contemporaneous misinterpretation of a genre. Such instances can shed fascinating light on a composer's success in communicating meaning through a given genre.

The assertion that a generic contract governs a particular interpretation of a work implies that the piece was planned to be heard in the tradition of previous works in that genre. How then are the *first* works of a genre to be understood? Clearly they cannot have been designed to fit with a tradition that they were retrospectively understood to have commenced; when the genre initially appeared, that tradition normally would have been an unforeseen consequence of the creative act. To the extent that they can be identified, then, the initial exemplars of a genre assume a special status. Designed by their authors to be interpreted under one set of circumstances, they are taken by later listeners to form part of an altered tradition. The first works of a genre, as Gary Saul Morson has observed, are normally interpreted according to an anachronistic set of conventions.[16] The diverse set of genres apparently used to measure the dramatic works of Peri, Caccini, and Cavalieri around 1600 was different from the idea of "opera" that composers in Venice applied in the 1640s.[17] When hearing initial works in a genre, later listeners ordinarily, rather than unusually, break the generic contract.

Works that seem to be anomalous with respect to a genre, that seem somehow to lie on the edge of it, can play a key role in generic studies. Such works expose the flaw behind viewing genre only as a classifying concept. The shared characteristics of the members of a genre can tell us much, but precisely in instances like the Nocturne in G Minor, where the search for common gestures yields a confused picture, we discover that such searches cannot inform us about the meaning of a genre. Unless, like Croce, we conclude from the lack of shared elements that the concept of genre itself is worthless, we soon realize that cases where the appropriate responses cannot be firmly fixed will figure centrally in our understanding of a genre. For in making us hesitate and waver in our responses, these works can reveal much about what these responses ought to be and what the real effect of them is in more clear instances of the genre. Marginal works focus our attention on interpretive decisions that ordinarily might pass without notice.[18] This is why it remains profitable to frame a discussion of the idiosyncratic Nocturne in G Minor in terms of genre.

Genres do not necessarily act in isolation from one another; relations among different genres also may affect the perceptions and conceptions of composers and listeners. Genres may interact in a number of ways. Hierarchical arrays are perhaps the most obvious of these interactions; much of the prescriptive writing about genre through the centuries has been concerned with the ranking of classes of art.[19] More provocative, though, are the various ways in which one genre can enter into the interpretation of another. Throughout history there have been groups of genres that overlapped perceptually, so that the meaning of one genre in part results from comparison with another. For example, the concert overture cannot fully be understood without knowledge of the symphony; its particular qualities tend to be measured against those of the symphony. The vocal romance was closely allied with the vocal nocturne in the nineteenth century, an association that continued in the piano transmutations of these genres.[20]

Composers often combined genres within a single work, a type of generic interaction that has a great tendency to promote change. Sometimes they merely alluded to a different genre in passing, leaving a short recollection of relatively minor significance in the piece. At other times they made more substantial reference to a foreign genre, so that a genuine mixture resulted. Mozart particularly enjoyed mixing genres in his instrumental finales: a number of his concertos finish with rondos that incorporate substantial references to different genres. (The foreign genre can come from the dance, as with the minuets Mozart interpolated in the Piano Concertos K. 271 and 482, and the gavotte in the Violin Concerto K. 218. In the Violin Concerto K. 219, he embedded "Turkish" interludes into the minuet finale, while in the Piano Concerto K. 415 he interleaved an adagio into the rondo structure.) Beethoven may have drawn upon this tradition of generically mixed finales when he conceived the complicated framework of the last movement of the Ninth Symphony; for many critics, indeed, the piece is baffling on any other assumption.[21] Generic mixture has long been employed to expand the range of possibilities in a genre, to communicate the unknown through the known.[22]

Genres may be mixed to form hybrid works in which no one type predominates. Often these hybrids are announced in the titles of the works: Sonata quasi una fantasia, Polonaise-Fantasy, Ode-Symphonie. But even when titles do not clue the listener in advance, hybrids can powerfully affect the experience of the work. Composers have often turned to generic hybrids at times when their personal styles were undergoing significant changes. Chopin's "last style," a significant departure in many ways from other works in the 1840s, coalesced in the Polonaise-Fantasy.[23] So too did Verdi fuse qualities of comic and serious opera in *Rigoletto,* and with this arrived at a new personal conception of musical drama.[24]

Genres may relate to one another negatively as well. That is, some genres are conceived in reaction to another genre; the choice of specific gestures is determined with the specific intention of refuting or contradicting another prevalent genre. Full understanding of these "countergenres," as Guillén has dubbed them, requires knowledge of the opposing genre.[25] Mendelssohn's *Variations sérieuses,* op. 54, though perfectly coherent when viewed in terms of traditional variation practice, should be taken in the context of the much-in-vogue *Variations brillantes* if their full significance is to be grasped.[26]

Countergenres are particularly prominent in the twentieth century, since the generic antitheses they depend upon have become more extreme. The *Orchesterstück,* for example, can be taken as a rejoinder to the nineteenth-century symphony; though it musters similar forces, it denies symphonic conventions of form, duration, melody, and tono. The extreme instance of this symphonic countergenre might well be John Cage's *4'33";* when "performed" orchestrally (as Cage permitted in his revision of the piece), it would refute nearly every expectation of the traditional genre, even the basic idea that players will produce sound with their instruments. Yet without these expectations, the effect of the piece—evidently to suggest that naturally occurring noises like coughing and rustling in one's chair can be cast in the willing listener's mind as "music"—would disappear. Cage's gesture was polemical—whatever instrumentation one selects for the piece, it will remain so—and meant as much to challenge received notions of what constitutes "music" as to question "symphony" or any other genre. But even in confronting these traditions, he was compelled to acknowledge the force of them. The past may be contradicted, but it cannot be obliterated.

When the workings of genre in the experience of a musical work are likened to a contractual agreement where *some* of the conventions will be employed, and *some* granted more central perceptual status than others, generic change is a likely result.[27] For if some conventions appear intact, others are altered; the alterations assume importance as potential models for future works in the genre. And this change may occur in any number of ways and at any rate of time. To some degree, every work written alters the genre to which it belongs. Even the most derivative hackwork can by the very baldness with which it imitates a conventional gesture weaken the attraction of that facet of the genre for a composer of skill. This is merely to state that the notions of stylistic change that underlie the history of music apply to genre as well.

That the nature of generically encoded information changes does not mean that communication will necessarily be hindered, only that the perception of the genre may be in some way different. And since this kind of variability in generic encoding would seem to be basic to the concept of genre, both the listener and the composer are accustomed to adjusting their expectations. In any epoch there develops a continual play between the evolving expectations for a genre and the evolving departures from these expectations. Part of the historian's task in exploring genres is to ferret out the specific ways in which this interchange between expectation and departure from norms affected the conception and perception of a genre at a given historical moment. This may be why the most useful statements about a genre tend to be rather closely circumscribed in time. More meaningful remarks may be made about the piano sonata from 1825 to 1850 than about the piano sonata over the entire nineteenth century.

To recapitulate: if genre conditions the communication of meaning from the musical work to the listener, if it is a rhetorical technique, then the proper concerns of generic studies are the manifold means by which this process occurs. The focus should include interpretation as well as the cataloguing of shared characteristics. Hence topics like responses—past and present, appropriate and inappropriate—signals, traditions, neighboring and contrasting genres, mixture, and mutability will all figure centrally in a study of genre.

The preceding discussion can no more than suggest the power of a properly conceived generic study: in effect, it serves as a generic signal in its own right, included to inform a fuller account of the nocturne. What are the appropriate responses to the genre "nocturne"? The search for these responses often most productively commences at borderline works. The Nocturne in G Minor sits as few other nocturnes do on the edge of its class. With the model of genre just proposed in mind, then, let us return to the piece to learn how decisions about genre affect the interpretation of Chopin's idiosyncratic composition.

Genre and the Interpretation of the Nocturne in G Minor

> We are accustomed to judge beforehand objects in
> and of themselves by the names they bear; we make
> certain demands of a "fantasy," and others of a
> "sonata."
>
> —Robert Schumann, reviewing the *Symphonie
> fantastique*[28]

Two pathways initially present themselves to the critic of the Nocturne in G Minor. One follows from a literal reading of the title of the work—an interpretive course determined by the conviction that Chopin planned the work to be heard in the tradition of earlier nocturnes. The other issues from a figurative understanding of it—the exegetic way guided by the sense that Chopin intended the piece to be taken as opposed, in some way, to its apparent class. Neither of these critical approaches is privileged, for the Nocturne in G Minor has been understood, at least in part, differently than its title might indicate. The two pathways, in other words, merge into one line of inquiry.

From the time of its publication in 1833, the Nocturne in G Minor struck listeners as being extraordinary. A review in the journal *Le pianiste* provides interesting contemporary testimony of its generic peculiarity. The anonymous critic opened with a complaint:

> These nocturnes are charming, and they contain the virtues and faults of this young and skillful composer. Why are ideas so fresh, so gracious often fettered, spoiled—we are obliged to say it—by intolerable harshness, and by a sort of affectation to write music almost as one should execute it—(we say *almost* because *entirely* is impossible)—to write in this wavering, languid, tentative fashion *[genre]*, this fashion that no arrangement of known note values can express well; *Rubato* in short, this *Rubato* the terror of girls, the *Bogeyman* of fumblers!

The reviewer went on to compare Dussek's use of rubato with Chopin's, and faulted Chopin for not performing more in public so that others might imitate his execution of the technique. After a pair of mostly favorable paragraphs on the first two Nocturnes of the set, the critic commented on the Nocturne in G Minor:

> The third nocturne is the most original, and cannot do without a great deal of dexterity in its execution. It is in *rubato* from one end to the other. It incorporates tied notes in the middle of the left hand that are a new effect. The first four lines of the second page [mm. 53–80] are rather tormented with modulations; but the plainchant that follows them seems perfect to us. The manner of returning to the key of G to conclude is as new as unexpected.[29]

The comments on rubato magnify a common response to Chopin's music during his lifetime: that the composer's own rhythmically inflected manner of performing was unique, and nearly impossible to reproduce—perhaps even completely impossible if one had not heard him play. The idea of rubato was closely linked with Chopin in the minds of many in the 1830s and 1840s; in a glossary of Italian musical terms printed two issues later in *Le pianiste*, Chopin is identified as the composer who made the most frequent use of the technique.[30]

The critic's fixation on rubato gives us our first clue to the generic idiosyncrasies of the piece. Although his opening gambit seems to suggest that rubato permeates the entire set, the remarks on the third nocturne make clear the real source of the complaint. In fact, the Nocturne in G Minor is the only one in op. 15 marked "rubato." Whatever degree of rhythmic modification the reviewer thought to be implied in the first two Nocturnes must have been deduced from the indication in the third.

"Rubato," however, was not a common prescription to performers of nocturnes; Chopin only marked it one other time in this genre, and then only at the end of a piece—in the coda to op. 9, no. 2, in E-flat Major (m. 26). The identification of "rubato" with Chopin's mazurkas was far stronger, some three-fourths of its appearances occurring in this genre (Chopin stopped using the term after 1835).[31] The heading "languido e rubato," in other words, might have conjured up associations that more normally arose in the context of mazurkas.[32] (This is particularly true when the term appears at the beginning of the piece, presumably applying to the entire Nocturne—in op. 9, no. 2, its application would seem to be more local, perhaps even limited to the measure in which it is written.)

Moreover, the generic signal "mazurka" sent by the rubato rubric seems to be amplified by other features of the opening of the work (Ex. 1.1). First, of course, the triple meter suggests a mazurka. Second, the accentual structure conspires to stress the second and third beats in a manner common in a mazurka, and unusual in a nocturne (compare the opening of op. 15, no. 1, also in triple meter). Third, Chopin's tempo marking of "Lento ♩. = 60" falls into a range faster than most nocturnes (though the tempos of these should not be nearly so slow as the way they are usually performed today), and more in keeping with mazurkas. Far from unambiguously evoking the mood of earlier works in the nocturne tradition, in other words, the opening of op. 15, no. 3 instead calls to mind a genre not usually considered to be closely related to the nocturne.[33]

And the foreign associations did not stop here. The critic went on to praise the perfection of the "plainchant" in the third Nocturne, a reference to the section Chopin marked "religioso," mm. 89–152. The aura of plainchant obviously arises not from any monophonic texture, but instead from the "modally" inflected harmonies and the block-chordal groupings in the right hand (Ex. 1.2).[34] "Plainchant," in short, refers to music with the quality of an archaic chorale, a genre about which a fair amount had been written in the first decades of the nineteenth century.

Example 1.1   Nocturne in G Minor, op. 15, no. 3, opening.

Example 1.2   Nocturne in G Minor, op. 15, no. 3, mm. 97–105.

From these accounts we learn just how closely Chopin's *religioso* section corresponds to contemporary ideals of chorale writing. The choice of key, the unadorned melodic style, the lack of dissonance, the imitation of organ swells and diminuendos, and the "modal" sound—all of these are textbook features of the archaic style.[35] As Nicholas Temperley has remarked, the harmonies of the *religioso* section are similar to those recommended for the accompaniment of plainsong by French church musicians like Niedermeyer.[36] In any case, however convincing an imitation of a chorale it is, the *religioso* section initially confounds expectations based on the traditions of both the nocturne and the mazurka.[37] Its anomalous status will require special interpretive efforts whichever initial generic pathway one takes.

Our exploration of these generic pathways may best begin with a discussion of this concluding section. The only surviving sketch for the Nocturne concerns just this section (Fig. 1.1).[38] It conforms in most respects with the version published. But at the very end, it departs significantly: the final four measures hover around the dominant of G minor, and then go into a "da Capo" repetition of the opening (Ex. 1.3). Chopin normally wrote "da Capo" when he intended a literal repetition of an entire opening section; this notation stood in place of a tedious rewriting of that section. Hence the sketch packs a surprise: Chopin probably once conceived of the piece in ternary form.

That said, the sketch still poses certain interpretive problems. For one, it leaves unanswered how much of the opening section is to be repeated. Were the whole section reprised (to measure 50), the Nocturne would end in D minor. More likely is either that the piece stopped around measure 37, or that Chopin planned a coda after measure 50 that would lead back to the tonic G minor.

Moreover, we cannot unequivocally presume that this sketch was planned for a piece whose opening was identical to op. 15, no. 3. The

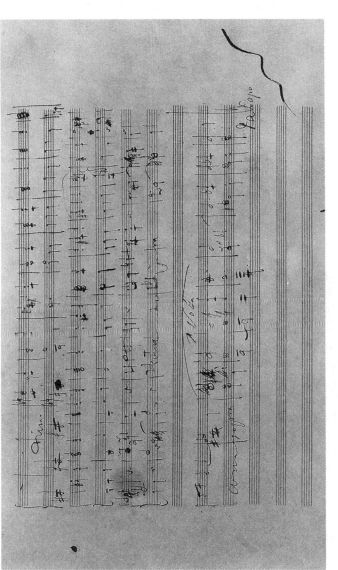

Figure 1.1 Chopin, sketch of the Nocturne in G Minor, op. 15, no. 3, mm. 86–152. Collection of Robert Owen Lehman, on deposit in the Pierpont Morgan Library. Except for its final four measures, the sketch corresponds relatively closely with what Chopin eventually published. In the second system, the slur (over the third and fourth measures from the right margin) is an abbreviation for "1. Volta."

Example 1.3   Ending of sketch, compared to ending of published edition.

C♯ – C in the bass at the opening suggests it, but the final b♭′ in the melody casts some doubt. I have suggested an alternate reading of d″ on the grounds that the note was a hurried last stroke of the pen. But it remains possible (though not terribly likely) that the b♭′ points to a different interpretation of the sketch from what I have offered.

While the final, truncated version of the piece remains idiosyncratic in any generic tradition with which Chopin was familiar, the earlier "da Capo" shape in 1832–1833 would have been more closely associated with the mazurka than the nocturne. Literal return, whether stated expressly with a "da Capo" or not, occurs frequently in the mazurkas of Chopin's youth and in the first two sets he published in Paris (opp. 6 and 7). The only earlier nocturne to feature anything like a literal return of the opening section was the F-major op. 15, no. 1. Ordinarily the return of the main theme was heavily ornamented and shortened.

So the literal ternary shape, too, was at odds with the tradition of Chopin's nocturnes. His decision to excise the return therefore affirmed the actual generic title.[39] Yet at the same time, the form suggested by the sketch underscores in one more way the ambiguous generic roots of the piece. Without necessarily suspecting that Chopin actually conceived the work as a mazurka, we can see how the original formal scheme demonstrates again how this genre had insinuated its presence in the ordinarily foreign territory of the nocturne.

The sketch also confirms the dual function of the F-major section in one's actual hearing of the piece. In prospect, the *religioso* functions as a middle section. It bears the hallmarks of the center of a ternary form in the nineteenth century: contrasting themes and textures, a reduction in harmonic tension, and a general relaxation in structure. All of this is no surprise, since we know it probably *did* once serve as a middle section. But in the final version, the *religioso* concludes the piece—a fact we learn retrospectively after it is concluded. This conflict between prospective and retrospective hearing first surfaces in the last four measures of the piece, which Chopin had to revise after he lopped off the ternary return. The powerfully abrupt quality of this ending depends not only on the brevity of the modulation from F major back to G minor/major, but also on the wrenching of formal expectations. (Like the decision to trim the "da Capo" return, the revised ending of the piece, with its rather incomplete sense of closure, reaffirms the nocturne tradition. Earlier nocturnes often undercut the strength of the final cadence, frequently by means of a blurred pedal. Mazurkas, by contrast, tend toward more secure, dominant-tonic final cadences.)

Despite some of the links to the nocturne heard in the *religioso* passage, two elements of the section still scan convincingly when taken as a mazurka. First, the modal quality of the "chorale" fits well with the folkloristic background of the mazurka, whereas the genre of the nocturne lacks a tradition of modality. To be sure, the "modal" sound of the early mazurkas, with their emphasis on sharpened fourth scalar degrees and hollow fifth accompaniments (see op. 7, no. 1, mm. 45–52, for a fine example), differs from that of the *religioso* Nocturne, with its mediant stress and flattened leading tones. But the archaic quality suffices to articulate once again the connection between this Nocturne and the genre of mazurka.

Second, the last half of the *religioso* introduces new, sharply defined melodic and rhythmic motives that frequently stress the second beat, an effect that comes right out of the tradition of the mazurka (Ex. 1.4). This change in the accentual structure, which more immediately brings to mind the genre of the mazurka than the "modality" of the chorale, seems partly conceived in order to balance the references to

Example 1.4   Nocturne in G Minor, op. 15, no. 3, mm. 121–136.

the mazurka at the opening of the Nocturne. It is as though Chopin sought to compensate for the lack of formal return by substituting a clear generic return: the piece begins and ends with plain invocations of the genre of the mazurka.

The fundamental generic ambivalence of this piece emerges as strongly in its first half as in its second. I have already described how aspects of the opening conspire to evoke the mazurka: the triple meter, rubato heading, accentuation, and tempo all agree with the tradition of that genre. Yet the nocturne also asserts itself, particularly in the relative stasis of the accompanying harmony. Harmonically static beginnings occur often in the nocturne, though the tonic pedals that create the sensation of stasis are usually balanced by florid melodies that grow even richer ornamentally as the opening evolves. In the Nocturne in G Minor the melody is gaunt and austere throughout: the sole capitulations to ornamentation are the short figures woven on the fifth scalar degree in measures 35 and 36 (Ex. 1.5). A tension arises between the two sets of generic conventions: the result is an opening that fits convincingly neither set of expectations.

Certainly the phrase structure of the first fifty measures would be idiosyncratic in either genre. The section falls into two large strophes of nearly equal length, the two strophes subdividing into two roughly equal parts (12 + 12 + 12 + 14 [=12+2]). This evidently symmetrical design is masked somewhat by overlappings between the parts (prospectively, the first measures of parts 2 and 4 sound as if they conclude parts 1 and 3). And in any case, the design reveals an odd sense of parallel structure, for the subdivisions break into units of 7 + 5 measures (7 + 7 in the final subdivision). In both the nocturne and mazurka, equal divisions of phrases would be expected: Chopin preferred four-bar units in both genres. The only work remotely to anticipate the uneven division of a twelve-measure opening phrase is the Mazurka in B-flat Major, op. 7, no. 1, where an overlap between a phrase ending and a phrase beginning in measure 4 creates a brief stammer in the otherwise even rhythm of subphrases.[40] But the uneven gait of the G-Minor Nocturne is at once more pervasive and more peculiar, the peculiarity resulting in no small part from the near cessation of forward motion when the melody lingers again and again on a high f″.

Chopin appears to have used the generically ambivalent opening of this Nocturne as a means to introduce and experiment with irregular phrase designs. And once admitted to the genre, the idea would resonate in later nocturnes like the two in B Major, opp. 32, no. 1 and 62, no. 1. This ambiguity widened the range of structural possibilities for the nocturne.

Likewise, the whole second portion of the opening section (mm. 51–88) fits neither the structural expectations for a nocturne nor those for a mazurka. Formally, it at first echoes measures 17–24 of the preceding Nocturne in F-sharp Major: a passage that commences with a new lyrical tune and then leads into the middle section proper (Ex. 1.6). Yet it quickly counteracts this impression. By subverting the mellifluousness of the theme through deceptive cadences (mm. 57–58), by

Example 1.5   Nocturne in G Minor, op. 15, no. 3, mm. 31–38.

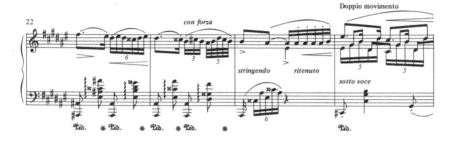

Example 1.6   Nocturne in F-sharp Major, op. 15, no. 2, mm. 17–25.

employing descending semitone sequences, by modulating to the distant key of F-sharp major (established through its dominant pedal),
and by coupling a long accelerando with an even longer crescendo—
by the use of all these ploys, the section takes on a dynamic sheen
wholly unlike the passage in the F-sharp-Major Nocturne (Ex. 1.7).
What it *is* like is the thematically profuse and harmonically mobile
middle sections that sometimes arise in the mazurka: measures 24–76
of op. 7, no. 3, in F Minor, measures 25–78 of op. 30, no. 3, in D-
flat Major, and measures 37–78 of op. 59, no. 1, in A Minor provide
excellent examples.

   Paradoxically, though, the immediate function of the section in
op. 15, no. 3 is precisely that of its progenitor in op. 15, no. 2: it serves
to lead from the main theme to the prospective "middle section," or
chorale. In this sense, it denies expectations associated with the mazurka. Form and function point generically in different directions, and,
just as in the phrase structure of the opening, the structural possibilities of the nocturne were broadened. This particular echo of op. 15,
no. 3 sounds two years later in the long "Più mosso" transition of the
Nocturne in C-sharp Minor, op. 27, no. 1.

Example 1.7   Nocturne in G Minor, op. 15, no. 3, mm. 51–72.

Rhetoric Redux: Chopin and Polish Romantic Nationalism

> You know how I have wanted to feel and in part
> have approached the feeling of our national music.
> —Chopin, in 1831[41]

Two pathways, I suggested above, were open for the generic interpretation of the Nocturne in G Minor. Not only has it become clear that neither the literal nor figurative readings of the piece are privileged, it has emerged forcefully that both must be taken into account if a deeper understanding of op. 15, no. 3 is to be reached. The generic ambiguity that results from the elastic play of expectations of the nocturne, mazurka, and chorale is integral to the meaning of the piece. Without an understanding of the rhetorical force of these genres, even these resonances of the piece would be lost.

But another interpretive course is suggested by the interplay of genres. Our entrée into this realm may be through some other contemporary responses to the Nocturne in G Minor. The most interesting reaction was a composition written by the little-known Polish composer Edward Wolff. Wolff's life and art paralleled his compatriot's in many ways. Six years Chopin's junior, Wolff studied composition with Józef Elsner in Warsaw and Wenzel Würfel in Vienna, both of whom figured prominently in Chopin's education as well. Elsner taught Chopin composition at the Warsaw Conservatory, and Würfel, who had lived in Warsaw during Chopin's youth and was a friend of his family, published a number of piano pieces that helped shape Chopin's style. In 1835, Wolff too emigrated to Paris, where he settled as a pianist and composer and remained for the rest of his life (he died in 1880).

The two composers apparently made their acquaintance in Warsaw; the first letter of Chopin to mention Wolff, in 1830, speaks of him with an air of familiarity.[42] Wolff, however, seems not to have counted as one of Chopin's intimates in Vienna or in Paris. His name turns up now and then in Chopin's correspondence, but never as more than a passing mention.

Musically, though, Wolff clearly felt strong affinities with his compatriot. A letter of 1835 testifies to his enthusiasm for Chopin and his music; Wolff even remarks that he is writing mazurkas "à la Chopin."[43] Wolff's admiration for Chopin's style was recognized by their contemporaries; a review of Wolff's music in *Cäcilia* in 1842 devoted space to the clear stylistic affinities of the two composers.[44]

Hence we might expect a general similarity to Chopin in almost any work by Wolff. But at least once these expectations would be surpassed, for Wolff in 1841 borrowed specifically from Chopin's Nocturne. Wolff's title immediately reveals his source: *Nocturne en forme de Mazurke*.[45] A glance at the beginning shows that it was cut from the same cloth as op. 15, no. 3 (Ex. 1.8a): the G-minor tonality of the main theme (which follows an introduction that itself appears modeled on the opening of Chopin's Mazurka, op. 24, no. 4), its prominent stress on B-flat major, its melodic descent from D to G at the start of the tune, and its decorated melodic Ds, all recall Chopin's Nocturne. As the piece continues, other similarities emerge. But the most striking emulation of the Chopin model occurs at the very end

Example 1.8 Edward Wolff, *Nocturne en forme de Mazurke*, op. 45.

(Ex. 1.8b): Wolff concluded with a completely new passage in G major, in a slower tempo ("Andantino"), and marked "Religioso." The homage is touchingly complete and frank. Like Chopin, Wolff evoked the mood of an organ chorale in his brief *religioso,* though without the modal tinges of his model.[46]

However, the fascination of Wolff's borrowing lies not in his appropriation of these specific elements from Chopin's Nocturne, but rather in his reflection, expressed in the forthright title of his piece, of contemporary comprehension of Chopin's work. Wolff sensed the generic ambiguity in his model, and in his own piece he opted to make the hybrid explicit. In other words, Wolff was struck with the generic originality of op. 15, no. 3—so struck, in fact, that he tried to imitate it in his own music. And just as in Chopin's piece, the vacillation between "nocturne" and "mazurka," along with the admixture of *religioso* music, in part accounts for the meaning of the *Nocturne en forme de Mazurke.*[47]

The second reaction to Chopin's Nocturne is more problematic. Around 1880, an anecdote began to surface in the literature that Chopin had written the Nocturne in G Minor while influenced by a recent performance of Shakespeare's *Hamlet.* The story exists in slightly different versions. The first, offered by the early Chopin biographer M. A. Szulc, asserts that the composer, returning from a performance of *Hamlet,* wrote the Nocturne and inscribed on the manuscript the heading "na cmentarzu" ("at the cemetery"). Then, when he prepared the work for publication, he canceled the inscription, saying "let them surmise it themselves."[48] Later versions report the inscription as reading either "after a performance of *Hamlet*" ("po przedstawieniu Hamleta") or "after (or according to) *Hamlet*" ("Podług Hamleta").[49] In every instance, however, Chopin was supposed later to have removed the reference from the manuscript.

Other than the sketch for the F-major section, no manuscript of the Nocturne survives against which to check the truth of this story. Chopin mentioned attending only one performance of *Hamlet,* in Warsaw in the summer of 1830, at least two years before the composition of op. 15, no. 3.[50] However, as Jean-Jacques Eigeldinger has observed, Chopin might well have seen *Hamlet* around 1832–1833; this was the period during which Chopin was close to that notorious Shakespeare enthusiast Hector Berlioz.[51] With Berlioz, Chopin might have viewed

Hamlet, starring Harriet Smithson as Ophelia, either in her public performances with her English troupe on 15 and 19 January 1833, or in private renditions for friends.[52]

Even so, the story rings false. First, the anecdote only came to light some half a century after its supposed occurrence. Second, Szulc, responsible for its initial publication, was by no means a trustworthy biographer. Finally, attempts to draw parallels between Shakespeare's play and Chopin's Nocturne—such as suggesting similarities between the hesitant and dolorous sound of the first part of the Nocturne and the general quality of Hamlet's monologues—seem forced.[53] The kind of overtly programmatic conception of art that the story implies was more in keeping with prevailing currents at the time the anecdote was published than with Chopin's own aesthetic.

But the stylistic trends of the 1880s suggest why the story still bears repeating. Its interest lies not in its accuracy, but in the fact that it arose for precisely the Nocturne in G Minor, and no other. For programs tended to be attached to compositions whose musical structures resisted understanding by audiences grounded in "classical" works. We have seen the ways in which Chopin's Nocturne departed from the models of its forebears; clearly its peculiar nature in comparison to these works did not diminish as the nineteenth century passed. In other words, the generic idiosyncrasy of op. 15, no. 3 continued to be perceived strongly enough so that, some fifty years after it was written, a literary association could be invoked to "explain" its peculiarity.

These two reactions to Chopin's Nocturne confirm—the *Hamlet* anecdote in a general way, Wolff's piece more particularly—the generic ambiguity that lies at the heart of the work. Yet while we can no longer doubt that Chopin sought to confuse the expectations of his listeners, we have not explained all that he hoped to achieve through this particular blend of genres in 1832–1833. At one level, the fusion of the nocturne, the mazurka, and the *religioso* into one heterodox work can be understood as an experiment in the combination of seemingly uncombinable types, one designed to broaden the expressive range of the genre of the nocturne. But there may be other resonances in the choice of precisely these kinds for mixture. What might these be? In particular, given the capabilities of at least two of the genres to convey extra-musical associations—the mazurka might evoke thoughts about Poland and the chorale would obviously bring to mind religion—could Chopin have intended the genres to stand metaphorically for some kind of intellectual subject matter? Said another way, was there a context that could account for the striking generic amalgam in the G-Minor Nocturne?

I want to suggest that there was just such a context, and one with which Chopin was inextricably bound: Polish romantic nationalism. The complex ethos of this nationalism will seem puzzling unless seen in light of developments in Polish history.[54]

The 1830 Polish revolt against Russian domination, the "November uprising," was the decisive political event in the young Chopin's life. The defeat of the Poles led to their massive exodus in what has come to be called the "Great Emigration," which encompassed almost the entire political elite of the Congress Kingdom, and a large segment of its intellectual and artistic population as well. Since the majority of these émigrés settled in France, throughout the 1830s and 1840s the center of Polish political, intellectual, and cultural life lay not in Poland, but in France, and specifically in Paris.[55]

Despite being divided by a number of ideological quarrels, nearly all the exiles were bound together by their devotion, in principle at least, to the cause of independence for Poland, and to the preservation of the idea of the Polish nation until such time that independent statehood could be regained. In this sense, "nationalism" was a concept espoused by most of the exiles in Paris.[56] Certain other beliefs were common coin as well. Among these was the adoption of a philosophy of history that imbued the Polish cause with a special mission: it aspired to no less than the realization of universal ethics in the sphere of politics, or what came to be known as the "Christianization" of politics. Poland's struggles would lead to the redemption of mankind. The coming war to liberate Poland would be the final war, after which everlasting peace would reign. This universal scope contributed to the particular character of Polish romantic nationalism, as did the notion of the eventual dominance of Christian morality in politics. Andrzej Walicki points out that although these notions were common enough in the 1830s—variants of them could be found in the writings of Kant, Saint-Simon, Fourier, and Mazzini—in no other group was their popularity as great as it was among the Poles.[57]

It was the Christian angle that gave rise to the great flowering of messianism among the Polish émigré community. "Messianism," Walicki proposes, refers first to a belief that the calling of one's nation would lead uniquely to the salvation of mankind. Second, and more specifically, it refers to an expressly religious consciousness closely associated with millenarianism, or the quest for total and imminent collective salvation. This narrower definition of messianism implies a belief that a redeemer, individual or collective, will mediate between heaven and earth in the process of history, and that a second coming of the Messiah will provide a second collective and terrestrial salvation of all mankind.[58] Polish romantic messianism may be viewed as a type of social utopianism, though religiously inspired and associated with millenarian beliefs. This close relation of messianism and social utopianism is crucial, for when the exiles arrived in Paris, French utopian socialism was in its heyday: the new Parisian soil proved to be fertile ground for the growth of messianic thought.[59]

One of the clearest articulations of Polish romantic messianism came with the publication of Adam Mickiewicz's *The Books of the Polish Nation and of the Polish Pilgrims* in 1832, that is, at just the time Chopin was composing the Nocturne in G Minor. Upon his arrival in Paris, Mickiewicz was dismayed by the numerous factions that had developed among the Polish exiles. He wrote the *Books* in an effort to reunite them by recalling to them the universal mission of Poland and of her exiles. In order that the *Books* would be taken as a prophetic utterance, he couched them in a biblical style. Mickiewicz's remarkable work portrays vividly the distinctive ethos of Polish romantic messianism—its idiosyncratic blend of nationalism, universalism, religion, traditionalism, and radicalism.

What has all of this to do with Chopin and the message communicated by the mixture of genres in the Nocturne in G Minor? The central tenets of the messianic brand of Polish romantic nationalism practically read like a description of the piece, particularly in its blend of the "nationalistic" mazurka and the "religious" chorale. Chopin's choice of the nocturne as the "host" genre for the blending might even have arisen from its lack of a clearly defined national identity: its relatively neutral character in this sense might have been perceived as "universal" or "international." (Moreover, by unexpectedly embedding nationalist and religious sentiments in the "neutral" genre of the nocturne, Chopin cast these ideas into sharper light than they might have attained in, say, a piece called "Mazurka," where they might have seemed commonplace.) He can scarcely have avoided the nationalist sentiments current in 1832–1833; since he had just barely begun to make his way in French circles, his ties with other Poles in Paris were especially strong at this time. His correspondence is characteristically mute on the specific subject of messianism and its relation to nationalism.[60] But more general clues from his letters suggest that during his first two years in Paris he was more aware than usual of nationalist concerns.

This awareness developed partly in response to urgings from various quarters that he compose an opera on a Polish national subject. These exhortations began already during his last days in Vienna. The poet Stefan Witwicki devoted most of a letter to Chopin extolling the composer's talents and his suitability to be the creator of Polish national opera, in terms that sound almost like a nationalist manifesto.[61] But the main pressure seems to have come later, from Chopin's teacher Józef Elsner, himself a composer of Polish opera.[62] Chopin obviously resisted these suggestions, displaying a characteristic resolve about his career (as when he referred to his wish "to create for myself a new world").[63] Nevertheless the hints that, as one of the most prominent artists of Poland, he owed some kind of creative duty to his homeland must have exercised his imagination.

Some further measure of support for reading nationalistic significance into Chopin's Nocturne in G Minor may come from Wolff's *Nocturne en forme de Mazurke*. That it was another Pole who chose to imitate Chopin's peculiar generic blend, and not a Frenchman, German, or Italian, implies that the cultural message of op. 15, no. 3 was one that Poles were most apt to understand. When Wolff composed his piece in the early 1840s, the messianic species of Polish nationalism was by no means passé. If anything, it was more prevalent; at this time, Mickiewicz commenced his lectures on Slavonic literature at the Collège de France, the bizarre Lithuanian mystic Andrzej Towiański created a stir in Paris, and important publications were issued by two poetic and dramatic rivals of Mickiewicz, Juliusz Słowacki and Zygmunt Krasiński.[64] Whether Wolff meant specifically to tap into the émigré intellectual milieu with his piece, or whether he meant it simply as an act of homage to his creative compatriot, is not clear. But in either case, Wolff's composition underscores the nationalistic scope of Chopin's Nocturne.

None of these observations securely establishes that Chopin was an ardent messianist. Indeed, given his lifelong avoidance of political activism, it would be surprising if they did. Still, the pervasiveness of the messianic ethos in Paris in the early 1830s, the composer's own heightened awareness of nationalist concerns at this time, and above all the striking parallel between the generic content of Chopin's Nocturne and the idiosyncratic beliefs of the Polish romantic nationalists together bear witness that Chopin was receptive at least to the cultural aims, if not to the political program, of the messianists. Opera was not his *métier;* yet Chopin did not need to compromise his artistic intention to "create a new world" in his chosen medium in order to express his nationalist sympathies.

Chopin expanded the range of expression of the genre with the composition of the Nocturne in G Minor. The work seems to teeter precariously at the edge of its ostensible genre, so bold was its experimental and virtuosic combination of kinds. But its marginal generic status was to serve an important purpose for Chopin: the articulation of his kinship with the Polish romantic nationalists. This was a goal very much in keeping with the intellectual and emotional leanings of a young man freshly separated from his homeland. As Chopin grew more at ease in his Parisian surroundings and more concerned to address this new audience, the need to identify with the aims of the messianists would not be as pressing (though he obviously would continue more generally to evoke nationalist sentiments through his mazurkas and polonaises). Hence political and cultural identification was not to be the legacy of the Nocturne in G Minor for Chopin. Rather, its message was to be specifically generic, broadening the means by which the composer could hope to move and persuade his listeners.

Examination of this legacy must wait for another time. Still, enough gauge has been taken of the piece to show the power of the rhetorical concept of genre discussed above. When we employ genre primarily to classify through the cataloguing of shared characteristics, it would inevitably cease to be useful after identifying the Nocturne as unusual. But when we grasp its persuasive and communicative capabilities— when, in other words, we restore its full rhetorical potential—genre allows the understanding of the meanings the idiosyncratic Nocturne might have, to Chopin and his contemporaries as well as to us.

≀ 2 ≀

The Harmony of the Tea Table: Gender and Ideology in the Piano Nocturne

In the flourishing but fledgling literature on constructions of gender in music, instrumental music reposes in relative neglect. Guided by the premise that (in Teresa de Lauretis's words) "gender is both a socio-cultural construct and a semiotic apparatus, a system of representation which assigns meaning . . . to individuals within the society,"[1] and nourished by theoretical models developed by critics of literature, art, and film, music historians have most readily gravitated toward explorations of the ramifications of gender in opera and song. The attraction is obvious. The feminist topic may initially be broached through the semantic content of the text, which then serves as a kind of lens through which is filtered the critic's reading of the music. Instrumental music, on the other hand, poses its ever-familiar quandary: lacking an evident semantic content, it would seem to stymie efforts to understand "systems of representation" at work within it.

Music historians have shied away from trying to recover and explicate these gendered systems partly because the idea that instrumental music occupies an autonomous realm still remains a powerful ideological force in the discipline. Those of us who would seek to lessen the stranglehold of this ideology on modern discourse encounter particular difficulties. We might recognize that the language of formalist musical criticism—a twentieth-century stepchild of the aesthetics of autonomy—does not adequately serve the purposes of an inquiry into gender.[2] But shorn of this customary prop, we face an apparent conceptual void, for the ideology of autonomy still seems to command our linguistic possibilities. How can we speak of gender when constrained by the analytical demands of "the music itself"?

The few efforts to discuss gender in instrumental music all seem most awkward precisely when the discourse shifts from feminism to traditional musical analysis. We can trace this sense of incongruity primarily to an implicit dissonance between the aims of the two systems of thought. The vocabularies of musical analysis—whether they label harmonic and contrapuntal processes, detect Schenkerian *Urlinien,* or identify pitch-class sets—typically represent implicit or explicit distillations of *individual* viewpoints, usually those of a composer, analyst, or "ideal" listener. (And assertions that these analyses are or were generally perceived by audiences usually remain in the realm of the ideal.) But the feminist projects in which these analyses occur generally stake wider *societal* claims, ones validated (in principal) by a network of historical contexts. The goals of the feminist critiques and the musical analyses apparently clash.[3] As yet unresolved, this discord has resulted in a sense of aporia that has rendered the historical traces of gender in instrumental music almost unrepresentable and has caused us to concentrate on more pliant texted repertories.

Yet a nocturne or a ballade was no less a cultural construct than *Carmen* or *Frauenliebe und -leben,* and in principal should have been no less (and no more) given to gendered meanings. If music historians are to detect and interpret these meanings, we need to seek alternative conceptual frameworks for use in discussing instrumental music. But this task, so smugly exhorted, is formidable: at the present time, we might at best hope for partial results. Thus, although I venture two alternative models of explanation in this chapter, neither of them breaks decisively with conceptual tradition. First, I examine the consequences of trying to understand historical constructions of gender in instrumental music without undertaking a close reading of the musical notes. Here I seek to cast off the burden of instrumental "autonomy"—of the "work itself." But second, and in some ways contradictorily, I assess how, if we filter our received analytical systems through a social-historical net, studying the notes of a piece might indeed contribute to our understanding of gender.[4]

My approach hinges on a crucial methodological move. Rather than studying instrumental music from the traditional horizon of form, I suggest instead that we focus on its constituent genres. To do so directs our critical attention away from a composer-centered notion, form, and onto a societal concept, genre, that displays more than just an etymological affinity with the idea of gender.

I first understood the significance of this methodological shift while thinking about Chopin's nocturnes and the problem of genre in the nineteenth century. As we saw in Chapter 1, having rejected the notion that genre functions only as a classificatory category located solely in compositions, I adopted instead an understanding of genre as a communicative concept shared by composers and listeners alike, one that therefore actively informs the experience of a musical work. Construing genre as a social phenomenon requires an investigation into the responses of the communities that encountered a particular genre. And it was the investigation of such responses to the nocturne that eventually led me to ask just who made up these communities in Chopin's day.[5]

The answer is: women, mainly. But this simple response masks a number of more complex meanings. For when we understand genre as a communicative concept, it makes us aware of ways in which music interacts with society. In particular, as literary critics and historians often remark, an examination of genre frequently uncovers otherwise hidden ideological agendas.[6] In Chapter 1, I began the process of exploring the societal constraints governing the perception of genre in an examination of Chopin's early Nocturne in G Minor, where the mixture of gestures from the mazurka, chorale, and nocturne genres seems calculated to articulate his kinship with the cultural goals of the Polish romantic nationalists. In this chapter I want to take the process one step further, to address a question that is basic to the understanding of the nocturne. What did it mean—culturally, historically, and musically—that the nineteenth-century audience for this genre was understood as primarily female?

An Archive of Musical Difference

I am not the first to observe that nineteenth-century listeners to the genre of the piano nocturne often couched their reactions in feminine imagery. Christoph von Blumröder, in his excellent article on the nocturne for the *Handwörterbuch der musikalischen Terminologie,* includes documentation of this "feminine topos" in his discussion of the "poetic idea" of the genre.[7] But von Blumröder's stance toward the topic (perhaps constrained by his format) remains neutral; he does not explore the critical, historical, and ideological implications of these gendered responses.

Since these reactions took many forms, we ought first to consider some representative samples of criticism in which feminine tropes were invoked. G. W. Fink's brief review of Chopin's Nocturnes, op. 15, written in 1834 for the *Allgemeine musikalische Zeitung,* drew attention to the unmediated, spontaneous quality of the feminine response:

> The Nocturnes are really reveries of a soul fluctuating from feeling to feeling in the still of the night, about which we want to set down nothing but the outburst of a feminine heart after a sensitive performance of the same: "These Nocturnes surely are my entire life!"[8]

In the following impressions of Chopin's Nocturnes, op. 27, penned in 1836, an anonymous critic limned a feminine genre associated with both darkness and pain:

> The names of the creations, Nocturnos, . . . admit nothing else but a fancifully dark hue . . . It is the dream, which celebrates its round dances with longing, longing which chose pain on its own, because it could not find again the joy that it loves. For that reason these new Nocturnes, like the old ones (as different as they are from them), will again always be most attractive to all hearts inclined toward the feminine.[9]

Sometimes the feminine topos broadened out to include allusions to effeminacy. (I will explore more fully in Chapter 3 the particular valences of "effeminacy" as a conceptual category applied to Chopin and his music.) Ferdinand Hand, in his discussion of the nocturne in the *Aesthetik der Tonkunst* (1841), introduced effeminacy as a potential expressive deficit in the genre:

> In the notturno, grace balances everything that is characteristically brought into prominence and surrounds it with tender mildness. But this can lead to a twofold error. With level bearing, which here generally is signified by a fixed soul-state, the composer falls into the prolix and dawdling [*in's Breite und Schleppende*] . . . On the other

side the representation of sentiment in the notturno runs the danger of falling into the effeminate and languishing, which displeases stronger souls and altogether tires the listener.[10]

Carl Kossmaly voiced similar opinions in 1844 in the *Allgemeine musikalische Zeitung*. His comments occur in the midst of a lengthy overview of Schumann's piano music; the subjects at hand are the *Arabeske* and the *Blumenstück*:

> [The *Blumenstück*] is in some measure impaired by an occasional, prominent family likeness to Mendelssohn's "Songs without Words" and J. Field's notturnos and romances. Both pieces remind us unequivocally of the soft [*das Weiche*, also "effeminate"], the rapturous, the tender, lyrical, almost womanly character of the Fieldian cantilena.[11]

In many of these passages, direct references to the perceived feminine quality in the nocturne were accompanied by other figural language. "Feeling," "dream," "longing," "sentiment," "tender"—all of these affective terms were linked to, and surely in different degrees meant to complement, the primary image of the feminine. And often, when these analogous terms appeared in other criticism independent of any explicit citation of the feminine, they were understood as code words for overtly feminine imagery. The feminine slant of Maurice Bourges's 1842 review of Chopin's Nocturnes, op. 48, published in the *Revue et Gazette musicale de Paris* is clearer than most. In fact, its title, "Letters to Mme la Baronne de *** on Some Modern Pieces for Piano," already frames the feminine image. (Although such rhetorical strategies were ubiquitous in nineteenth-century criticism, this does not weaken their ability to dispose a reader toward interpreting some of their tropes in terms of the gender of the addressee.)[12] In the following excerpt, the gender-typing behind the critical language explicitly reveals itself in the final sentence:

> Each note should be rendered with intelligence, should conceal a sense, an intimate expression. The material part is subordinated to the spiritual element. For the music of M. Chopin demands on the part of the performer if not soul, then at least imagination, and that naive finesse, next of kin to the spirit. That is why, madame, I have some reasons to think that Mlle Brigitte will not content herself with only rendering the letter of this charming production.

And it is not hard to sense a subliminally gendered message in the following passage from Schumann's 1838 critique of Count Joseph von Wielhorsky's Nocturnes, op. 2:

> Even though not highly original, the talent seems manifest. To be sure, it could also by no means become evident in such strongly drawn out form. But the composer also has experience on approval with a less sentimental genre where imagination can stretch more.[13]

Likewise, we can without difficulty construe the sex of the "heart" in the following anonymous critique of Chopin's Nocturne in B Major, op. 32, no. 1, subtitled "Il Lamento" by Chopin's English publisher, Wessel:

> "Il Lamento," an *andante sostenuto,* is a *morceau* in the style of Bellini's graceful and pathetic melodies; and may, without much stretch of imagination, be taken as a faithful portraiture of a heart pouring forth its feelings of "sweet sorrow," in strains of intense feeling and affection.[14]

All of these reviews and discussions date from the 1830s and 1840s, the period during which the piano nocturne first began to flourish as a genre. (It took a decade or so for John Field's activity in the teens and twenties to spawn sustained interest among other composers.) Feminine imagery did not cease after this point; indeed it continued with something of a vengeance. Rather than immediately quoting some of these later nineteenth-century formulations of the feminine topos, though, I want to consider some of the historical and critical ramifications of the evidence we have seen thus far.

Demography and the Feminine

What can have prompted a gendered response to the piano nocturne? Demography offers one obvious answer: women were far and away the primary consumers of piano music in the first half of the nineteenth century (just as they had been of keyboard music generally in the eighteenth century). Any number of sources confirm this. We have known for some time, through the work of Arthur Loesser, William Weber, and Judith Tick in particular, that women played most of the keyboards found in middle-class homes throughout Europe and the

United States in the eighteenth and nineteenth centuries.[15] A pair of citations culled from periodicals in the two decades of concern to us suggests the ubiquity of female pianists in Paris. First, the journalist Henri Blanchard in 1843:

> Since it is recognized that the professor of the piano has a high public usefulness, we must be permitted to inquire what are the qualities most suitable for properly fulfilling this important mission. Since he often has to do with young girls, it is necessary, so far as this is possible, that he be married, in the interests both of morals and of the security of parents.[16]

Second, an even more direct correspondent, writing in 1835 for the periodical *Le pianiste:*

> The piano today shares popular favor with singing, and that is true because, though I do not wish to favor other instruments, the two specialties are exclusively the province of women.[17]

Stunningly, Loesser also deduced, from a statistical survey printed in the *Revue et Gazette musicale de Paris* in 1845, that the presence of some 60,000 pianos in Paris at that time meant that something like one woman out of five living in the city had some kind of facility at the keyboard.[18] Even allowing for some exaggeration in Loesser's estimate, it still suggests that a remarkable percentage of the female population was engaged in music making at the piano.

Iconographic evidence further bolsters this written and statistical testimony. Writing about the eighteenth century, and surmising from evidence found in paintings from the time, Richard Leppert has suggested that keyboard instruments were conceived as "both signifiers and insurers" of the domestic role of women. He has also demonstrated the currency of this conception in the early nineteenth century, as embodied in portraits of British subjects in India, and as reflected in aspects of the physical design and function of pianos from the period.[19] Engravings and paintings of the sort reproduced in Figure 2.1 were common coin in the first half of the nineteenth century, suggesting that the association of the piano with the domestic world continued unabated from the previous century. The comments of Henri Blanchard in 1847 leave no doubt about the matter:

> Cultivating the piano is something that has become as essential, as necessary, to social harmony as the cultivation of the potato is to

Figure 2.1 Karl Eduard Süffert, *Hausmusik am Abend*, ca. 1840. Historisches Museum Basel.

the existence of the people . . . The piano provokes meetings between people, hospitality, gentle contacts, associations of all kinds, even matrimonial ones . . . and if our young men so full of assurance tell their friends that they have married twelve or fifteen thousand francs of income, they at least add as a corrective: "My dear, my wife plays piano like an angel."[20]

Beyond Demography: The Feminized Detail

But demography by itself cannot explain the affinity of feminine imagery to the nocturne. While women and the piano were clearly paired in the general consciousness of many nineteenth-century observers, the feminine topos did not extend to all genres of piano music. We rarely encounter it, for example, in treatments of polonaises and scherzos. This begins to suggest that demographic factors might primarily have provided a conducive atmosphere for the trope, and that other cultural constructions impinged on the nocturne in such a way as to help reinforce its characterization as a feminine genre.

Perhaps the most obvious of these ideas was the ancient association of women with notions of darkness and night.[21] Less intuitively apparent, but playing just as significant a constructive role in the musical culture of the time, was the persistent alignment of the idea of detail with the feminine. Naomi Schor has drawn attention to the marking of detail as a feminine aesthetic category.[22] She observes a pattern of associating particularity with the feminine extending at least as far back as Aristotle. The very antiquity of the association ultimately lent it the status of a semi-scientific fact, which could then be mustered, along with other unchallenged tropes like the presumed close affinity of women and nature, to help "explain" and evaluate the respective contributions of men and women to the creative arts.

Schor finds support for her reading of detail in scholarship on the visual arts. Thus Ernst Gombrich's observation that associations of crowded detail with feminine taste can be traced to the rhetorical manuals of classical antiquity leads Schor to see a similar alignment of sexual and aesthetic categories informing Sir Joshua Reynolds's critical evaluations of artistic schools.[23] This in turn helps account for Reynolds's slight preference for the sublime Roman art of Raphael and Michelangelo over the ornamental Venetian art of Titian and Veronese.

And the cultural resonances of this alignment were not limited to the art of the Italian peninsula. Rather, in the dominant Southern view, they mirrored what was perceived as a larger opposition between the universalist Italian tradition of art and the particularist Dutch tradition. Svetlana Alpers cogently argues that the persistent privileging of Southern over Northern art, and the consequent exclusion of Dutch art from the "great tradition," derive in large part from covert associations of Dutch art with the feminine.[24] From the Renaissance on, Italians had difficulty coming to grips with Dutch art, and often expressed this by calling Dutch art an art for women. For example, a remark attributed to Michelangelo dismisses Flemish painting as appropriate only for certain classes of viewers: "Flemish painting . . . will . . . please the devout better than any painting of Italy. It will appeal to women, especially to the very old and the very young, and also to monks and nuns and to certain noblemen who have no sense of true harmony."[25] Alpers remarks that "to say an art is for women is to reiterate that it displays not measure or order but rather, to Italian eyes at least, a flood of observed, unmediated details drawn from nature."[26] And, as Schor notes, the problem of this flood of details for Italian observers was that they threatened the relationship of the periphery to the center. They seemed to subordinate the background to the foreground.[27]

Schor's analysis of the gendered role of detail in Western culture is suggestive for our discussion of the "feminine" nocturne. The brevity of a nocturne, along with its typically ornate melodies, would presumably have led nineteenth-century listeners to focus more on momentary surface details of its construction than on the sorts of larger-scale processes that might enter into their experience of a more expansive work. And if this were so, their preoccupation with such details would help to reinforce the sexual characterization of the genre.

An article by August Kahlert from an 1835 issue of the *Neue Zeitschrift für Musik* supports this contention. The title, "Genre Painting in Modern Music" *(Die Genrebilder in der modernen Musik)*, reveals its goal: to articulate an explicit link between French genre painting (which grew out of the Dutch tradition) and the recent glut of short instrumental compositions.[28] Kahlert drew what he saw as alarming parallels between the situation in contemporary art, where genre painting seemed to profit at the expense of historical subjects, and that in music, where small instrumental genres gained with a resulting loss of larger kinds. And what is more important, the criticisms he leveled at the smaller "genre-pieces" drew on the same kinds of gender-based rationalizations that Alpers and Schor documented in Michelangelo and Reynolds:

> Genre painting has also become visible in music. It is characteristic that enthusiasm for the great, the far-reaching, the deep must make way for a multitude of small designs, accomplished forms for the graceful, charming, coquettish [gefallsüchtigen]. The lowest and most popular music genre, dance music even, must have recourse to the most expensive finery in order to corrupt the meaning. Dramatic music is with the greatest of pleasure composed of nothing but small forms (Romances, Couplets, Lieder, etc.). The catalogues swarm with Sketches, Eclogues, Impromptus, Bagatelles, Rhapsodies, Etudes, etc. One wants as much variety as is possible, however nothing but the small. Because however the newer art works are too weak to represent themselves, a content is therefore pressed upon them, and thus arise instrumental pieces with literary titles [Ueberschriften].[29]

Kahlert's descriptive language reveals the role of gender in the formulation of his aesthetic stance. The notion that "finery" might "corrupt the meaning" of a genre piece already deflects judgment onto a gendered criterion. Still more telling in this regard are his polar oppositions that pit "far-reaching" and "accomplished forms" against "coquettish" and "small designs." Later in the article he mentioned Chopin as one of the purveyors of musical genre pictures, even including Chopin, with Paganini, among those whose use of the concept struck Kahlert as "pathological" (krankhaft).

Kahlert confirms that the gendered resonances of detail as outlined by Schor also were felt in the world of music. Hence, we can securely assert that, in addition to the demographic environment of the nocturne, its very brevity and ornateness also encouraged its perception as "feminine" music.

Gender and the Devaluation of the Nocturne

The significance of this assertion goes beyond its affirmation of the historical affinity of the nocturne and the feminine. For to be associated with the feminine was also often to be devalorized.[30] How did this side of the aesthetic equation affect perceptions of the nocturne? We have already witnessed in Kahlert's commentary a general censure of Chopin on grounds that had partly to do with feminine associations (although in other forums he praised the composer).[31] And recall these words of Ferdinand Hand: "The representation of sentiment in the notturno runs the danger of falling into the effeminate and languishing, which displeases stronger souls and altogether tires the listener."

The negative tone should not surprise us. Indeed, given the prevailing attitude of the time in which affiliation with women and with effeminacy usually led to a lesser ranking in the aesthetic hierarchy, it would have been odd if the nocturne had escaped unscathed. But what is striking is how what was only an occasional trope in the criticism of the 1830s and 1840s grew to an almost obsessive preoccupation of writers in the second half of the nineteenth century. They theorized the feminine as a lack. A relatively mild sample of such disapproval comes from an article on the nocturne in Arrey von Dommer's *Lexicon* of 1865:

> NOTTURNO: The character of this piece of music is usually given to a gentle and quiet rapture, without thereby excluding cheerfulness, however elevated ideas and artful arrangement of the same remain distant from it. The whole amounts more to an agreeable amusement and awakening of a mellow frame of mind [*milder Gemüthsstimmungen*] than to an energetic stimulation of deep feelings and passions. For that reason, modern piano music, like other so-called character pieces as well as the notturno, is precisely suitable to sentimentalize and gush over [*empfindeln*] as much as possible, without worry of encroachment on the harmony of the tea table [*der Harmonie des Theetisches*] by awakening strong feelings and thoughts.[32]

Von Dommer did not directly invoke the feminine, but his aesthetic categories nonetheless can be read as covertly representing sexual differences. He distinguished the "gentle and quiet rapture" of the nocturne from the "elevated ideas and artful arrangement" that might be encountered in other, unnamed genres. The passive categories of "agreeable amusement" and "mellow frame of mind" run up against the more active "energetic stimulation" and "deep feelings." He labeled "sentimentality" and "gushing over" as characteristics of the genre: two more feminine categories in the minds of listeners in the late nineteenth century could hardly be imagined. By the time we reach the end of von Dommer's definition, we have little doubt as to which sex might be sitting about the tea-table avoiding "strong thoughts."

Later nineteenth-century critics—*male* critics, I should now begin to stress—obsessively disparaged music that they associated with femininity and effeminacy. It should therefore come as no surprise that this was the only time in which Chopin's nocturnes were frequently reproached, even by critics who were otherwise well-disposed toward the composer. Frederick Niecks, who authored the first great biography of Chopin in 1888, had this to say about the nocturnes:

> Among Chopin's nocturnes some of his most popular works are to be found. Nay, the most widely-prevailing idea of his character as a man and musician seems to have been derived from them. But the idea thus formed is an erroneous one; these dulcet, effeminate compositions illustrate only one side of the master's character, and by no means the best or most interesting.[33]

Earlier in the same work, Niecks had remarked on the qualities that gave variety to the compositions he admired more than the nocturnes:

> Another prejudice, wide-spread, almost universal, is that Chopin's music is all languor and melancholy, and, consequently, wanting in variety. Now, there can be no greater error than this belief. As to variety, we should be obliged to wonder at its infiniteness if he had composed nothing but the pieces to which are really applicable the epithets dreamy, pensive, mournful, and despondent. But what vigor, what more than manly vigor, manifests itself in many of his creations![34]

If Niecks's "epithets" here are not precisely those he used in his discussions of the individual nocturnes, they revolve in the same expressive orbit. What the nocturnes lacked, in his view, was "manly vigor," a quality he located elsewhere in the composer's oeuvre.

A few years later, James Huneker contributed these rambling thoughts on the nocturnes:

> Chopin is so desperately sentimental in some of these compositions. They are not altogether to the taste of this generation; they seem to be suffering from anæmia. However, there are a few noble nocturnes; and methods of performance may have much to answer for the sen-

timentalizing of some others. More vigor, a quickening of the time-pulse, and a less languishing touch will rescue them from lush sentiment . . . Most of them are called feminine, a term psychologically false. The poetic side of men of genius is feminine, and in Chopin the feminine note was over emphasized—at times it was almost hysterical—particularly in these nocturnes.[35]

By now, the construction of gender behind Huneker's repeated use of such adjectives as "sentimental" is clear. But it is interesting to witness Huneker's reaction to these and other "feminine" traits. He did not, like Niecks, simply consign the nocturnes to a lesser hierarchical category. Rather, he tried, in Judith Fetterley's clever neologism, to "immasculate" some of the nocturnes.[36] First Huneker urged a less "sentimental," more "vigorous" performance of them. And then he attempted to co-opt altogether the explicit characterization of them as "feminine" by questioning the psychological validity of the concept. If (in a common romantic trope) "femininity" is the "poetic side of men of genius," then it becomes somehow less related to actual sex, and more a "neutral" (or neutered) feature of gifted men.[37]

Devaluations of Chopin's nocturnes were usually framed in terms of general praise for his output as a whole and at least guarded recognition of his achievements in the nocturnes themselves. Nonetheless, in these negative judgments we can still detect the reflection of a larger issue in women's history. For throughout the nineteenth century, and in many different spheres of creative work, genres that were primarily the purview of men (as producers and/or consumers) were privileged. Genres cultivated by women, on the other hand, were relegated to the margins of the aesthetic horizon. Writing of an earlier period, Janet Todd has argued that the belittlement of sentimental writing in the late eighteenth century derived in part from its association with women readers and writers; reactions against it were often framed in terms of manliness, of men speaking to men.[38]

These are precisely the terms we encounter a century later in the criticisms of Niecks and Huneker.[39] Each in his own way longed for "masculine vigor" to conquer the "feminine" qualities he found in Chopin. In adopting this outlook, Niecks and Huneker took part in the broader cultural project that granted privileged status to the larger musical genres practiced by men. This attitude too would work against Chopin in the late nineteenth and early twentieth centuries, in the commonplace derogation of his efforts in larger genres like the concerto and sonata. Critics of the time found it simply implausible that the "feminine" Chopin could craft a sonata that measured up to the great tradition of Mozart and Beethoven.

If we in recent times have repressed most of these explicit associations of feminine imagery with the nocturne, then by what process was the genre "retrieved" from the feminine sphere early in the twentieth century? A shift in thinking about the genre—at least as it related to Chopin—can be detected early in the twentieth century in diverse sources, including pianists and analysts. Artur Rubinstein frequently gave himself credit for steering interpretations of Chopin away from the "salon style"—itself an encoded reference to "women's music"—of the late nineteenth century. In his memoirs, Rubinstein disparaged the performances of Chopin he attended as a youth, which led him initially to adopt, as he wrote, "the generally accepted opinion of Chopin as the young, sick, romantic figure who wrote sentimental music for the piano." But his epiphany came when he was able to hear "Chopin's music as it should sound," that is, expressing, among other virtues, "dignity and strength," qualities found in his favorite composer of the time, Brahms.[40]

Theorists did not state their positions quite so baldly, but the very fact that the likes of Heinrich Schenker and Hugo Leichtentritt devoted serious analytical attention to the nocturnes of Chopin served to "validate" the genre by negating its gendered past. Analyses like Schenker's that sought to lay bare the background structure of a musical work glossed over the same sense of detail that helped link the nocturne with the feminine in the first place. Analytical detail remained, of course, but of a "deep," not "surface" variety, and of a sort that commentators like Kahlert already in the nineteenth century would have found appropriate to "great, German" art.[41]

The first genre Leichtentritt examined in his analytical overview of Chopin's music was the nocturne, and his introductory comments are instructive for the way in which they situate Chopin's contributions to the genre in history. Leichtentritt cited Field and Schubert as progenitors of the Chopin nocturnes. He also specified generic, formal, melodic, and harmonic ties to works of Mendelssohn, Schumann, Liszt, Rossini, Bellini, Grieg, Brahms, and Wagner.[42] But he nowhere linked the genre to women; his language avoids even covertly feminine imagery. In effect, his chronicle of affiliations asserts that Chopin's nocturnes took part solely in the great tradition of male masterworks. Yet by stressing ties with other composers and neglecting associations with women, Leichtentritt told only part of the story: he neutralized the past. By such routes the nocturne eventually lost much of its explicit affinity to the feminine.

Nocturnal Love Songs and the Female Listener:
"Voice" and the "Double-Voiced Discourse"

While I have thus far stressed only the tendency toward feminine imagery in reactions to the nocturne, this was not the only type of response to the genre in the nineteenth century. The generic origins of the piano nocturne, which grew out of the vocal kind of the same name, also led to a situation in which both the conception and perception of the nocturne were bound to metaphors associated with "voice"—by which term I refer collectively to figures that evoke vocal music rather than to Edward Cone's concept of musical personae.[43] In 1839, Carl Czerny described the expectations many listeners brought to the genre:

> The *Notturno* for the Pianoforte is really an imitation of those vocal pieces which are termed *Serenades,* and the peculiar object of such works—that of being performed by night, before the dwelling of an esteemed individual—must always exercise an influence upon its character.[44]

Czerny implied that many listeners understood the piano nocturne to be roughly equivalent to its vocal counterpart; they viewed it quite literally as a "song without words." And Czerny's identification of the piano nocturne as a transmutation of its vocal namesake receives confirmation from another, very different source. The frontispiece to the Hofmeister edition of Ignacy Felix Dobrzyński's *Trois Nocturnes pour le pianoforte,* op. 21, sports an engraving (see Figure 2.2). A man, accompanying himself on a guitar, sings the nocturne to his beloved, who watches from her window.[45] Another amorous couple strolls in the darkened street in the background. Cupid, silhouetted by the moon, surveys the entire scene, arrow ready to fly from his bow. This narrative alone would suggest that vocal associations were part of the

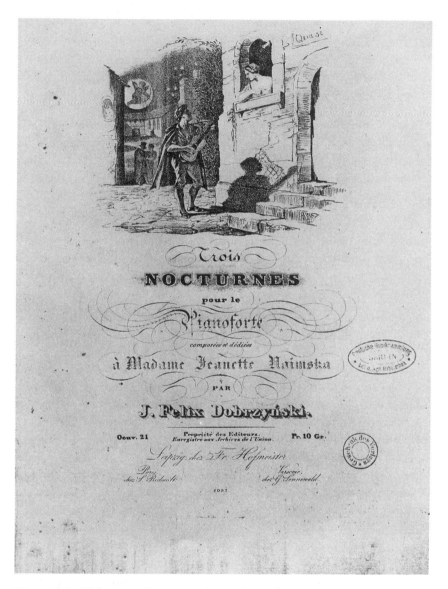

Figure 2.2　Title page, [Ignacy] Felix Dobrzyński, *Trois Nocturnes pour le pianoforte*, op. 21, ca. 1835. Staatsbibliothek Preussischer Kulturbesitz.

piano nocturne; it seems to translate graphically Czerny's words about the "peculiar object" of nocturnes, "that of being performed by night, before the dwelling of an esteemed individual." And a quick survey of some poetic texts for vocal nocturnes, which tend to be addressed from men to women, confirms the ubiquity of the performing situation represented in the engraving.[46]

But if a nocturne in one sense represented to nineteenth-century minds a kind of love poem sung by a man to a woman, how could it also be perceived, to recall our earlier discussion, as a mirror of the feminine spirit? On the one hand, a nocturne found its embodiment in the actions of a man; on the other hand, it expressed the soul of a woman. The genre appears to have been engendered in contrary ways. How can we account for this contradiction?

Again, we need to remind ourselves that both of these visions of the nocturne were articulated primarily by men. Thus, as Ruth Solie has suggested in connection with the impersonation of women's experience in Schumann's *Frauenliebe und -leben,* the disparity mostly informs us about the mindset of men at the time: it cannot be taken as an accurate representation of feminine response to the genre.[47] Instead, we can see in it an idealized conception of women of the sort that proliferated in the late eighteenth and nineteenth centuries (Solie mentions Goethe's *das ewig Weibliche*). Through the simultaneous portrayal of the nocturne as a woman's "entire life" (to quote again Fink's review of Chopin's Nocturnes, op. 15), but a life somehow oriented toward being courted by a man, the message of the genre served to reinforce a widespread ideological stance.

But what of the responses of women to this ideology? How might a female pianist of the time have reacted to what must have been a typical situation for her performance of a nocturne? Here again, the same environment that Ruth Solie imagined for a singer of *Frauenliebe und -leben* must also have existed for a pianist performing a nocturne (see Figure 2.1). She likely played in a house in front of men; the nocturne was probably written by a man; its expressive message was determined by men, and the ultimate point of the message was the satisfaction to be gained in being wooed by a man. To be sure, for some such pianists the situation would have seemed entirely "normal," and not worthy of reflection.

But just as surely, for others the asymmetry in this state of affairs

would have seemed anything but normal. I make this assertion for
two reasons. First, the rising subculture of women's movements across
Europe in the nineteenth century suggests that the mainstream ideological message of the nocturne cannot have had an absolutely secure
hold on all listeners. And second, scholars of women's history have
uncovered instance after instance of women challenging a pervasive
mode of interpretation forced upon them by men. Two particularly
moving examples concern artistic portrayals of male sexual aggres-
sion. First, Mary D. Garrard convincingly shows that the expressive
core of Artemisia Gentileschi's painting of *Susanna and the Elders*
resides in the victim's plight, not the villains' anticipated pleasure as
in other, more familiar versions of the subject.[48] Garrard further argues that Gentileschi's sympathetic treatment of the Susanna theme
owed much to her own feelings of sexual vulnerability at the time of
the painting, a year before she was actually the victim of a rape. And
second, Janet Todd records the outrage of one of Samuel Richardson's
first readers, Lady Echlin, upon reading *Clarissa*. So disturbed was
Lady Echlin that she composed a new ending to protect herself against
"those passages so horribly shocking to humanity."[49]

All of this suggests the likelihood that some listeners (lay and professional alike) might not have entirely accepted the prevalent image
of the nocturne in the nineteenth century. Surely some performances
of nocturnes encountered listeners who at least partially resisted the
ideological message of the genre, who questioned the need to "listen
like men" to this "feminine" kind.[50] (If we grant this point, we can
further imagine the possible variety of experiences enfolded in performances of nocturnes: male composers impersonating female experience, men listening to women, women listening like men [listening
to women], women trying not to listen like men [listening to
women]—everything, it would seem, but women listening like
women.) And to judge from evidence in the representational arts of
the nineteenth century, we might expect that the listeners who challenged or questioned the patriarchal tradition may well have found
themselves in a particularly ambiguous relationship to this practice.

But we need to go beyond speculation. For the instrumental nocturne, can we uncover traces of female listeners who, although depen-
dent upon a patriarchal frame of reference, nonetheless intimated
woman-centered meanings? Or, said another way, can we find

evidence of a "double-voiced discourse" in the realm of the nocturne?[51]

The Composer as Listener: Two Nocturnes by Women

At the present time, we have only limited documentation of specific feminine responses to music. Whereas one can investigate the reactions of men of Chopin's time with relative ease—men were the critics for the newspapers, and the correspondence and diaries of well-known male composers tend to be published in some form—the responses of women, who were for the most part excluded from journalism and were not well-known composers, are not as directly retrievable.

For a few notable figures like Clara Wieck Schumann and Fanny Mendelssohn Hensel, however, we have excellent access to their correspondence and diaries.[52] Occasional passages in these published sources support a tentative hypothesis that some women were trained to "listen like men," and moreover, that this experience led to a conflict or internal division. Clara Wieck's diaries and correspondence provide good examples. As is well known, she held contradictory feelings about her work as a composer, at times she was very happy with her efforts, at times quite displeased. But the terms in which she expressed her displeasure could be revealing. For instance, on 11 November 1839 she wrote in her diary:

> I once believed that I possessed creative talent, but I have changed my mind about this idea; a woman [*ein Frauenzimmer*] must not wish to compose—no one has yet been able to do it, should I be destined for it? that would be arrogant, something with which only my father once tempted me in earlier times, but I soon changed my mind about this belief. May Robert only still create; that should always make me happy.[53]

And about her own Trio, she wrote in her diary on 2 October 1846:

> There is no greater pleasure than composing something oneself and then listening to it. There are some nice passages in the Trio, and I believe it is also rather well done in its form, naturally it still remains women's work [*Frauenzimmerarbeit*], which always lacks force and here and there invention.[54]

Wieck deprecated herself in terms drawn directly from the prevailing male ideology of the day. Particularly striking is her definition of "women's work" as that which "lacks force," for the description could be transferred intact into many of the reviews and descriptions of the nocturne cited earlier.

Yet another means of understanding how women in the first half of the nineteenth century might have listened to nocturnes is to examine nocturnes composed by them. This is both to view these composers as a special category of listener and to treat their nocturnes as responses (at least partly) to the predominantly male generic tradition. And it is also to invoke, for the first time in this chapter, the vocabulary of traditional musical analysis. But while the jargon may be familiar to musicologists, the use to which I put it differs in one crucial way from ordinary musicological practice: I explicitly mean my analytical observations to serve as representations of documented early nineteenth-century perceptions of the genre. Because all representations of this sort are incomplete translations of the past, heavily burdened by and implicated in the present, it might therefore seem that I am guilty of mere sleight-of-(critical)-hand, promoting as new method the same tired bag of analytical tricks. But this undervalues the significance of the move from understanding familiar analytical idioms as expressions of an ideal or individual listener to grasping them as socially constructed representations. Shifting from a univocal to a polyvocal analytical discourse at least raises the possibility of bringing the aims of feminism and those of musical analysis into a similar critical orbit.

I want to focus primarily on a *Notturno* by Clara Wieck, and to a lesser degree on one by Fanny Hensel. These two stunning examples of the genre stand in some interesting ways apart from the efforts of Field and Chopin.[55] The Wieck *Notturno* forms part of her *Soirées musicales,* op. 6, which was composed in 1835–1836, and published in 1836.[56] The autograph manuscript of Hensel's *Notturno* bears the date 15 October 1838; the work, which she withheld from publication, was first printed only in 1986.[57]

In musical outline, including its harmonic inventiveness, treatment of dissonance, rhythmic variety, clever disposition of form, and wistful coda, the Wieck nocturne is an extraordinary work. But our main concern here is what the piece might tell us about Wieck's reading of the generic tradition. In this regard, two excerpts seem particularly noteworthy: the opening measures of the piece, and its middle section

(Examples 2.1a and 2.1b). In both of these passages, Wieck revealed herself as a progressive. Rather than following the model of Field, she instead adapted innovative gestures introduced into the genre by Chopin only a few short years earlier.

First the opening. Beginnings are strategically crucial to any genre, for along with the title, they can establish the appropriate mental frame for the apprehension of the generic codes of the work. In the first few measures of nocturnes, Wieck's included, several features generally help evoke the gentle and ethereal spirit that commentators (and presumably listeners) of the day identified with the genre.[58] But like only the nocturnes of Chopin before, the Wieck piece at the same time

a.

b.

Example 2.1   Clara Wieck, *Notturno,* op. 6, no. 2.

seems surreptitiously to subvert the feeling of surface stability at the start. We can detect two elements of the opening that undercut stability: (1) the tonic pedal (that is, the reiterated F in the left hand), which, occurring so early in the piece, produces a feeling of anticipatory tension—we expect change, not stasis, at this juncture of a work—and (2) the cunning placement of the dissonant and unstable augmented triad (f–a–c♯) as accompaniment for the first notes of the melody. (The augmented triad becomes a kind of reference sonority in the piece, recurring in each statement of the primary tune as well as in the transition back to the reprise and the coda.) Hence the opening measures of the Wieck nocturne subtly undermine the "normal" associations of serenity that attached to the genre and substitute in their place a kind of latent dynamism.

The functionally contrasting middle section of the Wieck nocturne (it projects a different mood from the opening section) again runs counter to Field's conception of the genre, and instead sides with Chopin's—but only to a degree. Before Chopin, middle sections themselves were infrequent in nocturnes, and when they did appear, they mostly left undisturbed the generic mood of tranquillity. Chopin however introduced radical shifts in mood in his middle sections; initially he did so chiefly by importing techniques from a foreign genre, the etude (good examples occur in the middle sections of the Nocturnes in B Major, op. 9, no. 3, and F Major, op. 15, no. 1).

These agitated middle sections departed so sharply from the Fieldian tradition of the genre that a wide spectrum of Chopin's listeners, including the progressive Robert Schumann, doubted the propriety of the gesture.[59] Yet no other innovation was so quickly recognized as deriving specifically from Chopin. Wieck's decision to adopt a contrasting middle section would plainly have linked her with Chopin in the minds of her contemporaries.

Nonetheless, the middle section in the Wieck nocturne sounds different from the typical example in early Chopin: the sense of contrast with the opening section seems more muted. It is as though Wieck decided to take a position midway between the older Fieldian tradition and Chopin's recent challenge to this tradition. Through her nocturne, she seems to assert that, although the addition of functional contrast adds positively to the generic tradition, this contrast needs to be kept in check so that it does not upset listeners by apparently referring to foreign genres like the etude.[60]

From these passages we gain a sense of Wieck's precarious struggle with the prevailing discourse on the nocturne. (Her diaries have already framed this characteristically ambiguous stance for us.) On the one hand, undermining the calm of the opening in favor of a latent dynamism suggests a rebuttal to (or a complication of) the notion that only placid sensations are appropriate to the opening of a "feminine" nocturne. On the other hand, muting the vigor of the Chopin-like middle section suggests a fear that such assertiveness, left unchecked, might ultimately co-opt the nocturne out of the feminine sphere, and so deprive women of one of the few genres deemed appropriate for them. Wieck faced a powerful predicament, both straining against and constrained by the culturally constructed values of musical "assertiveness." And only in some idyllic realm of fantasy could she have found a homogeneous resolution to this predicament. Hence, just as the genre transmitted a message of conflicted identity of gender, so too Clara Wieck must have been divided against herself in her response to the "feminine" nocturne.

The story of Wieck's nocturne does not end here, for the piece also figured as an encoded sign of Robert Schumann's love for Wieck during their clandestine engagement. On 6 February 1838, Robert wrote to Clara about his recent burst of creative activity:

> And then I have also been composing an awful lot for you in the last three weeks—jocular things, Egmont stories, family scenes with fathers, a wedding, in short extremely charming things—and called the whole Novelettes [sic], because you are named Clara and Wieckettes does not sound good enough.[61]

Imagining Clara, but unwilling to name her publicly, Schumann drew his title from the name of another well-known musical Clara, the singer Clara Novello. And five days later, with the *Novellettes* still fresh on his mind, Robert let slip, unconsciously perhaps, the presence of another covert musical signal to Clara:

> Do you know what the most precious thing [*das Liebste*] of yours is for me—Your Notturno in F Major in six-eight time. What do you think about that? It is sufficiently melancholy [*Schwermüthig*], I think. Then the Trio from the Toccatina.[62]

(That Schumann also loved the Trio from the *Toccatina*, the first piece in the *Soirées musicales*, is not surprising, given that it practically du-

plicates the melody and harmony of the opening theme of the following *Notturno*.) When Clara finally saw the completed *Novellettes*,
however, the signal became clear, for Robert had incorporated—without attributing it (contrary to his practice with other borrowings from
Wieck)—the opening tune of the *Notturno* into his eighth *Novellette*.
Schumann first introduced the theme as an eerily interruptive "distant
voice" *(Stimme aus der Ferne)* at the end of the Trio II, and then
recalled it twice in varied form (the variations are substantial enough
that we might better say that he transformed the expressive character
of Wieck's theme—see Examples 2.2a–c).

This tale of the immediate reception of the *Notturno* bears telling
for two reasons. First, and most directly related to the argument of
this chapter, Schumann's identification of the *Notturno* as Wieck's
"most precious" work shows yet one more way in which the genre
served both to shape and to reinforce commonly held ideas of femininity. In other words, I think it significant that he prized precisely a
nocturne and not a ballade, mazurka, polonaise, impromptu, or piano
concerto (to name other genres in which Clara had worked to that
point). For Robert, the *Notturno* not only embodied a generalized
feminine spirit, it also represented quite literally his beloved Clara. We
can therefore read his favoring of it as a sign that the piece did not
significantly upset his musical expectations for a nocturne. And should
Robert have sensed any generic dissonance arising from Clara's au-
thorship in a genre that ordinarily was understood to recall the love
song of a man to a woman, his appropriation of her principal theme
in the *Novellette* effectively reversed the direction of the address: now
the nocturne—its theme, at least—did quite literally transmit a message of love from a man to a woman. Robert's act of quotation would
have served in part to redress the balance of gender in this nocturne,
and so to lend it a kind of cultural value ordinarily hard won by
"women's" music.

Second, the nature of Schumann's quotation itself may well bear on
Wieck's ambivalent self-image as a composer. For careful comparison
of Clara's theme with its representations in Robert's *Novellette* shows
that even on its initial hearing, Schumann altered Wieck's theme in
several ways. In addition to the obviously disjunctive rhythm of the
accompanimental pattern, which in large measure conveys the effect
of "distance" Schumann wanted, I would note in particular the subtle

harmonic change Schumann made at the moment the melody begins.[63] What had been a straightforward (if unstable) augmented triad in Wieck now becomes, with the addition of the mid-range c♯, a harmonic entity that is a good deal more complicated (it may be scanned either as an F-sharp major triad over a D pedal or as an augmented D triad with a dissonant c♯ appoggiatura). It is difficult to imagine any strong contextual reasons why Schumann would have opted for this c♯; a d may be substituted, restoring the unadulterated augmented triad, without disturbing the framework of the phrase. Rather, as becomes clear in the two variations *cum* transformations of Wieck's theme, neither of which preserves the augmented harmony, Schumann simply "composed out" Wieck's distinctive triad on personal aesthetic grounds.

My point here is not to argue the relative merits of Wieck's harmonization against Schumann's. Rather it is to contemplate the effects that Robert's revision of Clara's theme—and this is not the only instance of such retouching—might have had on her creative psyche.[64] As is the case in so many other facets of Wieck's life, the situation seems fraught with ambiguity. On the one hand, we surely must concur with Nancy Reich's reading of Robert's quotations as evidence of the "uncommon unity" and "extraordinary sharing and flowing of ideas" between the two lovers.[65] On the other hand, we cannot help wondering if Robert's rewriting contributed to Clara's basic indecisiveness over the worth of her own compositions. When quotation becomes transformation, it suggests at the very least a kind of exertion of Robert's self over Clara's, an "authorizing" of the feminine work. And it calls into question the propriety of maintaining, as has one writer, that the two "enjoyed a complete dialogue, made possible by a shared musical heritage."[66] Wieck wrote to Robert that she harbored "a peculiar fear of showing you any of my compositions, I am always ashamed of myself"; and we know that she objected to alterations Schumann suggested for the third *Romance* from her op. 11.[67] When we note in addition that Wieck's sole quotation of Schumann, in her "Variations on a Theme of Robert Schumann," op. 20, is almost entirely faithful to its source (the first *Albumblatt* in Schumann's *Bünte Blätter*, op. 99), we sense that the "dialogue" may have seemed more complete from Robert's side than from Clara's.[68] With such basic asymmetry in compositional outlooks confronting her at every turn,

a.

b.

Example 2.2   Robert Schumann, *Novellette,* op. 21, no. 8.

c.

Example 2.2   *(continued)*

it is no wonder that works such as the *Notturno* seem to emanate conflict.

Fanny Hensel's G-Minor *Notturno* provides a different reading of the tradition of the nocturne. It directly engages the Fieldian model, avoiding the type of contrasting sections imported into the genre by Chopin. Instead its formal process develops out of the juxtaposition of short thematic phrases, the accompaniments of which remain mostly unchanged in style (Example 2.3a shows the opening of the piece). In writing this way, she may have followed a family prejudice: as writers in the 1830s and 1840s noted, her brother Felix Mendelssohn's "Songs without Words" are similarly rooted in the Fieldian nocturne.[69]

Yet Hensel's nocturne at the same time departs from the Fieldian model in one essential way. Roughly two-thirds of the way through the piece, the opening theme returns with sufficient weight as almost—but not quite—to suggest a reprise (Example 2.3b). What gives the

Example 2.3   Fanny Hensel, *Notturno.*

moment its import is that it marks the first unambiguous dominant-tonic cadence in the piece. Earlier, every apparent cadential progression proves to be a deceptive feint, along the way sliding through some fairly extraordinary chromatic byways (Example 2.3c). Chopin, in *his* Fieldian nocturnes, was up to similar tricks (somewhat tentatively in the D-flat Major op. 27, no. 2, and more emphatically in the E-flat Major op. 55, no. 2). But if the first of these pieces at all influenced Hensel (the second had yet to be written), then she plainly went be-c.

Example 2.3   *(continued)*

yond the Chopin model in more decidedly imposing a sense of higher-level structure, of formal return, on the processive phrases.

Like Wieck's *Notturno,* Hensel's at once confronts the generic tradition and is implicated in it too. In itself, this combination of innovation and tradition might not seem noteworthy: the new always comes with an admixture of the old, and a similar pattern could undoubtedly be detected in any competent work in any genre. Yet a common gesture need not arise out of common motives. We need also to consider Hensel's peculiar status as a woman composer. The published correspondence with her brother Felix often reveals a profound ambivalence about composing and publishing, as in this passage written on 22 November 1836:

> With regard to publishing I stand like the donkey between two bales of hay. All the same I have to admit honestly that I myself am rather neutral about it; Hensel wishes it, you are against it. I would of

course comply totally with the wishes of my husband in any other matter, yet on this issue alone it's too crucial for me to have your consent, for without it I might not undertake anything of the kind.[70]

The implied comparison (a manifest one in other letters) of her own talents to those of her brother and the lack of self-confidence that expressed itself through the conscious stifling of her artistic impulses together cast the formal experiment in the *Notturno* in a different light. In other words, to view Hensel's nocturne as simply another exemplar in the great tradition of the genre is to whitewash the most essential feature of its relationship to this tradition. For her experience with the genre plainly differed from that of her male contemporaries. In the end, her challenge to it remained a personal battle; she never published the nocturne.[71] Can we imagine Chopin making the same decision with a piece of this high quality? The message from Fanny Hensel seems to be that challenges to tradition must be confined to private musical statements, that for a woman there lurked unstated dangers in publicly confronting the orthodoxy.

To investigate women and the piano nocturne in the nineteenth century is to uncover stories of devaluation, marginalization, and sometimes outright exclusion—but also to discover intimations of individual voices questioning the patriarchal tradition. We have learned that the association of femininity with the nocturne served to reinforce an idealized male view of womanhood, one that may have had little connection with the perceptions of women themselves. Signs of challenge on the part of female composers were at best muted and ambiguous, at worst held from public view. And when a reaction to the prevalence of this "femininity" in the nocturne began in the second half of the century, the affiliation with women acted like an aesthetic lead sinker on the nocturne, pulling it swiftly down the hierarchy into the murky depths of sentimental salon music.

What do these stories lead us to conclude about the potential of musical analysis for a feminist musicology? On the one hand, I think we still must be wary of the music historian's reflex to analyze. Projects that veer toward a note-by-note mapping of musical discourse onto structures of feminist thought may, by privileging composer-centered concepts over societal ones, unconsciously promote the patriarchal agendas they ostensibly would deny. I have not entirely escaped this tendency here. Yet in the process of examining the nocturnes of two women composers, I have shown how, if situated historically, analysis (or at least close working with the notes) can aid our formation of past musical ideologies. So something like analysis might be of some service to a feminist music history after all. I realize this falls short of a ringing endorsement of the concept. But to wish otherwise is to risk slighting the more significant insights into constructions of gender in music that are likely to follow from the exploration of alternative epistemologies.

⁊ 3 ⁊

Small Fairy Voices:
Sex, History, and Meaning
in Chopin

Ariel, Queen Mab, Trilby, a coterie of unnamed fairies, elves, and
angels: through much of Chopin's life and for generations after he
died, his name and his art were styled metaphorically using these en-
twined terms and others like them. Manifestly a mode of praise, a
means of drawing attention to the ways in which Chopin transported
the purveyor of the metaphor into transcendental and ethereal realms,
these configurations performed another kind of cultural work as well:
they enabled the subject of sex to figure into the understanding of
Chopin.

Sexual meanings in music have lately concerned a number of musicologists. But particularly when they have attempted interpretations
that have to do with "sexuality" and "desire" in instrumental works,
the results of their studies have generally been disappointing.[1] Three
problematic suppositions derail them. First, they assume that the
methods of formalist analysis allow unmediated access to the notions
of "sexuality" and "desire" that are supposedly embedded in the
works under discussion. That is, they equate desire for, say, harmonic
closure with desire for, say, orgasm. Such historically and critically
unfiltered homologies yield crudely literalistic readings of both sex and
music. Second, they tend unreflectively to establish "sexuality" and

"desire" as universalist discourses. In so doing, they risk imposing present-day structures of understanding on cultures in which these concepts, when they were deployed at all, may have been construed differently. And third, they take as the point of departure for their interpretations of individual works the composer's presumed sexual orientation. They then read the composer's "sexuality" as a text that is somehow composed out in a score, and thus discernible through formalist analysis. But this is to allow the figure of the composer to police interpretation in a way that does not stand up to historical or hermeneutical scrutiny.

In this chapter, I want to address these methodological issues by restoring history to the critical matrix. The concern that motivates me is not how music "speaks" sex, how the formal dimensions of the score articulate both a sexual orientation (presumably that of the composer) and sexual experiences. Rather, I want to investigate how sex "spoke" music, how (and if) sex entered into the reception of music at a given historical moment.[2] In what follows, I will outline the history of the otherworldly metaphors that were applied to Chopin, trace the mechanics by which, through multiple deferrals and deflections of meaning, these metaphors were understood to invoke sex, and explore some of the images hazily limned through this unsteady historical process: Chopin as androgyne, Chopin as hermaphrodite, Chopin as sodomite.

Otherworldly Metaphors

People who heard and saw Chopin play the piano, who encountered his music, or who made his acquaintance repeatedly tried to share their experience by evoking various otherworldly beings, in particular fairies, elves, sylphs, and angels. The metaphors first began to attach themselves to accounts of Chopin soon after his immigration to Paris, and continued to configure him not only for the rest of his life, but through the nineteenth century and well into the twentieth.

Chopin's idiosyncratic manner of performing served as one of the most powerful stimuli to flights of otherworldly metaphor. Hector Berlioz, writing in *Le Rénovateur* in 1833 and himself no stranger to associating music with elves and fairies, offered one of the earliest such descriptions, moving beyond the general to compare Chopin to a particular sprite, the title character of Charles Nodier's *Trilby ou le Lutin d'Argail* (1822):

> There are unbelievable details in his Mazurkas; and he has found how to render them doubly interesting by playing them with the utmost degree of softness, *piano* to the extreme, the hammers merely brushing the strings, so much so that one is tempted to go close to the instrument and put one's ear to it as if to a concert of sylphs or elves. Chopin is the *Trilby* of pianists.[3]

In 1836, the young Charles Hallé, recently arrived in Paris, described his first audition of Chopin in a letter to his parents. To the otherworldly menagerie of elves and fairies, Hallé adjoined angels, a particularly common displacement that would also be used to characterize Chopin's personality:

> The same evening [30 November 1836] I went to dine with Baron Eichtal, . . . where I heard—*Chopin.* That was beyond all words . . . Chopin! He is no man, he is an angel, a god (or what can I say more?). Chopin's compositions played by Chopin! That is a joy never to be surpassed. I shall describe his playing another time . . . During Chopin's playing I could think of nothing but elves and fairy dances, such a wonderful impression do his compositions make. There is nothing to remind one that it is a human being who produces this music. It seems to descend from heaven—so pure, and clear, and spiritual. (Eigeldinger, p. 271)[4]

The journalist and founder of *La France musicale,* Léon Escudier, lit upon a particularly felicitous version of the trope in his review of Chopin's Paris recital of February 1842:

> A poet, and a tender poet above all, Chopin makes poetry predominate. He creates prodigious difficulties of performance, but never to the detriment of his melody, which is always simple and original. Follow the pianist's hands, and see the marvellous ease with which he performs the most graceful runs, draws together the width of the keyboard, passes successively from *piano* to *forte* and from *forte* to *piano!* . . . Listening to all these sounds, all these nuances—which follow each other, intermingle, separate and reunite to arrive at the same goal, melody—one might well believe one is hearing small fairy voices sighing under silver bells, or a rain of pearls falling on crystal tables. (Eigeldinger, pp. 293–294)

Chopin's Parisian recital of February 1848 occasioned otherworldly outpourings from diverse critical pens. Commenting in the pages of *La Presse* on the electrifying rumor of Chopin's upcoming concert, Théophile Gautier described the heavenly sensations that Chopin conveyed at the piano:

> Chopin means melancholy elegance, dreamy grace, virginal sensibility, everything that the soul possesses that is delicate, tender, ethereal. He modulates, he sighs on that rebellious instrument and, under his fingers, the keyboard seems brushed by the wing of an angel.

And feeling unconstrained by his failure to attend the actual concert, Gautier continued in a similar vein in his review of the event:

> Chopin, seated between his two wings, pale as a shadow, diaphanous as a sylph, played on a crystal keyboard melodies that have no name in any language, and that musical notation can never have fixed on paper.[5]

A review printed in the *Revue et Gazette musicale de Paris* essayed an especially elaborate Shakespearean version of the supernatural trope:

> A concert by the *Ariel* of pianists is something much too rare to be treated like any other concert where the doors are open to anyone who wants in . . .
>
> That being the case, it was only natural that Pleyel's rooms should have been filled on Wednesday with a select flowering of the most distinguished aristocratic ladies in the most elegant finery. In addition there was also present another aristocracy, that of artists and music lovers, all overjoyed to catch the flight of this musical sylph . . .
>
> The sylph has kept his promise and with what success, what enthusiasm! It is easier to recount the reception he received and the delirium he aroused than to describe, analyze, and reveal the mysteries of a performance that has no equal in our earthly realm. Even if we possessed that pen which traced the delightful marvels of Queen Mab (hardly bigger than the agate which gleams on the finger of an alderman) and her chariot drawn by her diaphanous steeds, it would still be impossible to give an accurate impression of such a talent—one so ideal it hardly seems to belong to the crass world of material things.[6]

This vision of Chopin as the Ariel of the piano resonated strongly among cultural observers of the time, and touched a particular nerve upon the composer's death in 1849. The trope figured centrally in the recollections of his playing that were recounted in several obituaries:

> Perhaps never has any artist more than he had a physique that corresponded to his talent. As frail as he was in body, was he delicate in style: a bit more, he evaporated into the impalpable and imperceptible. His manner of playing the piano resembled no one's: it necessarily disappeared in a vast hall; within reach of a confidant, it was something delicious. One nicknamed Chopin the Ariel of the piano. If Queen Mab had ever wanted to pass herself off as a pianist, it is assuredly Chopin she would have chosen, and only the divine pen that described the fantastic retinue of the dream fairy could analyze the complicated, infinite, and yet as-light-as-lace tangle of that phrase charged with notes, in the folds of which the composer always enveloped his ideas.[7]

> He has been styled the *Ariel* of the piano; but he was also its *Prospero*—a mighty magician, inventing imagery, flowing like an impetuous torrent, whilst his hands were a tornado aggregating the subjects and investing them with piquant and picturesque colouring, alternately pathetic and gay, as his fancy dictated.[8]

Jules Janin explicitly linked the appellation to Chopin's status as an exile, and moreover went on to suggest that this "Ariel" was comprehended most acutely by women:

> Only those who heard him could conceive an idea of this talent so fine, so delicate, so varied, who addressed that which the human soul holds most honest and most charming. He avoided, as others sought to, noise, fanfare and even fame. One called him the Ariel of the piano, and the comparison was just. He grew up in exile, he died there, surrounded by exiles like him, for whom he called to mind the absent country . . .
>   Of all the artists of our day, it is Chopin who most took possession of the soul and spirit of women. His students, and he produced students worthy of him, loved him with a quasi maternal tenderness; they surrounded him with an enthusiasm mixed with veneration, his music so spoke to them an honest and chaste language. Alas! they have lost him, and they cry! They have watched him pass away, they have closed his eyes.[9]

The imagery evoked in Chopin's obituaries continued to color recollections of the Pole's remarkable pianism long after his death. An-

toine-François Marmontel's discussion of Chopin is thoroughly suf-
fused with otherworldly metaphors, the evocation of which leads
effortlessly to the afterworld:

> Fabulous [*romanesque*] and impressionable to an excess, Chopin's
> imagination loved to haunt the world of spirits, to evoke pale phan-
> toms, frightful chimeras. The poet-musician delighted in improvising
> in a penumbra where the indecisive glimmers added a more thrilling
> element to his dreamy thoughts, elegiac plaints, sighs of the breeze,
> somber terrors of the night.
>
> Death, often so prompt to crush stronger organizations, took
> twelve years to destroy, fiber by fiber, the frail nature of Chopin.[10]

Chopin's compositions as well as his style of playing doubtless
played a role in all these recollections, since he typically was heard
performing his own works. Other writers more explicitly deployed
otherworldly metaphors to describe Chopin's compositions. This occurred occasionally during the composer's lifetime, as in the following
comments by J. W. Davison from 1843:

> In taking up one of the works of Chopin, you are entering, as it were,
> a fairy land, untrodden by human footsteps, a path, hitherto unfre-
> quented, but by the great composer himself.[11]

The habit of invoking otherworldly metaphors in order to explain
characteristics of Chopin's compositions grew more common after his
death. Thus Franz Liszt, in his 1851 monograph on the composer,
depicted by means of the supernatural trope the airy fragility of many
of Chopin's works—a fragility that, in his view, also embodied qualities of frustration and aversion:

> In most of Chopin's *Ballades, Valses,* and *Études,* as well as in the
> pieces just mentioned [i.e., the mazurkas, preludes, nocturnes, and
> impromptus], there lies embalmed the memory of an elusive poesy,
> and this he sometimes idealizes to the point of presenting its essence
> so diaphanous and fragile that it seems no longer to be of our world.
> It brings closer the realm of fairies and unveils to us unguarded se-
> crets of the Peri, of Titanias or Ariels or Queen Mabs, of all the genii
> of water, air, and fire, who are also the victims of the most bitter
> frustrations and the most intolerable aversions.
>
> At times these pieces [i.e., the mazurkas] are joyous and fanciful,
> like the gambolings of an amorous, mischievous sylph.[12]

Some half a century later, W. H. Hadow drew on images of fairies in summarizing and evaluating Chopin's creative output. Having averred that Chopin could not be counted among the greatest composers, Hadow instead placed him in a unique realm, attractive only to listeners of "certain moods and certain temperaments":

> We hardly think of him as making a stage in the general course and progress of artistic History, but, rather, as standing aside from it, unconscious of his relation to the world, preoccupied with the fairyland of his own creations. The elements of myth and legend that have already gathered around his name may almost be said to find their counterparts in his music; it is etherial [sic], unearthly, enchanted, an echo from the melodies of Kubla Khan. It is for this reason that he can only make his complete appeal to certain moods and certain temperaments. The strength of the hero is as little his as the vulgarity of the demagogue: he possesses an intermediate kingdom of dreams, an isle of fantasy, where the air is drowsy with perfume, and the woods are bright with butterflies, and the long gorges run down to meet the sea.[13]

We will see below what the lack of "the strength of the hero" meant for Hadow's interpretation of Chopin's creative output.

The otherworldly imagery was also at times mediated through visions of another party playing Chopin's music. The Reverend H. R. Haweis, after first touting music's function as a restorative outlet in the life of women, next turned to the dreams that music might arouse in them. In the following passage, just as remarkable as the embodiment of the "angel of music" in a "weird *nocturno* of Chopin" is the sensuous mood evoked by Haweis's prose style:

> That poor lonely little sorrower, hardly more than a child, who sits dreaming at her piano, while her fingers, caressing the deliciously cool ivory keys, glide through a weird *nocturno* of Chopin, is playing no mere study or set piece. Ah! what heavy burden seems lifted up, and borne away in the dusk? Her eyes are half closed—her heart is far away; she dreams a dream as the long, yellow light fades in the west, and the wet vine-leaves tremble outside to the nestling birds; the angel of music has come down; she has poured into his ear the tale which she will confide to no one else, and the "restless, unsatisfied longing" has passed; for one sweet moment the cup of life seems full—she raises it to her trembling lips.[14]

In the rich imagery of Haweis's rumination, we begin to sense that the angelic trope resonates in ways other than the religious. When angels come to mind, devils often linger at the edges of consciousness as well. This sensuous, sexual side of the supernatural metaphor was drawn upon by Thomas Mann in *Doctor Faustus*. The narrator, Serenus Zeitblom, quotes a youthful letter by the protagonist of the novel, the composer Adrian Leverkühn. Leverkühn turns in his last paragraph to the subject of Chopin:

> Playing much Chopin, and reading about him. I love the angelic in his figure, which reminds me of Shelley: the peculiarly and very mysteriously veiled, unapproachable, withdrawing, unadventurous flavour of his being, that not wanting to know, that rejection of material experience, the sublime incest of his fantastically delicate and seductive art.[15]

That Leverkühn should first sense the angelic in Chopin's persona, and only later in the "sublime incest" of his music, draws attention to another stimulus for the supernatural trope. Chopin's distinctive character occasionally led the composer's associates to employ otherworldly imagery, as for example when Astolphe de Custine signed off a letter with "Farewell, terrible year 1839! and you, inconstant Sylph, allow me a better one!"[16]

George Sand returned almost obsessively to supernatural and especially angelic configurations of Chopin in the early stages of her relationship with the composer.[17] Sand frequently deployed the metaphors in ways that linked Chopin's physical being to his spiritual sensitivities. Thus Sand's marvelous letter to Wojciech Grzymała in which she debates the merits and repercussions of entering into a physically intimate relationship with Chopin—a superb document that sheds real light on the personalities of both Sand and Chopin—is dotted with references to "this angel" and "poor angel."[18] Later, after the two lovers arrived for their storied stay in Majorca, she wrote to her friend Charlotte Marliani about the tenuous state of Chopin's health, and noted: "I care for him like my child. He is an angel of sweetness and kindness!"[19] Writing again to Marliani on 26 April 1839 about the progress of Chopin's recuperation in Marseilles from the illness that struck him in Majorca, Sand invoked the trope in a particularly moving and prescient context:

This Chopin is an angel. His kindness, his tenderness and his patience disquiet me sometimes, I imagine that this organization is too fine, too exquisite and too perfect to exist long in our vulgar and heavy earthly life. Being sick to death at Majorca, he made music that fully smelled of paradise. But I am so used to seeing him in the heavens that it does not seem to me that his life or his death bears witness to anything for him. He does not rightly know himself on what planet he exists. He does not take any account of life as we conceive it and as we feel it.[20]

Sand did not entirely abandon the sobriquet *"un ange"* as the years passed, although it gradually gave way to her favorite affectionate diminutive, *"le petit."* When Sand did refer to Chopin as an angel later in their romance, the term often continued to resonate with concern and sympathy about his health, only now it was modified with an adjective: *"pauvre ange."*[21]

What most strikingly, if perhaps enigmatically, emerges from Sand's reflections on Chopin's character is the way themes of the angelic and the heavenly are juxtaposed with the pathological and the diseased. To begin to understand what was at stake in the conjoining of these concepts, we need to shift our attention away from a chronicle of the trope and explore the diverse and changing cultural significance of it.

The Literary Otherworld and the Ambiguity of Sex

At about the same time that otherworldly metaphors began to attach themselves to Chopin, many of the same symbols enjoyed a vogue in literary, philosophical, and artistic circles throughout Europe, and especially in France. The chronological overlap is not coincidental, and it goes a long way toward explaining some of the particular implications these terms took on for Chopin. For metaphorical representations of him as an angel, sylph, fairy, and elf did not function solely as religious, otherworldly, or supernatural figures of speech. These terms also engaged a complex of unstable meanings having to do with sex and gender, and so ultimately helped forge a changing image of Chopin as an androgynous, hermaphroditic, effeminate, and/or pathological being.

The wide cultural dissemination of otherworldly and androgynous figures having been thoroughly rehearsed in a number of studies, we may forgo a detailed tour of their particular manifestations.[22] It will suffice here simply to recall some of the more consequential invocations of the tropes in two different spheres of activity. The first of these was a body of work, mostly philosophical and religious but encompassing also visual art as well as a handful of fictional writings, that deployed the androgyne in order to represent symbolically higher ideals of unity and integration. Although one can trace this line of thought at least as far back as Plato's *Symposium,* the more relevant tradition dates back to the late eighteenth century, its German branch including such figures as Franz von Baader, Friedrich Schlegel (particularly in the novel *Lucinde*), and Novalis, and its French trunk encompassing Antoine Fabre d'Olivet, Pierre-Simon Ballanche, Prosper Enfantin, Pierre Leroux, Honoré de Balzac *(Séraphîta),* Paul Chenavard, and Gustave Moreau. As A. J. L. Busst notes, this religious-philosophical sphere of thought generally conceived the androgyne in optimistic terms, indeed as symbolic of human brotherhood and solidarity and the original goodness and purity of mankind.[23] Certainly these connotations carried over into the metaphorical configurations of Chopin, particularly in their overt function as a means of praise.

But also conditioning the formulation of metaphors around the composer was a variety of literary constructions of otherworldly and sexually ambiguous characters, many of whom have already been signaled in the quotations gathered above. While some of these figures preserved the general sense of optimism that attached to the religious-philosophical androgyne, others offered a more tempered vision of sexual ambiguity.

These fantastic characters came from diverse sources. The works of Shakespeare, enjoying a newly heightened presence on the early nineteenth-century stage, placed a host of airy sprites before the imaginations of *literati* throughout Europe. Charles Nodier did not admit to direct Shakespearean influence in crafting the eponymous elf of his *Trilby,* but he did allow in his preface that the initial inspirations for the story came from an unnamed work by Sir Walter Scott (an author not far removed, either topically or geographically, from Shakespeare in the minds of many nineteenth-century French), and from a poem by Henri de Latouche entitled "Ariel exilé" (the Shakespearean connection here being explicit).[24] Latouche in turn, through his 1829

novel *Fragoletta,* served as a point of departure for a number of French
fictional works dating from the 1830s that treat themes of otherworldly and sexual ambiguity, including Balzac's *Sarrasine, La Fille
aux yeux d'or* and *Séraphîta,* Théophile Gautier's *Mademoiselle de
Maupin,* and George Sand's *Gabriel.*[25]

The Arch-angel Gabriel

It is worth lingering over the last of these titles. Not only is *Gabriel*
less well known than any other work I have mentioned (none of the
studies I have cited so much as lists its title), but Sand drafted this
roman dialogué in April 1839 in Marseilles during Chopin's recovery
from their harrowing sojourn in Majorca, and hence precisely during
the period when she was most inclined to style the composer as an
angel.[26]

Set in the Renaissance, *Gabriel* tells the story of a young member
of the nobility whose "true" female sex has been disguised from her
since birth. (Following Sand, I will refer to the title character as "him"
when "he" plays a masculine role, and "her" when "she" plays a
feminine role.) This extraordinary state of affairs was orchestrated by
Gabriel's grandfather, Prince of Bramante. In order to ensure that the
family inheritance devolved to his granddaughter's branch rather than
to his grandson's (a violation of the inheritance laws, which favor
exclusively the masculine line), he took steps to raise the girl as a boy,
and, moreover, to train "him" to despise the trappings of the feminine
sex. When Gabrielle discovers her biological sex, the Prince gives her
the option of remaining male and living the life of a prince, or assuming a female identity and joining a convent. But Gabriel(le) rejects the
Prince, instead staking out his/her own existence by posing alterna-
tively as a man and a woman.

In leading the reader through these transformations, *Gabriel* in-
sightfully critiques received notions about gender. It claims that the
supposedly natural qualities that society felt distinguished men from
women were instead fabrications that society inculcated in its members from the earliest age.[27] And, to return to my concerns here, with
its abundance of imagery relating to angels and sexual ambiguity, *Gabriel* clarifies the routes by which metaphorical stylizations of Chopin
as an angel could take on sexual connotations.

Two of the more striking invocations of angels in this work occur in passages charged with ideas of sexual ambiguity. The first takes place in the third scene of the Prologue, where Gabriel's preceptor is attempting to prepare his pupil for the meeting with the Prince, his grandfather, where his "true" sex will be revealed. The early part of the scene revolves around a tension in the respective attitudes toward gender evinced by teacher and student. The preceptor takes care to delineate sharply qualities he presumes appropriate for the different genders (he remains keen to continue instilling a distaste for the feminine in Gabriel), whereas Gabriel seems more ambivalent (at one point he admits, "I do not feel that my soul has a sex, as you often endeavor to demonstrate to me").[28] Before the preceptor can tell Gabriel about the impending visit from the Prince, Gabriel relates a "bizarre" dream he had the previous night:

GABRIEL

In my dream I was not an inhabitant of this world. I had wings, and could fly high enough to traverse other worlds, towards I don't know what ideal place. Sublime voices sang all around me; I saw not a soul, but some light and fluffy clouds, which passed through the ether, reflecting my image, and I was a young girl dressed in a long flowing gown and crowned with flowers.

THE PRECEPTOR

Then you were an angel, and not a woman.

GABRIEL

I was a woman; because all of a sudden my wings became numb, the ether closed in around my head, like the vault of an impenetrable crystal, and I was falling, falling . . . and I had around my neck a heavy chain, the weight pulling me towards the abyss; and then I woke myself, overcome with sadness, weariness and fear . . .[29]

Gabriel's dream functions dramatically to foreshadow the tragic fate that awaits him as a result of assuming a female identity. But it also reveals some of the sexual uncertainty and confusion that surrounded the category of "angel" in 1839. Sand draws on this while a young man (who is "really" a young woman) narrates a dream of transvestism (though again, in "reality" he is cross-dressed as he speaks). And its meaning proves unstable even to the two characters: the preceptor understands the transvestite Gabriel to be an angel (and thus implies that angels are not women, but rather men in women's gowns), which interpretation Gabriel summarily dismisses (without clarifying what he understands an angel to be).

Gabriel's dream recurs later in a situation even more charged with sexual ambiguity, the remarkable mirror scenes of Act II.[30] The scenes take place in Florence during Carnival; Gabriel has been persuaded by his cousin Astolphe to costume himself in women's clothes for the festivities. Posing in front of a mirror after dressing himself, Gabriel "lets out a cry of surprise" and becomes utterly absorbed by the image he sees. When Astolphe, who as yet has no notion of Gabriel's "real" sex, enters, he too is transfixed by the vision of Gabriel in a white silk dress. Astolphe tells Gabriel, "If I were to see you for the first time, I would have no doubt as to your sex . . . In fact, I would fall head over heels in love with you . . . You would immediately become my mistress and my wife."[31] (Indeed, this is precisely what happens after Astolphe learns that Gabriel is "really" Gabrielle.) After telling Gabriel that he "plays his role like an angel," Astolphe goes on to question Gabriel about his costume:

ASTOLPHE

But who placed on your brow this crown of white roses? Do you know that you resemble the marble angels in our cathedrals? Who gave you the idea for such a costume, so simple and so refined at the same time?

GABRIEL

A dream that I had . . . some time ago.

ASTOLPHE

Ah-hah! You dream of angels, do you? Well! don't wake up, because you will only find women in real life![32]

The angel looms as a particularly vertiginous figure as we strain to grasp the dynamics of sex and gender in these scenes. In both instances, the men who interpret Gabriel's dream read into it a kind of transcendental transvestism: Gabriel garbed in a silky white dress represents an angel.[33] For Gabriel, reporting his dream in the Prologue, the angel would seem to denote an apparently unattainable ideal female identity. But in Act II, it signifies in a different way. Gabriel is brought to a kind of crisis of identity precisely at the moment when his male gaze fixes upon her female image in the mirror: the moment seems to wrench him/her free of the moorings of gender, such that he/she can only cry out in surprise—surely the literary envoicing of Michel Poizat's sexually nondifferentiated, operatic "angel's cry."[34] And if the depth of Astolphe's reaction to the mirror-bound Gabriel indicates that he has already guessed the "real" sex of the person in the dress, does the angel then somehow become doubly cross-dressed—a woman passing as a man passing as a woman?[35]

The play of interpretations can continue *ad infinitum,* which is precisely the point. Sand plainly meant the image of the angel in these scenes to act as a decentering device: it accentuates the wobbly basis of the edifice of gender, the critique of which serves as the principal message of this *roman dialogué*. As such, the angelic trope in *Gabriel* plumbs further reaches of sexual ambiguity than do other literary angels from the period.[36] Sand's Gabriel(le) instead seems to anticipate in literary form aspects of Judith Butler's recent challenge to the foundational status of the categories of sex and gender.[37] In Butler's bracing thesis, sex and gender are both performative effects that enact the identities they claim to be. Summarizing her arguments about gender in particular, Butler writes: "Gender ought not to be construed as a stable identity or locus of agency from which various acts follow; rather, gender is an identity tenuously constituted in time, instituted in an exterior space through a *stylized repetition of acts.*"[38] One might comprehend the mirror scene as a performance of Butler's performative theory: it so thoroughly demonstrates the contingency of the notion of being "in drag" as to undercut severely any fixed meaning that this term might have. *Gabriel,* much like *Mademoiselle de Maupin* before it, attacks the basis of commonly held distinctions between male and female by enacting the impossibility of locating any fixed essence in these categories.[39]

And the celebrated figure of the author herself must also have reinforced her challenge to sexual essence. As most readers surely grasped, Sand embodied some of the traits she ascribed to Gabriel(le). This reflexivity appears most obviously in connection with Sand's famous (and overemphasized) penchant for dressing in men's clothes. But more interesting is the case made by Leyla Ezdinli for Sand's literary transvestism.[40] Ezdinli argues that Sand was much the exceptional female writer of her period, not by virtue of her male pseudonym (these were common coin among women writers), but instead because of the public perception of her double gender identity. Among the authorial signatures adopted by women, only "George Sand" was recognized as female but categorized as male, in the sense that Sand possessed the social resources and cultural power of a man. And Sand regularly exploited the rhetoric of her double gender identity in her prefaces, constructing an elusive sense of her authorial persona. "George Sand" itself stood as a fictive category: it was a construct whose very name and whose very societal function worked to undo the fetters of traditional distinctions of gender. Thus *Gabriel* and "George Sand" reflexively frame one another, each buttressing the political and social message of the other.

This reflexivity brings matters back to Chopin. For not only does *Gabriel* inform us of the general means by which angels could take on sexual meanings during Chopin's time, it also tells us of some of the particular constructions implied by Sand when she described Chopin as an angel. Of course, this *ange* was as transgressive in its gender identity as the authorial "George Sand." As fictive, too: Sand's gesture would seem to construct a "Chopin" that mirrored "George Sand," setting in motion a potentially infinite regress of reflected identities akin to that experienced by Gabriel while transfixed by his image in the mirror.[41]

Supernatural Sprites

How did Chopin's becoming attached metaphorically to various elves, fairies, and airy sprites also bring with it implications of sexual ambiguity? At first glance the matter might seem more complex than for angels, since most literary elves, fairies, and sprites have determinate sexual identities (Ariel and Trilby are males, Queen Mab and Titania females).[42] But the issue is not so much the sexual identities of the airy sprites themselves as how a metaphorical affiliation with them might be wielded in interpreting the sexual tendencies of a human being.

Briefly put, although the interactions of literary fairies and elves with other fairies, elves, or even humans of the opposite sex (one of the first things we learn about Trilby is that he is in love with the brunette Jeannie) scarcely differ from those of literary humans, their small stature and high voices—their "small fairy voices"—lead us to think of them not as akin to adults, but rather as childlike.[43] Now if on the one hand children apparently inhabit a realm of innocence with respect to sex, it is also the case, as Michel Foucault has observed, that from the later eighteenth century onward, childhood came to be increasingly sexualized.[44] Thus children occupied a vexed position with respect to reigning ideas about sex: they were thought at once to be pure of it (and hence to a degree asexual) and utterly possessed by it (and thus the object of fierce campaigns against masturbation and other forms of precocious sexual activity). To label an adult male a fairy or an elf in the 1830s and 1840s was to invoke, besides the obvious qualities of lightness, charm, and magic, notions of a being at once removed from sex and possessed by a longing for it.[45] (It may well be through this dual construction that the English word "fairy" came, toward the last decade of the nineteenth century, to stand for a male homosexual, particularly one who, often in the role of prostitute, sought out men who otherwise engaged in sex with women—a figure who, although he stood outside the sexual matrix of the majority of society and was thus in a way inexplicable in its terms, was also clearly given over to a sexual way of life.)[46] To some degree, then, ambiguity for fairies and elves differs from that associated with angels: angels undermine an assured determination of sexual identity, whereas fairies and elves weaken a secure sense of the presence or absence of sexual appetite. Yet as with every other term under consideration here, these two forms of ambiguity cannot really be so neatly separated.[47] We will see that, as they cluster around Chopin, their distinctions readily blur.

Between Androgyny and Hermaphroditism

As we attempt to understand the perpetually shifting terrain of signification around Chopin and otherworldly images, we should examine one more curious bit of documentation from the composer's personal circle. This comes in a letter written in 1842 by the thirteen-year-old Solange Dudevant-Sand. Solange was responding to a missive from her mother, George Sand, who had reported news from their summer home in Nohant. In Solange's reply, after asking for correspondence from her brother, she added the odd request "also tell Sexless to write me" *(dis aussi à Sans-sexe de m'écrire)*—*"Sans-sexe"* would seem to refer jokingly to Chopin.[48] Solange's comment can be read in at least two ways. Most patently, her remark draws on idealized imagery in order to portray Chopin as an asexual being, an androgynous object for adolescent teasing. But *"Sans-sexe"* also invokes the category of sex even as it denies its presence: there do seem to be indications from a few years later that she entertained obsessively sexual feelings for the composer, and that these may have been reciprocated—vaguely, to be sure—by Chopin.[49] Since Solange's elliptical remark resists resolution to one interpretation or the other, *"Sans-sexe"* would then seem to waver between two different characterizations of the composer's sexual ambiguity, the one veering toward asexual and ideal realms, the other bound to the earthily experiential and (given Solange's age and status as George Sand's daughter) the morally divisive.[50]

In its unresolvable semantic slippage, *"Sans-sexe"* thus replicates the disorder that marks the relationship between the two key terms in nineteenth-century perceptions of sexual ambiguity: androgyny and hermaphroditism. As Kari Weil has persuasively contended, these terms have different histories and meanings with respect to the status of the body.[51] The conjoined female and male elements of the androgyne, according to Plato in the *Symposium*, stand for one of the harmoniously whole original states of human beings. The dual nature of the hermaphrodite, as described by Ovid in the *Metamorphoses*, represents the fall from grace of man. Having different histories, however, does not mean that the ideas existed independently from one another. Rather the two notions come to infect one another, the one present relationally to the other, whether this relation is spoken or silent. Already in Plato, at the very first invocation of the term "androgynous" in Aristophanes' speech, after saying that once the word "really meant something," Aristophanes admits that now it is "only used as an insult."[52] What once had delineated an ideal balance and symmetry now derisively and divisively configured a physical body—that of a man interested in same-sex love. This ironic coupling of the androgyne and the hermaphrodite, intertwining an ideal sexual past with an original chaos of the sexes, haunts several of the central Romantic portrayals of sexual ambiguity, as Weil demonstrates through readings of *Lucinde, Séraphîta,* and *Mademoiselle de Maupin.*

Weil's analysis suggests that the metaphors linking Chopin to an idyllic androgyny ordinarily deflect silently toward fragmentary hermaphroditism as well. Occasionally, the traces of this diffraction surface so that a plurality of sexual connotations loosely gathered around the androgyne/hermaphrodite becomes more explicit. Recall, for example, Liszt's evocation of the gauzy frailty of the essence of Chopin's art, an "elusive poesy" that "brings closer the realm of fairies . . . who are also the victims of the most bitter frustrations and the most intolerable aversions." In this formulation, Chopin's music evokes a realm of airy sprites at once magical and quarrelsomely strained and factional. A mystically ideal existence also summons forth an earthy fractiousness.

More commonly, though, the disorderly hermaphrodite remains an absent presence within the androgynous metaphors.[53] Hence the overtly innocuous import of Astolphe de Custine's "inconstant Sylph" was gently to implore more social contact with his distant friend, whose ethereal art and personality he enfolded under the rubric "Sylph." But Custine's imagery imparts another meaning, somewhat analogous to the dual sense of Solange's *"Sans-sexe"*: echoes of bodily frustration ring in his words. As a result of being the focus of one of the more infamous sexual scandals of the early nineteenth century, Custine himself occupied an ambiguous sexual space in the eyes of French society. In 1824 he suffered intense, public opprobrium (as well as a severe beating, which brought the matter to public attention) for apparently having made sexual advances to a young soldier.[54] Without making any suppositions about Custine's intent or about Chopin's response (and, indeed, recognizing the impossibility of discovering any essential position for either subject), "inconstant" and "Sylph" inevitably bear the trace of Custine's sexual history.

Between Hermaphroditism and Sodomy

Custine's brief remark draws attention to another significant deflection in the meanings associated with otherworldly metaphors. "Hermaphrodites" were not just mythological representations of notions of an earthy disorder; they also existed in the "real" world of Chopin's time. Indeed, they came under intense scrutiny in various medical and medico-legal texts that explored the phenomenon of hermaphroditism in what were understood to be its various physical and psychical manifestations. And in this medico-legal discourse, one of the figures to embody these psychical symptoms was the sodomite or pederast.[55]

By describing this figure as the sodomite or pederast rather than the homosexual, I mean to suggest that the culture that gave rise to the otherworldly metaphors around Chopin differed from ours with respect to the ways in which it configured the relationship between sexual practice and identity.[56] In our modern view—which we may trace linguistically and perhaps conceptually back to the later nineteenth century—the categories of "homosexuality," "heterosexuality," and, indeed, "sexuality" itself all ultimately read the genital proclivities of individuals as significant, if at times mysterious, determinants of their character, judgment, personality, taste, and so forth.[57]

The emergence of this modern view marked a significant and complex shift in ways of conceiving human individuals. Foucault famously described the nature of this shift:

> As defined by the ancient civil or canonical codes, sodomy was a category of forbidden acts; their perpetrator was nothing more than the juridical subject of them. The nineteenth-century homosexual became a personage, a past, a case history, and a childhood, in addition to being a type of life, a life form, and a morphology, with an indiscreet anatomy and possibly a mysterious physiology. Nothing that went into his total composition was unaffected by his sexuality . . .
>
> Homosexuality appeared as one of the forms of sexuality when it was transposed from the practice of sodomy onto a kind of interior androgyny, a hermaphrodism of the soul. The sodomite had been a temporary aberration; the homosexual was now a species.[58]

Before this shift, then, for someone of the dominant culture to label a man a sodomite or pederast was not to stake a claim about his fundamental mode of being, at least in ways that approach a late twentieth-century understanding of what a "fundamental mode of being" might resemble. Rather, it was to identify (again, from the perspective of the dominant culture) and ultimately control a pathological symptom of criminal and amoral behavior.[59]

The wish to subject hermaphrodites to juridical control animated Isidore Geoffroy Saint-Hilaire's influential text *Histoire générale et particulière des anomalies de l'organisation* (1832–1837).[60] Geoffroy Saint-Hilaire erected an elaborate forensic apparatus to enable physicians to diagnose properly the many kinds of hermaphroditism that they might encounter. He divided hermaphrodites into two classes, "without excess in the number of parts" and "with excess in the number of parts," which he then subdivided into four and three different orders respectively. The point of these diagnoses was less for the physician to offer therapeutic advice than to determine the "true" sex of the hermaphrodite for the sake of ordaining "his" or "her" civil status with respect to ownership or inheritance of property.[61] The mechanics of teratology, the study of malformations and monstrosities, thus served the same legal system that generated the ambiguities of Gabriel's sexual nature in Sand's *roman dialogué*. Gabriel's ambiguous status represented the kind of subversion of civic laws that Geoffroy Saint-Hilaire's teratological technology aimed to suppress.

Geoffroy Saint-Hilaire maintained for the most part a coolly objective tone throughout his scientific description and analysis. Only twice in the chapters on hermaphroditism did he give vent to moral outrage, both times when he considered the possibility that the abnormal construction of his subjects might lead to sodomitic practices. Under discussion is the second kind of feminine hermaphroditism, wherein the "clitoris is of considerable volume, and simulates a man's penis." According to Geoffroy Saint-Hilaire, this species of hermaphrodite was prone to a mode of behavior whose name he could not bring himself to utter:

> One only knows too well the compensation against nature that these women have sometimes sought in infamous pleasures. I will not soil this page by the picture of this depravation of morals, common enough in antiquity to have motivated the creation of a special word, by which some contemporaries have even wanted to soil our language. But I at least had to recall here the facts that, attested by all the historians, are the unfortunately too authentic proof of the influence exercised by hermaphroditism on the propensities [*penchans*] as well as on the physical organization.[62]

Geoffroy Saint-Hilaire here drew on a well-established specific tradition of labeling women who had sex with other women as hermaph-

rodites, as well as on a more general habit of referring to male sod-
omites by this term.[63] The difference in these traditions was that the
women were often understood to be physical hermaphrodites, while
the men were generally constructed as metaphorical hermaphrodites.

The history of such sodomitic or pederastic meanings attaching
themselves to metaphorical stylizations of Chopin seems to support
the Foucauldian contention that the shift to a modern view of sexuality
took place only in the second half of the nineteenth century. For sodomitic meanings applied to Chopin emerged unambiguously only
around 1900. To be sure, we have earlier hints of the possibility of
such meanings in such negative formulations as Haweis's "weird *nocturno*" from 1875. (Although momentarily taken aback by this adjective—how can a gently lyrical work be heard as "weird"?—we might
recall the long history of characterizing the nocturne as "effeminate.")[64] A few decades later, the implications grow somewhat louder
in the following scattered remarks of Hadow, comments that ultimately contributed to his construction of Chopin's "unearthly" musical "fairyland" that we examined above:

> If, in order to be a good man, it is first necessary to be a good animal,
> we may admit at once that Chopin's virility was imperfect. There is
> no doubt that, to the end of his life, he was characterised by a super-
> sensitive refinement, which, fifty years ago, would have been de-
> scribed as feminine . . .
>
> The want of virility, which has already been noted in his character,
> appears beyond question in his music; leaving untouched all the
> grace and tenderness, all the rare and precious qualities of work-
> manship, but relaxing into an almost inevitable weakness at any
> crisis which demands sustained force or tenacity . . .
>
> The want of manliness, moral and intellectual, marks the one great
> limitation of Chopin's province.[65]

But the insinuations become utterly clear only in a school of Germanic
criticism from the first decades of the twentieth century that eschewed
otherworldly metaphors, and turned instead to a deeply problematic
mixture of psychological and racial theories. Thus the notoriously
coarse Otto Weininger, after describing George Sand as "part bisex-
ual, part exclusively homosexual," later observed:

> The most famous of the many "relationships" of George Sand were
> with Musset, the most effeminate lyric poet known to history, and

with Chopin, whom one could even designate the only effeminate musician—so womanly is he.[66]

And Adolf Weissmann, in a chapter on Debussy where he earlier had described Debussy's physical nature in terms that seem copied from contemporary medico-legal portrayals of passive pederasts, explained Chopin's influence on Debussy as follows:

> Through strong racial feeling, Chopin's emotional, hermaphrodite nature had discovered new shades of sound, a new language of the soul, and a smoothly gliding technique, accentually weak, which was to serve Debussy for the expression of his moods, both as man and pianist.[67]

But in what seems to signal a markedly different climate as concerns sex and sexuality, sodomitic or pederastic references from Chopin's lifetime, and up to around 1875, arose only as distant and deferred linguistic allusions, in suggestions of the composer's affinity to women (which could carry a presumption of effeminacy), and in phrases like Custine's "inconstant Sylph." And one more way, perhaps: in the repeated coupling of otherworldly metaphors with ideas of sickness and disease.

Conclusion: Between Sodomy and Pathology

The issue of sickness and disease moves us back from otherworldly meanings and confronts us directly with Chopin's physical body. For (in the minds of the dominant culture) to be affiliated with notions of hermaphroditism was also to be conjoined to ideas of pathology, particularly in the nineteenth-century sense whereby the "pathological" and the "normal" were understood to exist on a continuum, with the former distinguished from the latter only by quantitative variations.[68] Hermaphrodites differed in numerical ways from "normal" humans (recall Geoffroy Saint-Hilaire's initial categorical division); their anomalies helped determine (through an often complex chain of reasoning) their pathological status.[69]

Viewed in the terms put forward in nineteenth-century treatises on pathology and juristic medicine, Chopin's very body could have reinforced a sodomitical interpretation of the metaphors of hermaphroditism that gathered around him. According to the forensic mode of reasoning that was then in place, if the sodomite/pederast was understood as a pathological figure, then physical symptoms of this pathology should be detectable to the practiced eye: the body should "tell" of its pathological defects.[70] As with all of the signs that we have been considering, instability reigned: the same symptom could tell of a number of different pathologies, depending upon what kind of explanatory narrative it was embedded within. Hence Chopin's weakness, pallor, and slight build, explicable as resulting from pulmonary or cardiac causes, could also have been read as a sign of sodomitical inclinations. So, too, his smooth skin and lightly developed musculature, when understood as indications of "effeminacy," were available as indices of sodomy. Even those who were led to read these symptoms as evidence of tuberculosis could not rule out sodomy. Tuberculosis was thought by many to be connected to the practice of masturbation, and, at least from the time of the great anti-onanism tracts of the eighteenth century, masturbation and sodomy had been understood as closely related practices.[71] In outlining these details, my purpose (I hasten to stress) is neither to demonstrate the "actual" conduct of sodomy, whatever that might have been, nor to foreclose such an investigation in the future. Rather I hope to indicate the cultural categories through which Chopin's pathologized body could have physically spurred the metaphorical enactments of hermaphroditism we have discussed.

The contiguity of ideas of hermaphroditism and pathology helps explain the conjunction of otherworldly metaphors and images of disease in accounts of Chopin. The affiliation occurs often enough that it cannot be understood solely as a response to his frail physical status. The linked *topoi* reverberate through Chopin's obituaries (as we would expect); they frame Marmontel's reminiscences of his playing (Marmontel's very first sentence about Chopin describes "this name . . . that has preserved over the years the double halo of poetry and suffering"); and they color George Sand's vision of his music ("being sick to death at Majorca, he made music that fully smelled of paradise").[72] The worlds of angels and fairies evoked through the metaphorical substitutions applied to Chopin were, at the most obvious level of perception, hallowed and magically charmed places. But we would be missing a key element of their signifying power were we not to recognize the diseased and disorderly images that also inhabit there.

How then did sex "speak" music—Chopin's music—during his lifetime and thereafter? I have suggested here that it did so through processes of linguistic deferral and deflection that took place around supernatural images that repeatedly attached themselves to Chopin. The
"sex" so constructed by these processes was messily contingent. The
sexual meanings, unstably concerned with notions of ambiguity and
pathology rather than with ideas of identity and desire, often stood as
shadowy presences beyond the foreground of awareness. At the same
time, these meanings touched a "Chopin" writ large; they inseparably
configured the performer, his music, his character, and his body.

We might readily continue to pursue the multiple refractions of the
supernatural trope. We might hear distant echoes of the "pathological
angel/fairy" in the occasional associations of Chopin's music with disease that took place in the 1830s and 1840s.[73] And we might also, as
I suggest in Chapters 2 and 5, investigate how the otherworldly, androgynous trope interacts with aspects of Chopin's musical produc-
tions: the perceived "feminine" nature of his nocturnes or the generic
uncertainty occasioned by his "concert" preludes.[74] (Such an investigation would require a deft interpretive touch if it would hope to parse
specific musical texts and procedures. For many of our analytical techniques, as valuable as they might be in other present-day intellectual
contexts, remain imbued with formalist ideals that firmly took root
only toward the latter half of the nineteenth century, and thus would
seem of questionable significance to an effort to elucidate values and
modes of understanding of the early nineteenth century having to do
with sex and music.)[75] These suggestions only begin to frame the possibilities for further research.

Yet we should not expect that such pursuits, or this pursuit for that
matter, will lead to a mastery of the systems of thought that gave rise
to the supernatural trope. Instead, we find ourselves confronting unresolvable limits to our knowledge similar to those described by Gary
Tomlinson in his superb account of Renaissance musical magic.[76] We
can partially construe that segment of a musical culture whose strategies for making sense of Chopin included invoking images of otherworldly figures of a sexually unstable nature. But in some ways the
epistemological premises that permitted the unsteady mapping of sex
onto music in the first part of the nineteenth century remain foreign
to our understanding: we cannot experience images of Chopin as hermaphrodite or sodomite as his contemporaries in the 1830s and 1840s

did. Far from leading to an appropriative control of the subject, then, following the refractive course of the otherworldly trope should suggest that we cannot continue blithely to enfold Chopin's musical culture into our own. Residues of difference and dislocation must surely remain as we strain to hear its voices—its small fairy voices—in some of their faintness, disorder, and strangeness.

II

Social Constructions and the Compositional Process

❧ 4 ❧

Chopin's Last Style

The story of Chopin's final years seems to be taken from the pages of a tragic Romantic novel. One wrenching event follows another: the debilitating attacks on his health; the rupture with his companion of nine years, George Sand; the outbreak of revolution in Paris; the subsequent months of self-imposed, lonely exile in Great Britain; and, upon his return to Paris, the protracted decline that culminated in his death in the early hours of 17 October 1849. So riveting is this downward spiral in Chopin's life that the music he wrote in these years has been neglected by comparison. But Chopin's crises at this time were artistic as well as personal. They are revealed not only in events of his biography but also in a few experimental works in which he sought to transform and alter basic tenets of his musical language. In these works we may detect the beginnings of Chopin's new style—his last, since he had scarcely established it before death intervened.

Chopin's personal difficulties in the years 1845–1849 resulted from problems of long standing, and so, too, the last style followed an extended period of stylistic reappraisal. Chopin's oeuvre resists rigid segmentation into periods; many stylistic traits appear in his earliest mature works and remain throughout his career. Nevertheless, reasons both documentary and musical suggest that a significant shift in his artistic direction began in 1842. General clues come from his rate of production, which in the years 1842–1847 dropped by nearly half.[1] Letters testify that he struggled with his musical ideas. George Sand refers to the phenomenon, always lightly, as on 29 August 1842:

> Chopin calls to you with a loud voice to return to him the musical faculty that he claims to have lost. So do not be late, dear.[2]

On 12 November 1844:

> Chopin is fashioning a small package of new compositions, all the while saying as usual that he can do nothing but the *detestable* and the *miserable*. The funniest thing is that he says it with the most sincerity in the world.[3]

And on 21 August 1846:

> Chopin still composes masterpieces, of which somebody will inform you, although he claims to do nothing that is any good.[4]

Chopin also assumes a matter-of-fact or humorous tone at first (18–20 July 1845):

> I do not play much—because my piano went out of tune, I write still less—which is why you have had nothing from me for so long.[5]

And on 8 July 1846:

> My good friend, I am doing everything possible to work—but it does not progress—and provided that this continues, my new productions will moreover remind you neither of the *chirpings of warblers* nor even of *broken china*. I must be resigned.[6]

But if he could invoke warbling birds and broken china to Franchomme in 1846, by the end of 1848, when the flow of compositions had slowed to a trickle, he would sum up his frustration with a far more poignant phrase, "Where has my art gone?"[7]

Composition had clearly become more difficult for Chopin, and in 1842 strictly musical, rather than biographical, reasons best account for the drop in output. A number of stylistic features came to the fore only around this time. Counterpoint, for example, played a more fundamental role. Canonic writing appeared frequently, and independent part-writing became the rule. Chopin began exploring elementary counterpoint treatises by Cherubini and Kastner.[8] Stylistic elements present since his early maturity took on different significance. Ornamentation, always central to Chopin's melodic style, was applied with greater restraint, often to articulate moments of structural importance. Non-pitched musical elements were explored for their capabilities in defining formal properties. Rhythm in particular was used to increase tension over entire sections of pieces. Harmony transcended the high sophistication of earlier works, either by probing more chromatic reaches, or by repeating, as a unifying device, the same chordal progressions throughout a work. New genres were essayed, old ones recharged by the admixture of elements from other forms.[9] What Chopin undertook from 1842 was no less than a complete critical reassessment of the nature of his craft—small wonder composing came slowly.

Chopin's late style, a compositional phase of general reappraisal, prepared the way for his last style, itself marked by aesthetic renewal. The essential distinction between these two styles is the discovery of new artistic methods versus the reshaping of familiar ones—in other words, the contrast of *vision* and *revision*. Neither this distinction nor the full ramifications of Chopin's final creative period have been adequately drawn in the literature, despite the notion of such a new period having almost achieved the status of a critical commonplace.[10] For all the critical remarks made about the last style and the few works that represent it, its fundamental musical significance remains obscure. Hence, Chopin's last style still deserves detailed consideration.

Central to Chopin's last style were two works, the Polonaise-Fantasy, op. 61, and the F-Minor Mazurka, published posthumously in an incomplete reconstruction as op. 68, no. 4. In differing ways, these two works illustrate the essence of the last style: in the one, the composer devised and successfully employed a new means of organizing formal shapes in a genre unique to him; in the other, he fell short in attempting to apply these means to a traditional genre. Successful discovery in novel circumstances, unsuccessful application in familiar situations—the last style is the story of unresolved artistic problems, of Chopin's search for a missing art. What was Chopin's discovery in the Polonaise-Fantasy, and how did it go awry in the F-Minor Mazurka?

The Polonaise-Fantasy

One of the most striking facts about the Polonaise-Fantasy is that Chopin labored for some time on the piece before he hit upon a title. Although he rarely hesitated over the name for a composition, in the midst of a long letter written to his family in Warsaw around Christmas, 1845, he offered the following report on his work in progress: "Now I would like to finish the Sonata for violoncello, the Barcarolle and something else that I do not know how to name, but I doubt whether I will have time, for already the bustle begins."[11] There can be no doubt that the unnamed work to which Chopin refers is the Polonaise-Fantasy. His uncertainty betrays the special nature of the piece; it provides a glimpse of Chopin's compositional outlook at the time and suggests a route by which we might come to understand the distinctive quality of the last style it exemplifies. While we will eventually want to explore the reasons why the name "Polonaise-Fantasy" was not from the first apparent to the composer, what is most immediately interesting is his decision to juxtapose precisely the polonaise and fantasy genres in his title. We wish to understand, in other words, what these titles represented to Chopin before he wrote op. 61, and thus to learn what he meant by joining them in this piece.

Toward the Last Style: Two Polonaises and a Fantasy

Chopin's first published piece was a Polonaise, and from the age of seven until well into his maturity, he adhered to a stable large-scale organization in this genre, with a few exceptions. Ternary form, whether a simple Polonaise—Trio—Polonaise design with the reprise marked through a da capo sign, or a more complex structure with a varied reprise, recurs from one work to the next.[12] Chopin tended to separate clearly the expressive functions of the principal sections: the Trio often represents a period of repose in comparison to the Polonaise. New, more lyrical textures are frequently introduced, harmony is often more regular, and the characteristic rhythms of the polonaise genre may be omitted. Toward the end of the middle years of his maturity, however, Chopin began to probe for ways to modify both the simple ternary design of the genre, and the functional qualities of the specific sections of the form, particularly the Trio. It is with these works that the polonaise tradition most relevant to op. 61 begins.

Perhaps the most significant of these mature polonaises is op. 44, in F-sharp minor, for Chopin not only experimented in interesting ways with its form, but also in reference to it he first juxtaposed the titles "Polonaise" and "Fantasy." In a letter of 23 August 1841 to the

Viennese publisher Mechetti, the composer reported a manuscript for
sale, saying, "It is a sort of fantasy in the form of a polonaise, and I
will call it a Polonaise," and the next day he wrote to his associate
Julian Fontana: "I offered him a new manuscript (a polonaise of sorts,
but more a fantasy)."[13] Although Chopin henceforth abandoned the
word "Fantasy" (it appears neither in the published title nor in later
references to the work in his correspondence), the early combination
of the two terms in op. 44 still can be suggestive for op. 61. What
aspects of op. 44 first suggested the appellation "Fantasy," and why
was it later dropped?

The fantasy—the "free" fantasy in particular—had long been
marked by its deviations from ordinary conventions of composition;
presumably Chopin invoked the term with respect to op. 44 to account for those aspects of the work that diverge from a typical polonaise. Most often, the early title is ascribed to the functionally peculiar
"Doppio movimento/Tempo di Mazurka" section (mm. 127–245).
Writers usually refer to the passage as an "interpolated" mazurka and
imply that this generically foreign material accounts for the title "Fantasy."[14] Now Chopin in fact rarely borrowed from the mazurka in his
polonaises (though the mixture of polonaise and mazurka had evidently occurred in polonaises by predecessors of Chopin).[15] But to
assign to this generic blend primary responsibility for the added title
obscures the role of other irregular elements of form that proved to
anticipate more clearly Chopin's future polonaises. For example, the
singularity of the "Tempo di Mazurka" section derives as much from
its placement after the beginning of what would otherwise have been
the usual middle section as from the ways in which it displays the
rhythm and texture of a mazurka. Chopin commences an orthodox,
if somewhat static, middle section—the Trio—at measure 83, only to
discontinue it with another completely different block of contrasting
material—the Mazurka—at measure 127. The generic quality of this
second block of music is significant, but no more so than the way in
which the section frustrates expectations of a formally orthodox Trio
for the Polonaise.

If Chopin's initial uncertainty over the genre of op. 44 was spurred
by aspects of the work not found normally in a polonaise, then the
formally unorthodox middle section surely must have contributed to
his doubt as much as did the incorporation of elements from the ma-

zurka.[16] Yet, as Chopin's ultimate title demonstrates, this unusual or unorthodox feature was not enough to weaken the generic identity of the work. The structural oddities of op. 44 do not really cloak its essential ternary shape; even though the Trio (when construed as mm. 83–245) contains two very distinct parts, the proportions between the section in its entirety and the outer portions do not diverge notably from those found in previous polonaises (compare, for example, op. 40, no. 1, in A major). Nor does the abandonment in the Mazurka of the conventional rhythmic and accentual patterns of the polonaise mask the overall genre, for the middle sections of earlier polonaises often lack the rhythmic and accentual identity of the polonaise proper. Unusual features may be found in op. 44, but when balanced against the other utterly conventional formal attributes of the polonaise, they could not on their own justify the added name of "Fantasy."

The F-sharp-Minor Polonaise marks the beginning of an experimental phase in Chopin's composition of polonaises; his next effort, op. 53 in A-flat major (published in 1843), also shows interesting divergences from the norm. As in op. 44, it is the central section of op. 53 that is most unusual; but now the novelty concerns the internal construction of the section, not its relation to the preceding music. The middle section divides into three distinct segments. Chopin commences with a bipartite section primarily in E major, though he invokes D-sharp major in the last four measures of each part (mm. 81–120). Despite these parenthetical harmonic excursions, the section sounds static, in large part because of the notorious ostinato that drums throughout in the left hand. Both the harmonic orientation toward E major and the sixteenth-note ostinato disappear at the start of the second section (mm. 120–128). Here Chopin shifts into an unsteady F minor, essays a new theme, and adopts a dactylic rhythmic ostinato in the left hand. The third section (mm. 128–154) introduces still more new thematic material, explores several different keys (G minor, B-flat major, F minor), and posits another persistent rhythmic pattern (now Chopin is not so insistent in his application of the pattern as in the preceding sections).

Three clearly demarcated segments in the middle section, none repeating: such linear thematic profusion is unprecedented in the polonaises (it does occur in earlier mazurkas—see the F-minor op. 7, no. 3 and the D-flat-major op. 30, no. 3). Just as in op. 44, Chopin blurs function as he clarifies form. By comparison with their predecessors in the genre, the irregular constructions at the centers of opp. 44 and 53 seem designed to increase musical tension. Middle sections (or Trios) in earlier polonaises had tended, instead, to ground the energy generated in the main section by shifting either to a much more lyrical and less rhythmically incisive setting (see op. 26, nos. 1 and 2) or to a relatively static, blocklike presentation (op. 40, no. 1). In fact, stable (or static) Trios were typical of the polonaise; to energize the central portion might weaken the identity of the genre. Chopin's problem was to incorporate, somehow, both stability and instability into the center of his polonaises, and his solution in the early 1840s was to juxtapose disparate and distinct segments. In the F-sharp-Minor Polonaise, the initial portion of the middle section responds to the need for a static Trio, the Mazurka to the composer's desire for instability. Likewise, the A-flat-Major Polonaise commences statically and moves on to instability in the later two portions.

In sum, two facts seem particularly significant about the two polonaises written immediately prior to the Polonaise-Fantasy. First, Chopin showed already in op. 44 an inclination to mix genres. Second, he sought in both op. 44 and op. 53 to increase musical tension in the middle section while still maintaining some of the qualities of stability that define this portion of the genre.

Although the name "Fantasy" was given to more than one type of work in the 1840s, Chopin clearly meant to invoke the free kind, not the species based on a tune or set of tunes borrowed from an opera or folk setting, when he joined the term to the title of op. 61.[17] The tradition of the free fantasy, however, poses two potential problems not encountered with the polonaise. First, the very adjective attached to the title creates difficulty: any free genre could resist efforts to generalize or sift out a tradition. Second, Chopin wrote only one free fantasy in his career, op. 49 in F minor.[18] One fantasy does not constitute a tradition, even a personal one; hence we need to consider, however briefly, the genre as a whole. Yet even though the F-Minor Fantasy differs markedly in overall form from the Polonaise-Fantasy, these problems do not really hinder the assessment of what the term "Fantasy" meant to Chopin. As free as the genre may have been, certain formal structures were carried over from the earlier work to the later, and some tonal procedures limned in op. 49 were influential in op. 61. The F-Minor Fantasy was fundamentally important to the birth of the last style.

Two formal attributes of op. 49 show striking parallels with op. 61. Both works begin with a lengthy introduction that sounds melodic motives used later in the piece (the link between the introduction and the remainder of the work is forged more patently in op. 61), and both works feature a contrasting thematic unit in B major and in a slower tempo roughly midway through the piece. These parallels illuminate the question of received tradition in the Polonaise-Fantasy, for precisely these structural elements—the lengthy introduction and the central slow theme—recur in fantasies throughout the first part of the nineteenth century and may have been fundamental for defining this slippery genre. That is, what determined the label of "Fantasy" for many composers seems to have been, in part, a lengthy opening section that showed subtle connections to the following material and a section placed near the middle of the piece that contrasted sharply in key, tempo, and mood with the surrounding music.[19] Of course, many other kinds of events could and did take place in fantasies; they were, after all, free forms. However, a long introduction and a suddenly inserted slow section stand among the most arresting aspects of a fantasy.

The importance of the shared idea of an introduction and a slow middle section in opp. 49 and 61 goes beyond the fantasy tradition; it begins to suggest how Chopin at this time understood generic hybrids. If we assume that Chopin actually merged the polonaise with the fantasy, then it seems doubly significant that the formal attributes these two genres share are exactly a substantial introduction and a contrasting middle section of a more lyrical character. Chopin did not title op. 61 "Mazurka-Fantasy," "Nocturne-Fantasy," or "Waltz-Fantasy," and for good reason: none of these genres share these two formal attributes with the fantasy. He chose instead to graft together two genres with significant archetypical similarities; it is as though, by analogy to the biological process, he felt that this kind of fundamental link was necessary for the graft to take.[20] Hybrid works, to Chopin, could not be formed casually from any two genres; rather the two had to be carefully weighed for structural compatibility.[21]

Tonality in the Fantasy presents something of a paradox: Chopin tends to explore many keys in each formal unit, yet the overall impression is of relative harmonic stability. For example, the principal thematic group, measures 68–142, rises rapidly by thirds from the tonic F minor to E-flat major. On the face of it, the modulations should weaken substantially any sense of stability. However, Chopin sets most of these keys within closed segments where their local stability is firmly, if temporarily, asserted. In these segments, he allows the minor and its relative major to function in effect as two sides of one key (this had long been a possibility in his harmonic vocabulary).[22] Hence the tonal progressions in the principal thematic group actually join two closed pairs separated by a fifth, one in F minor/A-flat major, the other in C minor/E-flat major; they may be viewed as a Romantic reinterpretation of the conventional tonal scheme for an exposition. Such a succession of self-contained units generates little tension.[23] Thus Chopin loosens tonal syntax considerably at the local level by admitting tonal pairs, but then treats these pairs in a conventional way at the higher level.

The oddly static quality of the tonality in op. 49 emerges in some of its large-scale harmonic relationships as well. When Chopin recalls in measures 235–309 the principal thematic group (mm. 68–142), he maintains precisely the same motion by rising thirds, only transposing the entire complex down a fifth (and so suggests, by the earlier analogy, a Romantic reinterpretation of the Classical recapitulation). The cause of symmetry is aided when, in comparison to the downward transposition of this third statement of the principal group, the shortened second statement (m. 135) begins a fifth up from the original (but soon diverges from it). Unusual or asymmetrical patterns are admitted into the framework of the piece, but in such a way that the stable or symmetrical elements remain most prominent. Chopin in 1841 clearly was not yet willing to allow instability to reign simultaneously on several levels; as a result, this fantasy carries with it an abiding sense of regularity even in the face of its unorthodox tonal structure.

The immediate traditions of the polonaise and the fantasy thus elucidate the formal problems Chopin faced in composing the Polonaise-Fantasy. In both genres, he had struggled with ways of shaping larger units of unstable and stable material into a coherent whole. Although he clearly wished instability to play a more significant part in his last two polonaises and the Fantasy than it had in his earlier works, he did not yet allow it a governing formal role. These shared formal concerns, as much as the shared structural characteristics, likely prompted Chopin to fuse these two genres in op. 61.

Traditions Transformed

Even cursory familiarity with the Polonaise-Fantasy reveals that the work inhabits a formal world new to Chopin. So many novel elements of form are explored in the piece that the task of a critic becomes quite complex. In the context of an examination of Chopin's last style, however, the most significant aspects of the piece are the composer's control over long passages of unstable material and his subsequent discovery of a new means of musical continuity.

Chopin avidly avoids closure in the Polonaise-Fantasy; the pervasive instability of the work represents a quantum change from the earlier Polonaises and the F-Minor Fantasy, and contributes a remarkably fluid sense of forward direction to the piece. Most commonly he proceeds in any given section from a point of relative stability toward one of relative instability; one way he does so is by deflecting the music away from tonic closure. The initial two statements of the principal Polonaise theme (mm. 24–65), for example, begin as a model of diatonic stability: the four-measure theme opens on the dominant and closes with a downbeat cadence on the tonic. But this stability proves illusory, for from this point until the onset of the following section (m. 66), Chopin skirts dominant-to-tonic progressions. He repeats the theme sequentially, extends it into the submediant (the key a third below the tonic), returns to it over a dominant pedal, and extends it once again into chromatic realms. Only four measures before the ensuing new theme in measure 66 does Chopin return to simple diatonic harmony. The first thematic block of the Polonaise-Fantasy thus moves from a standard diatonic opening toward progressively more unstable material so that a peak of instability is reached just prior to the conclusion of the section. Chopin had, of course, pursued this type of progressive instability in previous works; what is striking about the technique in op. 61 is the extent to which it permeates the piece as a whole.

The novel balance of stability and instability in the Polonaise-Fantasy emerges not only within individual sections, but across the boundaries between them as well. In working out solutions to problems of continuity from section to section, Chopin discovered a fundamental tenet of the last style: the unexpected juxtaposition of stable and unstable material. Fortunately, a full set of sketches for the piece graphically preserves his extensive struggles over just this issue. These sketches provide a rare glimpse into Chopin's aesthetic world at the time of the composition of the Polonaise-Fantasy, and an interpretive reading of significant excerpts from them will lay open the essence of his new style.[24]

To interpret the sketches for the Polonaise-Fantasy, we first need to understand something of Chopin's general sketching habits: when in the formulation of a work he began to put pen on paper, and what habitual procedures he ordinarily followed at this stage.[25] Although sketches contain the earliest written manifestation of Chopin's compositional thought, the essential creative act for most pieces was completed beforehand at the keyboard. Chopin himself asserted in letters, and George Sand seconded in her famous description of the composer at work, the necessity of having a piano to compose.[26] By the time he dipped his quill in ink, larger notions of structure and melody were likely shaped in his fingers and mind.

Chopin ordinarily sketched on pre-cut bifolia of music paper in oblong format. Sketchbooks were not used; collections of drafts for individual works are found on groups of loose bifolia or on individual leaves. He ordinarily notated music only on adjacent pages of the bifolio (that is, either folios 1ᵛ and 2ʳ or 1ʳ and 2ᵛ), leaving the reverse sides blank. (When he used both sides of a sketched leaf, the music on the two sides is rarely continuous; usually some amount of time separated the entries on one side from those on the other.) He first would write on the left-hand leaf of the open bifolio, next on the right. He nearly always sketched in piano score (except, of course, in the Sonata for Violoncello): even when he actually wrote down only one line, he still marked off measures in two-stave units. Ordinarily he filled in the staves on the page beginning at the top and writing continuously from the left margin to the right,[27] and while he occasionally jotted down ideas one or two measures long, on the whole his extant sketches survey longer portions of a piece. Since sketches were private documents, Chopin employed a whole range of idiosyncratic symbols and abbreviations.[28] Moreover, he felt no need to be neat: his musical script was often hastily and inaccurately scrawled, and he at times used sketch leaves as a blotter to daub off excess ink from his pen.

The main body of sketches for op. 61 survives in an unknown private collection (photographs of these leaves were taken before they disappeared from public view in 1957); a further short but significant draft rests in the Chopin Society (Towarzystwo imienia Fryderyka Chopina) in Warsaw.[29] The principal sketches fill eight sides of fourteen-stave manuscript paper; squinting at the photographs and generalizing from Chopin's ordinary sketching practices, we may safely deduce that these eight sides occur on eight leaves with blank opposite sides. The photographs furthermore suggest that six of the eight leaves are linked into pairs to form three separate bifolia. Each leaf is numbered in the upper right-hand corner; presumably these numbers were added by Chopin's friend Auguste Franchomme or by his descendants, who owned these sketches (and those for many other works) from Chopin's death until they passed into the private collection mentioned above. Since the leaves were not first arranged in the order of their composition, the numeration is unhelpful. I have therefore ordered the leaves and bifolia approximately according to the measures of the final version they contain (as we will see, this numerical order does not always correspond with the order in which the pages were notated), and numbered them 1–8. Table 4.1 provides a summary of the contents of each page.

The extant sketches present, in some form, the entire Polonaise-Fantasy except for measures 214–221 (and one could argue that these measures, which repeat music heard earlier in the piece, are implicitly represented in the sketches). Some sections were drafted in longer or shorter versions than occur in the printed score, and some sections differ in other interesting ways. Perhaps the most surprising revelation of the sketches is that Chopin first conceived the entire central lyrical theme and the 32-measure transition leading into it a semitone higher than in the final published version. Thus, the transition (mm. 116–147) began in B major, and the slow section (mm. 148–213) was in C major with its contrasting tune in A minor.[30] That C major originally was to have been the secondary tonal goal of the piece played an important role, as we shall see, in Chopin's search for a solution to the problems of continuity between sections.

A glance at the sketches also reveals one symptom of Chopin's early uncertainty over the title for the piece. Nowhere in any original layer in the sketches does the characteristic polonaise rhythmic figure occur; its rare appearances are always as additions or revisions to first thoughts. On page 1, staves 9–12, for example, Chopin changed what were originally undifferentiated eighth notes in measure 22, making them conform to the polonaise pattern, and he added a variant of the rhythm to the upper line in measure 23 (see Ex. 4.1). Clues of all sorts could be significant in identifying a work as a polonaise, but certainly none was more important than this rhythmic figure. All of Chopin's mature polonaises employ it. The absence of this pattern in the initial layer of sketching must be related to Chopin's early confusion over the genre of the work, and the omission of the name "Polonaise" from his first reference to it. ("Fantasy" admitted many more structural and gestural possibilities, and presumably came to the composer with less trouble.)[31]

Although the sketches differ in many particulars from the final version, the relatively minor adjustments that Chopin needed to make to bring them into agreement with the final version probably did not require another set of drafts. Despite the variants in the sketches, in other words, the work exists in a state sufficiently polished to posit that Chopin, who carped often about the drudgery of writing out his music and liked to minimize all copying, prepared directly from these sketches the first of the eventual three *Stichvorlagen* (manuscripts used as models for engraving) needed to publish the work.[32]

Example 4.1 Polonaise-Fantasy, op. 61, sketch for mm. 22–24.

Table 4.1 The Contents of the Polonaise-Fantasy Sketches

Page	MS numeration	Contents (measures)	Staves	Comments
1	165	1–38	1–14	A key signature of three flats is given in system 1. The first eight measures are sketched in C minor; a transposition signature of four flats is indicated by the title "Lento f mol[l]" in the left upper margin and by a melodic sketch on staff 3. The remainder of the sketch, from system 2, is drafted in an implied signature of four flats.
2	2	39–66	1–13	Measures 45–49 are not actually sketched, but that they should repeat mm. 25–29 is clearly implied. Measures [1–5] are presumably an alternate opening for the piece.
		[1–5]	12–13	
3	170	116–35	1–9	Measures 116–35 are drafted a semitone higher than the printed version and continue on p. 5, staves 8–9. Measures [116–19] are an elaborated version of mm. 31–34. Measures 116–17 in the third draft listed are sketched at the same pitch as the final version; mm. 114–17, on staves 7–8, are linked to the rest of the draft via two "x" marks. Measure 117 continues directly to the first system of p. 7.
		105/106–15, [116–19]	11–14	
		[106/107]–117	11–14	
			7–8	
4	171	70–105, [106–107]	1–14	Measures 136–43 are drafted a semitone higher than the printed version and are a continuation from p. 3, staves 1–9. Measures 182–94 and the various versions of [194–99] on staves 11–14 and 5–6 are drafted a semitone higher than the printed version. Measures [194–97] on staves 5–6 are linked to staves 13–14 via an "x." Measures [193]–206 are notated at the final pitch.
5	162	94–105, [106–108]	1–7	
		[106]		
		[106–109]		
		136–43	8–9	
		182–94, [195]	10–14	
		[195–98]		
		[195–99]		
		[194–97]		
		[193]–206	5–6	
		64–66	5–7	
			9–10	

⌊ 6	173	[152]–181	2–10	Measures [152]–181 and 148–52 are drafted in C major, a semitone higher than the printed version, and linked to p. 5, staves 10–14 via an "x." Measures [206–23] are drafted in C major, a semitone higher than the printed version (where it corresponds to mm. 206–13). Measures 144–47 are notated at the printed pitch.
		148–52	10–11	
		[206–23]	12–14	
		144–47	8–9	
⌈ 7	164	[118]–128	1–5	Measures [118]–128 are a continuation of p. 3, staves 11–14; 7–8. Measures 277–88 continue directly from p. 8, staves 11–12.
		277–88	5–8	
		221–41	9–14	
⌊ 8	167	242–59, [260–64]	1–10	Essentially a continuous draft with alternate versions of mm. 260–66. Measures 264–71 are linked by a line with m. [263] on staves 11–12. Measures 272–77 are linked by a line with mm. 264–71, staves 13–14. Measures 274–75 are indicated by "bis" written over mm. 272–73, staves 11–12. The draft continues on p. 7, staves 5–8.
		[260–66]	11–12	
		264–71	13–14	
		272–77	11–12	
	18	66–72	10–11	Chopin Society, M/1341. The remainder of the page is filled with inkblots. The manuscript numeration may be autograph.
		25–27	13–14	

Note: In the list of contents, measure numbers enclosed in brackets represent bars in which the music does not correspond to the published version. The contents of each page are arranged from top to bottom in my reconstruction of the order in which they were notated on that page by Chopin. Measure numbers not aligned with the left side of the column represent different versions of the bars immediately above them; in such cases, the initial measures of the first version—aligned with the left side of the column—apply also to the later versions. Page numbers joined by brackets indicate intact bifolia.

The comprehensiveness of the sketches masks the indirect progression of Chopin's thoughts. The physical organization of the individual pages and their respective contents reveal that the music was not all drafted consecutively through the piece, but rather was notated in two distinct ways. To state the matter simply, the music on some leaves runs continuously from one system to the next; on others it falls into separate segments.[33] Continuous pages predominate; in this category are pages 1–2 (which connect musically), 4, 6, and 8. Pages 3, 5, and 7 constitute the segmented leaves. Some of the drafts of individual segments on these pages are explicitly connected to music on the continuous pages, and two segmented drafts join to form one longer sketch (page 3, mm. 116–135; page 5, mm. 136–143). Still, each of these pages holds disparate sections of the piece. The continuous pages of intact bifolia (pages 4, 6, and 8) are all found on the right-hand leaf (or folio 2^r). Since Chopin ordinarily began a bifolio on the left-hand leaf, we may deduce that the continuous drafts appear where they do because he had already used the tops of the left-hand pages for fragmentary jottings. This would account for those continuous sketches that begin on a right-hand leaf and join with music on the middle or lower staves of a left-hand leaf.

Some significant conclusions about the composition of the Polonaise-Fantasy follow from this graphic evidence. All but one of the continuous pages contain precisely defined statements of complete sections of the piece, beginning with their first measures and ending on their last (the exception is p. 4). These pages present the introduction, the initial statements of the principal theme, the contrasting slow section, the synthetic reprise that unites the principal and slow themes, and the coda. Thus, included among the passages that flowed most freely from Chopin's pen are exactly those that constitute the most significant points of overlap between the genres of polonaise and fantasy: the long introduction and the lyrical middle section. The formal basis of the generic hybrid was therefore well-established even before Chopin began sketching, and well before he realized consciously that the piece bore any resemblance to a polonaise.

Moreover, the continuous pages contain sections that by themselves fall into a neat ternary form with an introduction and coda. Now Chopin cannot have viewed the completed work simply as some sort of expanded ternary form; in fact, as we shall see below, he took emphatic steps to blur any sense of ternary design in the piece. But in the written genesis of the work he labored least over the aspects of the form that were most familiar to him. These sections formed a sort of foundation that he could build upon and eventually conceal. Of course, Chopin did not notate the reprise and coda until after he had fretted over much of the preceding material, but this does not weaken the argument; he composed first at the piano, and certainly conceived the reprise before he wrote it down.

In essence, I am arguing that the written record in Chopin's sketches reveals something of the compositional process at the keyboard, that those passages showing the greatest continuity and the fewest corrections were those most securely fixed at the piano before sketching began. Again, when he labored over the Polonaise-Fantasy, Chopin doubtless followed a path far more complex than first formulating a ternary design and then fleshing it out. But the graphic evidence for the genesis of the piece points unmistakably to the enduring strength of ternary form in the initial compositional process.

If Chopin sketched with relative assurance those portions of the work that, taken by themselves, translate into ternary form, what stymied him elsewhere? Particular difficulties arose in composing the music that ultimately became measures 92–117 of the finished work, where two different and transformed versions of the principal theme and a transition to the contrasting lyrical section are heard. Chopin, in a gesture rare in his sketches, essayed multiple versions of this extended passage, considering on paper his various options for the transition from one section to another. I will examine in some detail the sketches for this structural link, for it is at just such boundaries that the character of his last style emerges most vividly.[34]

The opening of the passage presents the first transformation in character of the principal theme, from the original, assertive version to a more lyrical, nocturnelike statement. Chopin initially thought to present only one four-bar statement of the modified theme in the subdominant, or the key a fourth above the tonic (page 5, staff 1, mm. 1–4; see Fig. 4.1), but before he notated the accompaniment to these measures, he chose instead to commence the passage with two four-measure statements of the theme, the first a step higher than the second and in the dominant. This he notated directly beneath on staff 2 (see Ex. 4.2). He thus hearkened back to the sequence in the first eight

Figure 4.1 Page 5 of Chopin's sketches for the Polonaise-Fantasy, op. 61 (current owner un-known).

Example 4.2   Polonaise-Fantasy, op. 61, sketch for mm. 94–101.

measures of the principal theme (mm. 24–31), but modified it in service of his goal of transformation. In its first appearance, the sequence
rises stepwise from the tonic to the supertonic (the key area a whole
step above the tonic) and so increases the harmonic tension; in the
passage sketched, it descends stepwise from the dominant to the subdominant, and so diffuses harmonic tension in a manner familiar from
Chopin's nocturnes.

To sort out and make sense of the versions of the passage leading
away from the first transformation of the theme requires an aggressive
interpretation of the sketch. Following the single-line drafts at the beginning of staves 1 and 2, Chopin reverted to his normal two line
drafts, and added six measures in the first system, six in the second,
and one partial measure at the beginning of the third system. The first
three measures of system 2 are lightly cancelled with a wavy line. What
would appear visually to be a simple linear draft with one three-mea-
sure replacement vanishes upon performance; neither the first (cancelled) measure of system 2 nor the fourth (first uncorrected) measure
of the system will follow the last measure of system 1 without awkward harmonic and melodic shifts. Either system 1 stands completely
apart from systems 2 and 3 (which seems unlikely), or some other
explanation must be put forward.

The proper solution begins to emerge from close scrutiny of the last
two bars of system 1. All of the last measure and all but the first three
notes in the treble clef of the penultimate measure are written in a
darker, somewhat less precise hand than the preceding measures. Of
course, Chopin's pen could simply have run out of ink at this point;
but if we posit instead that the darker notes were entered later, then
a convincing link may be made between systems 1 and 2. According

to this interpretation, Chopin sketched this passage in three stages. First, he proceeded from the early version of the penultimate measure in the first system through the first three measures of the second (Ex. 4.3). Next, he cancelled these three measures and returned to the first system, penning the later version of the penultimate measure and the last measure (Ex. 4.4a). Finally, he decided to rewrite the last measure so that its opening rhymed musically with the penultimate measure, placing this revision in the fourth measure of the second system, although failing, as he did often in his sketches, to cancel the version of

Example 4.3 Polonaise-Fantasy, op. 61, sketch for mm. 94–[108].

Example 4.4 Polonaise-Fantasy, op. 61, sketch for mm. 94–[109] (mm. 94–103 as in Example 4.3).

the first system (Ex. 4.4b). Chopin continued this draft through the remainder of the second system and into the beginning of the third.

Chopin thus sketched two very different versions of the continuation. In the first, he stated the principal theme in G-flat minor over broken diminished chords, and then repeated this phrase transposed up a step to A-flat. In the second version, Chopin retained only the initial statement of the theme over diminished harmony and then extracted a motive from the theme and treated it canonically and sequentially until C minor is established. The thematic goal remains undefined in both versions: presumably Chopin sought here a means of introducing the second, agitato transformation of the principal theme (m. 108 of the published work), but there is no trace of this in the sketch. Whatever his goal, his choice of keys was significant, for at this point in the genesis of the work, A-flat and C constituted respectively the primary and secondary tonal regions of the piece (recall that the slow central section was sketched in C major). In the first version, Chopin probably meant the A-flat-minor passage to close out the first large unit of the piece, one that would comprise the introduction, the initial statements of the principal theme, the contrasting section (mm. 66–91 of the published piece), and the transformations of the principal theme. In the second, he established the key of the lyrical central section while still working out transformations of the first section. The first version synchronized tonal closure and thematic repetition to create a large, relatively stable formal unit. The second separated the two to weaken the structural articulation between two large sections.

C minor proved such a suggestive goal that Chopin sought three different ways of introducing it in the corresponding drafts at the conclusion to page 4 (see the end of Ex. 4.5). Chopin's concern here was essentially to solve small problems in chordal content. In all three cases he retained the ascending sequences and the canon of the later version on page 5. However, rather than allow the resolution to C minor to occur in the midst of the sequential and imitative phrase, Chopin deflected the resolution until the arrival of what presumably would be the agitato transformation of the principal theme. On the one hand, the shift in resolution underscored Chopin's general desire in the Polonaise-Fantasy to prolong and enhance instability, even at the level of the phrase; on the other hand, it demonstrated his sense that harmonic arrival and thematic repetition should be made to coincide. The one augmented structural instability at the level of the phrase, the other diminished it at the level of the theme.

By the time Chopin notated the agitato transformation of the principal theme on the bottom two systems of page 3, the harmonic goal of the canonic passage had been altered back to the tonic minor (Ex. 4.6). (On page 3, Chopin sketched two different links between the version on page 4 and the opening of the theme; the first rendition most closely resembles the route actually taken in the published work.) While tonality was clarified in the composer's mind, the proportions of this transformed statement were not, for the initial draft of the theme lasts a full eleven measures (as opposed to eight in the final version). Chopin simply quoted more of the principal theme in the

Example 4.5   Polonaise-Fantasy, op. 61, sketch for mm. 92–[108].

Example 4.6   Polonaise-Fantasy, op. 61, sketches for mm. 105/106–[119]; [106/107]–118.

Example 4.6   (continued)

sketch, and terminated the draft at the end of the page poised on the dominant of C. Again C is invoked, although here it has more to do with the composer running against the end of the page than with any genuine harmonic goal. Earlier on the page Chopin had drafted the transition to the slow central section (mm. 116–135, staves 1–9), beginning not in the final key of B-flat major, but instead in B major. When he entered measures 105/106-[119] at the bottom of the page, he had not yet decided to transpose the transition down a semitone; hence his immediate problem was to find his way from A-flat minor to B major. The pause on the dominant of C does not seem likely to have been related to this search, except perhaps in a negative way.

Chopin did shorten the theme to eight measures on page 3, but only after he opted to transpose the transition. Although this decision was reached relatively late in the evolution of the piece, it still betrays the same problems of how much and what kind of structural stress to place on the second transformation of the principal theme. His previous attempts worked in opposite directions: to promote internal closure by rounding off the first large unit of the piece with a statement of the transformed principal theme in the tonic minor, or to blur internal divisions with a recitation of the principal theme in the key of the main contrasting section. By extending the statement of the theme to at least eleven measures on page 3, Chopin initially advocated closure. The repetition of a lengthy segment of the principal theme marked these measures as the terminus of a large formal block, which, rounded off and securely closed, would be construed as the first leg of an expanded ternary design. But his final solution mediates between the formal stances described above. By trimming the agitato theme to eight measures (and rewriting substantially its eighth measure), Chopin initially nodded toward a rounding off of the first large unit of the work, but then deftly deflected the music into a foreign key and a new theme without actually closing harmonically or thematically the transformed principal theme.[35]

Chopin arrived at a new control over stability and instability at formal joins with this final version on page 3. In methodically working out on paper his options at this juncture of the piece, he wavered between stability and instability before settling on a blend of the two. The technique he evolved creates an impression of stability and clearly directed continuity (here toward large-scale closure of the first section of the piece) only suddenly to undercut both with the introduction of the transition theme. Chopin had adumbrated this technique in earlier works like the Mazurkas op. 59, nos. 2 and 3, where the reprise of a principal theme is cut short in order to introduce a developmental coda into a ternary piece. But the technique in the Polonaise-Fantasy differs in one important respect from that in earlier works. In the Polonaise-Fantasy, Chopin gave no clue that the shift to a new section would occur: he avoided tonic closure, and dropped no other hints that a formal divide was imminent. The earlier procedure would highlight the section break either through harmonic closure or by an alteration of tempo, dynamics, or texture.

Chopin exploited the new technique in order suddenly to deny expectations at another formal juncture in the Polonaise-Fantasy, in the passage leading from the slow middle section to the reprise of the principal theme, particularly measures 214–224. The composer recalled in rapid succession two ideas heard previously in the work: first the beginning of the introduction and then the contrasting theme within the slow lyrical section. Each idea sounds first in its original guise, and then is put to new use. The opening idea shifts from a harmonically vague, sequential figure to one with clear tonal implications (V of F minor), and the contrasting tune turns from a stable theme into an unstable motive. Again the sudden changes juxtapose the stable with the unstable, the inscrutable with the clearly defined.

These sudden juxtapositions allowed a novel solution to the problems of musical continuity that had been nagging Chopin in the recent polonaises and the Fantasy. Earlier I referred to his concern simultaneously to increase musical tension in the central portions of polonaises and to maintain some of the stability that generically typified such areas. His response in the F-sharp-Minor and A-flat-Major Polonaises was to join musical units of disparate functions within the central sections: a Trio with a Mazurka, or a static ostinato with an unsteady one. In the F-Minor Fantasy, too, he apportioned unstable and stable elements of the piece into separate compartments, taking care not to allow them to intermingle. But in the Polonaise-Fantasy he achieved a convincing amalgam of the stable and the unstable.

This, in turn, allowed Chopin to create large-scale formal relationships that earlier would have eluded him. After the conclusion of the slow middle section, fragments of two ideas originating in very different parts of the work follow in rapid succession, and their juxtaposition sounds convincing because of the successful merging of the unstable—that is, the harmonically vague quotation from the introduction—and the stable—its transformation into a motive with clear tonal intent. Our perception of overall proportions in the work is significantly affected as a consequence of this combination of functions (and of tunes as well) at this point in the piece. Just where we might expect an orthodox return to the principal material (a return evidently heralded by the onset of the introductory motive), instead we are surprised to hear music from the lyrical central section. Formal outlines are clouded: does the central section conclude irregularly, or does the return to the principal theme commence irregularly? Function is blurred, and along with it any secure sense of ternary form in the piece, for the end of the central slow section is as anomalous with respect to function as was its beginning.[36] At the two most significant junctures of a potential ternary form—the joins between the principal theme and the contrasting section—Chopin has frustrated our expectations, at the one link by introducing an entirely new theme in a new key, at the other by reusing elements from widely separated areas of the piece.

Such abrupt appositions lend to formal junctures a new kind of articulative significance, one that, when combined with Chopin's general tendency to conclude sections in an open-ended fashion, yields an extraordinarily forward-moving work, strongly directed toward terminal climax. Terminal climaxes themselves were nothing new to Chopin; rather it is the way in which he prepared the exciting finale that distinguishes the Polonaise-Fantasy. Prior to op. 61, Chopin typically shifted structural weight toward the end of a work by withholding the resolution to the tonic until the coda (for example, the G-Minor Ballade, op. 23), by telescoping the reprise of the main theme and following it with a developmental coda that compensates for the shortened return (A-flat-Major Mazurka, op. 59, no. 2), by following the relatively stable and diatonic body of the piece with a kinetic and chromatic coda (C-sharp-Minor Mazurka, op. 50, no. 3), or by some combination of these techniques. The Polonaise-Fantasy, however, creates its climax from different kinds of internal relationships. The fervor of the reprise of the chief theme in measure 242 derives in part from its transformation; this has led Edward T. Cone to cite it as an example of the device of apotheosis, which he defines as "a special kind of recapitulation that reveals unexpected harmonic richness and textural excitement in a theme previously presented with a deliberately restricted harmonization and a relatively drab accompaniment."[37] But the transformation carries the extraordinary expressive charge it does because it heralds the climactic point of arrival in the piece, an arrival finally announced transparently after so many opaque hints before.

Ultimately Chopin's ability to shift formal implication from one measure to the next made possible the successful fusion of genres in op. 61. Earlier I drew attention to the lyrical central section as a formal attribute shared by Chopin's polonaises and the Fantasy, and suggested that this fact likely weighed strongly in the composer's decision to join these two genres. But the broader formal context of these lyrical sections contrasted sharply in the two kinds of works: in a polonaise it appeared as part of a ternary design; in the Fantasy it came as an interruption of a more fluid, processive shape. Chopin's achievement in the Polonaise-Fantasy was to meld these two contexts so that the slow, lyrical section sounds at once like the middle segment of a large ternary form and, by virtue of the flexible formal allusions leading into and out of it, like an interruption in a processive shape. To continue the earlier analogy, what makes the generic hybrid in op. 61 take is more than the archetypical attributes that the polonaise and the fantasy share. It is also the merger of their contextual functions.[38]

Chopin's mastery of the new manner of continuity and his awareness of its implications for formal procedures set the Polonaise-Fantasy apart, not only from its antecedents in the polonaise and fantasy traditions, but also from other works of Chopin's late period. While it draws on techniques found in earlier polonaises and the Fantasy, and although it does not stand alone among works written after 1841 in mixing elements from different genres, the Polonaise-Fantasy makes a quantum leap into a new style. No other piece solves problems of musical continuity in the manner of the Polonaise-Fantasy; no other work blends formal implications as does op. 61. In essence, Chopin redefined his principles of musical form in the Polonaise-Fantasy. In so doing he established the basic mission for what was to be his new—and last—style.

The F-Minor Mazurka

Chopin developed his new style in creating a new genre, a hybrid of the polonaise and the fantasy. However, to judge from the surviving music after the Polonaise-Fantasy, further invention of new genres did not interest him. Rather he explored the possibilities of applying his new techniques within the context of already familiar genres. He did not pursue these experiments exclusively; several works written toward the end of his life draw comfortably and unadventurously on the general stylistic precepts of the late period. But in a few notable instances, he breathed into familiar genres the new air of the last style. One such work, left unpublished at his death, will concern us here: the so-called last mazurka, in F minor.

Since the discovery of a convoluted and chaotic sketch for the work among the composer's posthumous effects (see Fig. 4.2), Chopin's Mazurka in F Minor has suffered a troubled exegetic history. Numerous attempts have been made to decipher the document, none entirely successful.[39] Formidable problems confront the transcriber of the sketch; even such basic information as pitch, rhythm, and the order of sections is only vaguely specified in the composer's notation. As significant as these problems are, however, the inordinate attention focused on their solution has obscured other issues of central importance to the understanding of the work itself. Little consideration has been given to why the Mazurka survives only as a sketch, and, as a consequence, attempts to discern its place in Chopin's stylistic development have floundered. To be sure, an understanding of the textual problems posed by the work is essential; the relatively large body of work in this area will allow a simple summary of the basic points here. But an awareness of what the manuscript of the work represented to the composer—a work in progress or a work discarded—is needed in order to grasp the significance of the F-Minor Mazurka to Chopin's last style.

The history of the transcription of the Mazurka sketch falls into three stages. Two early and related versions, the first by Chopin's close friend Auguste Franchomme and the second by his former secretary Julian Fontana, constitute the first stage. Franchomme's transcription dates from 1852 and survives only in manuscript (Warsaw, Chopin Society, M/236).[40] Fontana's, based to some extent on Franchomme's,

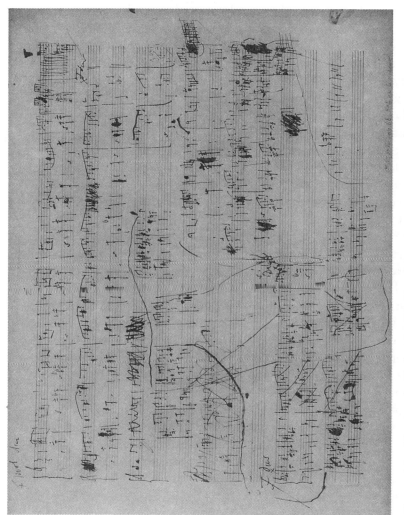

Figure 4.2 Chopin, sketch for the F-Minor Mazurka, op. 68, no. 4. Warsaw, Towarzystwo imienia Fryderyka Chopina.

dates from between 1852 and 1855, and was published in 1855 in his posthumous collection of Chopin's works as op. 68, no. 4; it was also issued separately under the title *Dernière Pensée musicale de Frédéric Chopin* by A. M. Schlesinger in Berlin.[41] Fontana's reconstruction of the piece is the one most frequently printed in modern collections of mazurkas. However, Fontana failed to include a substantial portion of the sketch in his transcription, either by choice or because of an inability to decipher portions of the document (Franchomme failed in this respect also). Thus, most current performances and analyses of the F-Minor Mazurka present just a torso.

Only in 1951, when Arthur Hedley examined the sketch, then in the possession of Franchomme's descendants, were the lacunae of Fontana's edition recognized. This realization initiated the second stage in the history of the work: the efforts to transcribe all of the music contained on the sketched leaf. Hedley attempted a reconstruction that until recently circulated only privately, although evidently it was employed for a few public performances in England in the 1950s; and Ludwik Bronarski, in a 1955 article devoted to the work, published transcriptions of a number of the passages omitted by Fontana.[42] However, it was Jan Ekier who, in 1965, first published a more substantial version of the whole Mazurka.[43] But even Ekier's edition, although advertised as a "complete reconstruction of the sketch," omits music: two substantial repeats, one in the middle section of the piece and one in the reprise of the main section. Another interpretation of the sketch was then offered by Wojciech Nowik. In two articles devoted to the Mazurka, he posited readings that differed in some significant internal details from Ekier's; unfortunately Nowik, too, missed the important clues in the manuscript that point to repetition.[44] His version is thus curtailed as well; indeed, it is slightly shorter than Ekier's (99 versus 101 measures).

In 1975 Ronald Smith detected most of the clues for repetition and insertion in the Mazurka; his version represents the third stage of interpretation of the sketch.[45] In Smith's reconstruction, the piece falls into a modified complex ternary form, ABA'CA". (Ekier's version is in the same form, but the central C section lacks a sixteen-measure repeat.) Only one formal marker escaped Smith's attention, a one-measure bass figure notated at the end of the sixth staff with "3ci," an abbreviation for *trzeci* (Polish for "third"), written above it (see

Fig. 4.2). Other commentators have noticed this indication, but none has publicly offered a convincing interpretation of it (only Hedley's private reconstruction apparently succeeded in this regard). Penned directly to the right of an alternate, or second, ending to the A section (itself notated directly beneath the first ending), "3ci" here must point to a third ending, one that by virtue of the implied continuity in the bass figure does not terminate the piece. Such a third ending may be derived most simply from the sketch if, after the central C section, one recapitulates the entire ABA complex, thus generating a third statement of A that continues into another section. The most complete reading of Chopin's sketch hence would yield a formal structure of ABACABA, a more substantial design than others have publicly suggested, but one with related precedents in earlier published Mazurkas (see op. 17, no. 3 in A-flat major and op. 50, no. 3 in C-sharp minor).

As the list of attempts to interpret it suggests, this single leaf is extraordinarily complex. One is tempted to burrow into the problems of interpretation of smaller detail and larger form in the sketch. But precisely because scholars have fretted intensely over the labyrinthine insertions and cancellations, the larger issues posed by this draft have not been addressed. Most discussions of the piece assume, explicitly or implicitly, that the F-Minor Mazurka survives only in a sketch because Chopin's health deteriorated before he could prepare an orderly manuscript of it. Had Chopin lived longer, so the thinking goes, he would have seen the work through to completion, in the process altering some of the details of the sketch. In essence, the sketch is generally taken to contain a version of the piece with which Chopin was satisfied, at least for the stage it represented in the genesis of the work. But why should we assume that this was the case?

The hypothesis that the progression of Chopin's diseases interfered with the completion of the Mazurka presumes that the work dates from 1848–1849, when his health was particularly poor. Evidence for this presumption traditionally derives, as Nowik points out, from three sources.[46] First, Franchomme noted on his 1852 transcription that the work was Chopin's last Mazurka, "composée à Chaillot," that is, 74, rue Chaillot in Paris, where Chopin lived from June to mid-August 1849.[47] Chopin's student, Jane Stirling, in close touch with Franchomme at this time, mentions Franchomme's transcription of "la dernière Maz[urka], écrite à Chaillot" in a letter to Chopin's sister,

Ludwika Jędrzejewicz, dated Paris, 18 June 1852.[48] Second, Fontana added a footnote to the date of 1849 in his published version of the Mazurka that reads: "This Mazurka is the last inspiration that Chopin jotted down on paper, a short time before his death:—he was already too ill to try it at the piano."[49] Third, Chopin's sister, in a list of unpublished works by her brother, grouped the incipit of the F-Minor Mazurka together with that of the G-minor Mazurka, op. 67, no. 2, gave them the heading "Mazourkas. two last," and dated them 1848.[50] The circumstances and date of the list remain uncertain; Kobylańska posits that Jędrzejewicz compiled it for Fontana to help in the planning of his publication of posthumous works.[51] If true, Fontana ignored her date, for, as we have seen, he placed the work in 1849.

Although all three witnesses agreed generally on the date of the Mazurka, their reliability is questionable. Two of them, Fontana and Jędrzejewicz, were physically far removed from Chopin during the period of composition they posited for the Mazurka (Fontana was in America, Jędrzejewicz in Poland); we do not know how they arrived at their dates. The third figure, Franchomme, dated the piece precisely to a period when he was at least some of the time in close contact with Chopin; yet, as Nowik has pointed out, Chopin's own letters from the summer of 1849 suggest very strongly that he was physically incapable of creative effort.[52] To cite only three examples, on 18 June he wrote to Wojciech Grzymała: "I have not yet begun to play—I cannot compose"; on 10 July he reported to the same: "I play less and less; I cannot write anything"; and on 14 August he indicated to Marie de Rozières that "I am very tired . . . I am weaker than ever."[53] In nearly every letter from his last summer, Chopin commented on his exhaustion, and his direct word must take precedence over Franchomme's later testimony.

Yet not only did Franchomme, Fontana, and Jędrzejewicz assign the Mazurka to the last year of Chopin's life, they furthermore designated it his last mazurka or composition (note that only Fontana identified the piece as the composer's final work of any sort). Given that they probably did not learn of the piece from Chopin, something else must have triggered the association of last work with the Mazurka. If we can understand the forces that led to their choice of adjectives, we might begin to see how it is that some long-standing assumptions about the piece came to be formed.

Consider for a moment the probable circumstances faced by our trio of witnesses. Among Chopin's posthumous effects appears a sketch for a work that the composer did not publish. The overall form of the work initially appears to be indecipherable, but parts of it are legible enough for Franchomme to reconstruct. The chromatic sequences of the opening clearly identify it as a relatively late work. Since Chopin presumably had continued to compose for a while after his last publications in early 1848, one of the several unpublished works contained in his posthumous portfolio must have been his last composition. There was even a mazurka that may have seemed later, one in G minor, for both Jędrzejewicz and Fontana assign a contemporary date to op. 67, no. 2. No record survives of any manuscript for the G-minor work; given, however, that the correspondence concerning the posthumous publication of Chopin's works does not mention it, we can assume that it was published either from a legible, finished manuscript or from a sketch that posed no problems in transcription. Contrast this with the known sketch for the F-Minor Mazurka: if it was thought that Chopin wrote two mazurkas in the last year of his life, then the one composed when he was most enfeebled would likely—so the reasoning might go—have been that which survived in the most chaotic state. A clear connection would have been drawn between Chopin's physical condition and that of the manuscript: from his body racked with pain arose the tortured document containing his last musical thoughts, ideas that themselves display, in their sinuous chromatic digressions, the soul of a man *in extremis*.

The Romantic hyperbole is intentional, for it was in just such a way that the last days of a creative artist engaged the nineteenth-century public. A special mystique radiated about a final artistic utterance, one from which publishers hastened to profit. Hence Schubert's *Schwanengesang* was advertised in 1829 as the "last blossoms of his noble strength" and published with an engraving of a dying swan on the title page. Likewise, his three final piano sonatas were published in 1839 as "Franz Schubert's last compositions of all." So too Beethoven's C major *Klavierstück*, WoO 62, apparently derived from an incomplete String Quintet of November 1826, was published by Diabelli in 1838 as "Ludwig van Beethoven's last musical conception [*Gedanke*]" (the manuscript for the work was sold at the auction of Beethoven's *Nachlass* for an "excessive" price, which suggests clear cognizance on the part of the publishers of the market value of a last work). A similar awareness must account for the competing versions of Bellini's "Dernière pensée." A spurious composition might even be provided if an authentic last work were not at hand: the piano piece issued throughout Europe as Weber's "Dernière pensée" actually was written by C. G. Reissiger.[54]

In short, the "last thought of the composer" represented a special category of music in the nineteenth century, one for which a strong tradition existed before the death of Chopin.[55] And I suspect the choice of the F-Minor Mazurka as Chopin's last work arose from the sense that last works were of a special quality. Tennyson, in his 1830 poem "The Dying Swan," evoked the ancient myth of the swan song, the wild bird whose

> awful jubilant voice,
> With a music strange and manifold,
> Flow'd forth on a carol free and bold.[56]

By no means do all *dernières pensées* qualify as "music strange" or "free and bold," but the association was there to be made nonetheless. The physical and musical circumstances of the F-Minor Mazurka seem tailor-made for the tradition of the "last work"; it took only a simple leap of the imagination to designate the work as Chopin's swan song.

Thus Chopin's three associates appear to have arrived at their dates and adjectives for the Mazurka not from evidence drawn directly from the composer but rather from an interpretation of the physical state of the manuscript and its (partial) musical contents, an interpretation strongly colored by the tradition of the *dernière pensée*. However, that they may have too readily fallen under the influence of this tradition does not in itself negate their datings. Only when we consider two other varieties of evidence—that of the paper on which the Mazurka is sketched, and that of the music itself viewed in comparison with another F-minor Mazurka—do we satisfactorily arrive at a new date for the piece.

Table 4.2 presents data on all the leaves of the same paper type as the F-Minor Mazurka. It evidently yields a straightforward conclusion: Chopin used this type of paper mostly during the years 1842–1844, not at the end of his life.[57] But this evidence needs to be interpreted with some caution. By the standards developed in research on

Table 4.2   The Paper Type of the F-Minor Mazurka

TS (mm.)	LS (mm.)	Works	KKp Number	Dates
178	232	50	709	fall 1842
		55	750	summer 1842
	233	65/IIsk	872	
		sketch	880	
		68/4 copy	982	1852
	234	65/IIsk	871	
		65/IIsk	874	
178 +	234	65/IIsk	870	
		65/IIsk	878	
178.5	232	50/3	718	summer 1842?
	232.5	58sk	783	late 1844?
	233–35	70/2	1015	late 1842?
	233.5	53	740	fall 1843
		56	761	summer 1844
		Draft for piano method	1371	
	239	61sk	816	
178.5 +	234	65sk	870	
	236	68/4sk	980	
179	232	50/1	710	1842?
	234–35	Largo	1229	"6.VII"
		Doÿna Vallacha	1402	
	235–37	72 copy	1063	23.XI.1849*
	237	69/1 copy	991	22.V.1850
179 +	234	sketch	1356	
179.5	234	65/IIsk	873	
		Draft for piano method	1371	
	236	Casta diva sk	1410	

Key: TS = Total span; LS = Length of staves; mm. = millimeters; 68/4 = Op. 68, no. 4; 65/II = Op. 65, second movement; sk = sketch; copy = scribal copy; KKp = Krystyna Kobylańska, *Rękopisy Utworów Chopina: Katalog.*
   Date in quotation marks is in Chopin's hand.
   *Date is to a mazurka by Kurpiński written on the verso of Op. 72.

Haydn, Beethoven, or Schubert, the shelf life for this particular paper type seems imprecisely defined: for the earlier composers, one may often pinpoint the date for a category of paper to within a year or less. Chopin, however, wrote far less than the earlier composers, and consequently exhausted his supplies of paper less quickly. The slower the turnover in paper, the longer the duration of its use. Moreover, since Chopin in the second half of his career employed exclusively machine-made paper with no watermarks, we must depend only on staff dimensions. The refinements in dating allowed by the decay of watermark molds cannot be employed here.

Chopin, furthermore, could have used a remnant from an earlier batch of paper toward the end of his life. Some evidence of this practice exists: a number of leaves used to sketch the Sonata for Violoncello, op. 65, a work begun no earlier than 1844, appear on paper that otherwise dates mainly from 1841–1843, and both a presentation manuscript dated 23 May 1846 containing the opening of the last movement of the B-flat-Minor Sonata, op. 35, and a *Stichvorlage* of the Barcarolle, op. 60, also prepared in 1846, are on twelve-stave paper used mostly between 1843 and 1845. And the presence in Table 4.2 of several leaves of sketches for op. 65 suggests that remnants of this variety of paper may well have been available after the principal period of its use. At best, then, the staff dimensions of the Mazurka leaf provide only a *terminus post quem*. But this paper evidence does at least broach the possibility that Chopin began the Mazurka earlier than traditionally assumed.[58]

An intriguing musical relationship provides further evidence for the date and context of the work. Chopin's final published set of mazurkas, op. 63, begun in 1846 and issued in 1848, contains another F-minor Mazurka (he wrote only three in this key—these two late ones and the early op. 7, no. 3). Now on the whole, the F-minor op. 63, no. 2 differs in nearly every way from the F-minor op. 68, no. 4. But surprisingly, two passages—a relatively diatonic section in op. 68, no. 4 and a relatively chromatic one in op. 63, no. 2—significantly reflect one another. That measures 24–39 of op. 68, no. 4 (the B section) can be perceived as relatively diatonic underscores the heavily chromatic framework of the entire piece, for in fact the section is unstable harmonically, passing initially from A-flat major through C minor to G major, and then descending by sequences, first whole-step, then half-step, back to the tonic F minor. The second part of the middle section of op. 63, no. 2 (mm. 25–40) sounds on the whole more stable than the passage in op. 68, no. 4, yet it is here that the parallels in internal structure occur (see Ex. 4.7). In op. 63, no. 2, Chopin moves, in eight measures, from A-flat major to a momentary and wistful pause on G major; in the sketch he does the same (semitonal modulation within a phrase is rare in his mazurkas). In op. 63, no. 2, he follows the caesura on G with four measures of descending whole-tone melodic sequences accompanied by D, G, C, and F harmonies; in the sketch he does the same. The parallels are not exact; in the sketch, Chopin reaches G via C minor, whereas in op. 63, no. 2 he shifts to it suddenly out of A-flat major; in op. 63, no. 2, the D, G, C, and F harmonies sound over a G pedal, whereas no pedal occurs in the sketch; and the sequences continue in the sketch beyond four measures, whereas they stop in op. 63, no. 2. Still, the two passages mimic one another closely enough to rule out chance.

These resemblances might well indicate common compositional origins; that is, the structural parallels are so idiosyncratic (I know of no other such example in the mazurkas) as to suggest that the two works were written at about the same time. But which came first? Given the evidence of the paper of the sketch, which points to a comparatively early date of conception, and the known circumstances of the published op. 63, which was not likely begun before 1846, the most convincing hypothesis—and the evidence permits no more than a hypothesis—is that the F-minor op. 63, no. 2 contains a residue of the earlier F-minor sketch. And if the structural resemblances arose in part because the dates of composition of these two mazurkas were close, a further consequence of this hypothesis could be that the sketch was originally intended for, but ultimately rejected from, the eventual op. 63. In short, I would suggest that the sketch represents not Chopin's last mazurka, or *dernière pensée*, but instead a work composed roughly contemporaneously with the Polonaise-Fantasy, in about 1845–1846.

What might have led Chopin to discard the sketch from op. 63? Aside from internal reasons, which I will consider below, considerations of the entire set could have played a role. As I wrote earlier, the sketch and op. 63, no. 2 seem markedly diverse; this very contrast might account for the substitution of the eventually published ma-

Example 4.7 Mazurka, op. 63, no. 2, mm. 25–40; Mazurka, op. 68, no. 4, sketch for mm. 24–39.

Example 4.7   (continued)

zurka for the sketched one. Chopin took great care in his published
sets of mazurkas to ensure what I have termed the "compatibility" of
the individual numbers when they are played in sequence.[59] Simple
matters of size concerned him: ordinarily the longest mazurka appears
last in a set. When the longest work is not last—as in op. 63—the last
work instead is both the most complex and the most securely closed.
But the sketched Mazurka exceeds op. 63, no. 3 in complexity. Instead
of the extended chromatic wanderings of the sketch, Chopin may have
opted for the restrained, relatively diatonic and understated op. 63,
no. 2, a piece not only more cohesive in its own right than the sketch
but one that better fits the needs of the set as a whole.

Internal problems in the sketch demonstrate even more compell-
ingly why Chopin may have decided against publishing the piece. The
most significant of these flaws are related directly to Chopin's new

style, and in particular to the ill-gauged application of one of its tenets in a familiar genre. In other words, just as the Polonaise-Fantasy reveals a successful working out of the ideals of the last style, op. 68, no. 4 may betray their failure. What marked the style of the Polonaise-Fantasy as new were the novel possibilities for musical continuity it explored through sudden juxtapositions of unstable and stable material. The F-Minor Mazurka similarly abounds in adjoining unstable and stable passages: the richly chromatic phrases for which the piece is famous lead invariably to diatonic ones (see Ex. 4.8a and b). Just as in the Polonaise-Fantasy, Chopin first implies a certain type of continuation of a pattern only to veer suddenly and sharply into unex-

Example 4.8   Mazurka, op. 68, no. 4, sketches for mm. 1–9; 62/63–70.

Example 4.8   (continued)

pected territory. The diatonic resolution of the chromatic sequences in the opening phrase already follows this procedure, but even more unexpected is the juxtaposition of contrasting elements in the repetition of this phrase. We expect the sequences to wend their way back to the tonic F minor as in the opening statement; instead Chopin directs them into a distant and stable A major before providing the expected tonic resolution.

Nevertheless, the placement of the unstable and stable material within the overall structure of the Mazurka differs strongly from that in the Polonaise-Fantasy. Rather than reserve the juxtapositions for structural seams, Chopin instead employs them only within sections. The structural divisions are all articulated cleanly. The technique that in the Polonaise-Fantasy allowed for a striking redefinition of overall musical form is constrained in the Mazurka to merely local applications. As a result, the work sounds strangely inconsistent in its intent, at once exploring unstable chromatic realms that would imply a more continuous kind of overall structure and retreading familiar (even banal) diatonic ground, all within an orthodox, complex ternary form. Perhaps it was this uncertainty of internal direction, even more than its proportions relative to the rest of op. 63, that caused Chopin to reject the F-Minor Mazurka for publication. In any case, these musical flaws stand, whether or not the suggestion that the sketch was meant for op. 63 proves true. In my view, the fundamental significance of the sketch lies in the fact that it was abandoned not because of Chopin's health but because it contained irreparable musical defects.[60]

Two antithetical notions collided in the F-Minor Mazurka: the desire to explore the new possibilities of musical continuity allowed by the new style, and the wish to maintain the generic, sectional integrity of the mazurka.[61] The one forged new pathways; the other communed with the past. Chopin allowed considerations of genre to rule, and consequently frustrated the effect of the new style. He succeeded with it in the Polonaise-Fantasy because there his fusion of two genres released him from the constraints of familiar types of pieces. But in the F-Minor Mazurka, Chopin fell short in his attempt to merge the experimental new style with an old genre.

Formal redefinition, stylistic experimentation, the clash between the aspirations of the new language and the constraints of genre, the development of new means of musical continuity—these central traits of Chopin's last style emerge from close study of the Polonaise-Fantasy and the F-Minor Mazurka. The exploration could continue, with the Sonata for Violoncello, op. 65, a fine work that nonetheless falters in attempting to integrate the newly developed style of musical continuity with its unstable, chromatic harmonies into a genre that normally for Chopin featured long passages of stable, diatonic material. We could probe the Nocturne in C Minor, op. post., an unsuccessful experiment at abandoning the large-scale structural contrasts that generically typ-ify the nocturne in favor of an additive principle of form at the local level. And we might investigate the song "Melodia" ("Z gór, gdzie dźwigali"), a superb blend of a familiar genre with a new formal scheme in which the through-composed, harmonically fluid body of the song is presented as a large parenthesis in the descending melodic sequence that frames the work. But the Polonaise-Fantasy and the F-Minor Mazurka lay bare the concerns of the last style; an examination of them suffices to underscore the extraordinary significance of this final, abbreviated creative period.

Chopin experimented widely, if not always successfully, in his last style, and so broke sharply with his own musical past: for the first time since the formation of his mature musical language in the late 1820s and early 1830s, he explored substantially new possibilities in his art. The last style thus affected crucially Chopin's compositional development, but this is not its only significance. Scholars have long argued that a fundamental caesura in European musical style begins around 1848–1849. On the one hand, they cite the new developments around this date: Wagner's cultivation of the music drama, Liszt's efforts in the symphonic poem, Verdi's increasing concern for more continuous operatic structures, the general fascination with distantly chromatic harmonies, the common interest in concise melodic mo-tives. On the other hand, the old guard faded from view around this time: the lives or active compositional careers of Mendelssohn, Cho-pin, and Schumann all ended near this date. The more probing his-torians draw attention to the important continuities that exist from the first to the second halves of the century—Carl Dahlhaus, for ex-ample, remarks that Liszt's novel procedures after 1850 mostly derive from aesthetic ideas of the 1830s and 1840s. But they argue, none-theless, that the essential difference between the two eras still stands—

Dahlhaus, again, writes that even had Schumann lived to Wagner's age, he would have done little but repeat himself: his musical style would have remained that of the first half of the century.[62] However compelling these arguments, one particular aspect needs to be reconsidered in light of Chopin's last style. If the search for new methods of musical continuity and the abandonment of or dissatisfaction with old conventions and genres are indeed fundamental to the definition of the new epoch beginning about 1848–1849, then Chopin—at least as represented in his last style—ought to be counted among the innovators rather than among the old order. Dahlhaus's arch observation about Schumann may be stood on its head for Chopin, whose date of death is less decisive than the stylistic changes he wrought before 1849. Had Chopin lived, the value of modernity expressed in Honoré Daumier's pronouncement "il faut être de son temps" would have seemed no less apparent to him than to Wagner, Verdi, or Liszt.[63]

Contemporaneity exacted a price, however. The stylistic changes of the day could not have seemed more poorly timed to Chopin, for just when he needed to muster all of his energy in service of his art, the structure of his daily existence collapsed. The meaning of the last style to the composer himself would have been altogether different from whatever general cultural message it communicated. Like nearly every facet of his life at the end, Chopin's aesthetic orientation was in flux. "Where has my art gone?" must be interpreted as more than the plaint of an artist faced with diminishing powers. It is also the cry of one who confronted change in his basic conception of composition just as unsettling as that in his love life, home, and health. And his anguish can only have increased as he realized he would be unable to see the last style through to fruition. Whereas in earlier years he could find in his music solace from the travails of his life, in the last period even this comfort eluded him. For all of its musical and cultural significance, the last style seems overwhelmingly poignant: at the end, the pages of Chopin's tragic story do not exclude his art.

⦃ 5 ⦄

Small "Forms":
In Defense of the Prelude

Chopin was a master of small forms. Few beliefs more centrally govern modern perceptions of Chopin than this one. It supports not only the myriad manifestations of his high stature in our culture (performances and critical analyses alike can be read as endorsements of the composer's extraordinary skill at miniatures), but also the occasional barbs that are thrown his way (some writers profess a complementary axiom that mastery of large forms eluded him).

But while the centrality of this belief may lend it the appearance of a timeless truth, it appears instead that the meaning of its fundamental term, *form*, has altered substantially over the past century and a half. When we unreflectively discuss form in Chopin's music as if its intent were self-evident, we therefore at least to some degree misrepresent its significance to his culture. All of us—pianists and amateur enthusiasts as well as musicologists—need to be aware of this disjunction between past and present: before we can probe aspects of form in Chopin's miniatures, we need to explore some of the ways in which the ideas of form and (to a lesser extent) smallness were construed in the first half of the nineteenth century. That these explorations can have very practical applications I hope to show in the second portion of this chapter, which will focus on Chopin's smallest forms, the preludes.

What then was meant by musical form in Chopin's day, and for whom was it an issue? While other interpretations are sometimes aired (these will be noted below), form in modern parlance most often refers to the structure, morphology, or plan of a musical work ("sonata form" and "binary form" are two commonly invoked examples in this sense). It is generally the concern of composers, performers, and listeners alike (the study of it has become, in the words of one authority, "a basic tool of musical analysis").[1] But this definition and this function only partially circumscribe the possibilities of what was a richly nuanced concept in the 1830s and 1840s. Two other senses of form prevailed during Chopin's lifetime, the first deriving from aesthetics and generally embracing all of the constructive means by which beauty might be expressed in music, and the second serving more particularly as a synonym for *genre* or *kind*. I will discuss these three meanings separately, beginning with the most general.

Aesthetic Form

One of the legacies of late eighteenth- and early nineteenth-century aesthetic debates about form was a profusion of definitions of the concept. While the general terms of the debate—ideas of order, proportion, coherence, pattern, and unity that dated at least as far back as the Pythagoreans and Plato—remained roughly the same, successive writers tended to characterize form somewhat differently. Most of them, however, did not react directly to Platonic or Aristotelian ideas about the concept, but rather to the notion, expounded by the eighteenth-century philosophers who founded the discipline of aesthetics (among them Baumgarten, Shaftesbury, and Hutcheson) that form was the means by which beauty was expressed in the arts.

In what did this form consist? Consider the following array of representative citations from philosophers, theorists, and critics:

> Beauty should surely be a question only of form . . . Any form of an empirically perceived object (whether external or internal) is either a *pattern* or an *interplay*. In the latter case the interplay is either of shapes (in space: mime and dance) or simply of emotions (in time). The *charm of* colors or the pleasurable sounds of instruments may also be involved; but in the first case the *design* constitutes the actual object of any pure judgement of taste and in the second, the composition. (Immanuel Kant, *Kritik der Urteilskraft,* 1790)

Musical form is a process whereby the infinite is embodied in the finite; hence the forms of music are inevitably forms of things in themselves. In other words, they are forms of ideas exclusively under a phenomenal guise.

Since this has now been demonstrated in the general sense, it must also be true of rhythm and harmony, which are the [platonic] forms peculiar to music. In other words, rhythm and harmony can express the forms of eternal things to the extent that those forms are thought of entirely as discrete entities. (Friedrich Schelling, *Philosophie der Kunst,* 1802–1803)

But what delights and enchants us is how the composer uses sound to create melody and harmony, thereby evoking a specific reaction: in other words, it is the *form* of the music . . . no piece of music should be loosely constructed from sections that effectively cancel each other out and neutralize the overall impression. Everything should possess unity in diversity. (Christian Friedrich Michaelis, *Allgemeine musikalische Zeitung* 9 [1806])

Form. In music, as well as in the other fine arts, there is often talk of the form of the art work, and by the form of a musical composition, one understands the way it is brought before the soul of the listener.

Daily experience indeed teaches that the different genres of musical compositions are distinguished merely by their forms; the symphony has a different form from the concerto, the aria a different one from the song; even so, if the aestheticians maintain that that which one calls the beauty of a musical composition is contained in the selfsame form, then there must certainly also exist an incidental [*zufällige*] form in which the beauty is contained, and that can just as well be present as lacking, otherwise, e.g., any rondo, if it conforms to its usual form, would maintain the character of beauty without further conditions.

If accordingly the discussion is of the form of art products in such a way that it is dedicated to the content of beauty, then one does not thereby understand that external [*äußerliche*] form of art works whereby the genres themselves may be distinguished, rather on the contrary the particular way in which variety is consolidated in unity, or the particular way in which the composer transmitted to the art work the moments of pleasure that were contained in his ideal. (Heinrich Christoph Koch, *Kurzgefaßtes Handwörterbuch der Musik für praktische Tonkünstler und für Dilettanten,* 1807)

[Music's] essence is play, through and through; nothing else. It has no content of any kind that men have tried to adduce from and give to it. It simply comprises forms, regulated combinations of sounds and sequences of sounds. (Hans-Georg Nägeli, *Vorlesungen über Musik,* 1826)

The idea of beauty . . . is expressed either completely, or at any rate in large measure, in form, and it awakens a pleasure that is in the highest degree disinterested . . . Now form is not merely a matter of the shape of a thing, nor can the uninterrupted contemplation of individual words, notes or ideas make them more or less beautiful, or more or less displeasing. Beauty of form really results from the ways in which variety is molded into a unity according to the rules of taste. (Gustav Schilling, "Beauty and the Beautiful," *Encyclopädie der gesammten musikalischen Wissenschaften* [Stuttgart, 1834–1838; 2d ed., 1840–1842])

Beethoven mastered these rich resources and exploited them as he strove so astonishingly to break the bonds of the traditional forms that his predecessors had established. What is musical form but the natural body that a piece of music must assume in order to establish itself as a living organism? The laws of nature apply just as much to what is heard as to what is seen . . . Mendelssohn showed a constant concern for organic construction, for form as it is called in short. (August Kahlert, "Über den Begriff der klassischen und romantischen Musik," *Allgemeine musikalische Zeitung,* 50 [1848])[2]

To search in the above accounts for a general meaning of form is to risk smoothing over disagreements among significantly distinct philosophical traditions.[3] Nevertheless, three ideas recur often enough to be worthy of note. First, most aestheticians included notions of pattern or design in their definitions. Kant stated this belief expressly (at the same time broaching the complementary idea of "interplay"), whereas Schilling admitted it while claiming that form should not be limited to design or morphology ("form is not merely a matter of the shape of a thing").

Schilling's last assertion alerts us to the second important trend in aesthetic discussions of the period: the constructive features that constitute form usually remained rather loosely defined. Hence Michaelis vaguely located form in melody and harmony, while Nägeli more ambiguously thought that forms were "regulated combinations of sounds and sequences of sounds." And Michaelis, Koch, and Schilling all took refuge in the hackneyed aesthetic dictum of form as unity in diversity (more on this formula below). Kahlert's conception of form as "the natural body that a piece of music must assume in order to establish itself as a living organism," as "organic construction," lies somewhere between the view of form as pattern ("the natural body") and form as a broader constructive entity that gives the work life ("a living organism"). Kahlert's theories bear the strong imprint of Hegel (compare the latter's statement in his *Aesthetik* that "the inner consciousness itself thus becomes the form in which music contrives to embody its content").[4]

We find the third significant idea broached in Koch's distinction between form as a schematic "incidental" or "external" concept, and form as the manifestation of the content of beauty, represented by the consolidation of variety in unity. Koch's opposition draws on the previous two notions about form, and assesses their respective worth. Composers and dilettantes help distinguish genres through a form both "incidental" and "wanting." The form revealed in "particular" mixtures of diversity in unity or feelings of the composer helps elucidate the "content of beauty," a positive goal.[5] This distinction between "outer" and "inner" form recurs, expressly or implicitly, in later aesthetic discussions. Thus when Schelling identified "rhythm" as one of the "forms peculiar to music," he understood "rhythm" (by which he meant "the periodic division of something uniform") to express some of the "inner" meaning of the work (rhythm "constitutes the concept of unity expanding into diversity"; its "beauty is not material").[6] Likewise Schilling's remark, cited above in a different context, that "form is not merely a matter of the shape of a thing" hinges on this opposition between "outer" and "inner."

In practical forums (such as composition manuals or newspaper criticism) from Chopin's time, the precise philosophical lineage of citations of aesthetic form cannot usually be determined. Most often, writers who invoked the concept referred generally to the entire organization of the composition, and the ways in which all of its parts related to one another.[7] These references nonetheless demonstrate that at least a general, sometimes casual, cognizance of the positions of the aestheticians reached the populace at large. At the same time, the very broadness with which form in the aesthetic sense was cited suggests that the idea did not occupy a particularly prominent niche in the minds of this populace.

Generic Form

Far more significant in musical circles was the second pervasive sense of form, meaning genre or kind.[8] The quotation from Koch already introduced us to this usage, which is still with us today: when we hear talk of, say, nineteenth-century Polish dance forms, we understand this to refer to such genres as the mazurka and polonaise. But we have repressed and even reversed the understanding held in musical cultures of Chopin's time of the relationship of this meaning of form, and form meaning *structure* or *plan*. For form as a synonym of genre was by far the more common of the two; indeed, for most composers, critics, and listeners, structural form was widely considered but one of many constructive and affective features that might enter into the composition and perception of genres.

When the word "form" appeared in journalistic criticism from Chopin's day, it usually meant genre or kind. The following excerpts show this clearly:

> The true Polish mazurka, such as M. Chopin reproduces for us here, carries so particular a character, and at the same time adapts with such advantage to the expression of a somber melancholy as well as to that of an eccentric joy—it is suitable as much to love songs as to war songs—that it seems to us preferable to many other musical forms. (a review of the Mazurkas, op. 17)[9]

> The form of the sonata maintains its authority amid the countless small forms of salon pieces occasioned by the taste of fashion. Because it traverses in its three or four movements a whole scale of sentiments, it offers the composer not merely occasion to verify his richer and persistent ingenuity, rather it also demands great mastery in the accomplishment of extended forms. (a review of the Sonata in B Minor, op. 58)[10]

Here too, as in its aesthetic guise, form as genre admitted a much wider variety of musical experience than did the simpler notion of schematic form. For as we saw in Chapter 1, the concept of genre (when properly understood as extending beyond a simple classificatory notion derived from a list of shared characteristics) involves the conceptions and perceptions of composers, performers, and listeners.[11] Social constructions lie at the heart of genre: the composer employs some of the conventions and gestures of a genre in writing a piece, and the listener (or the performer) interprets certain aspects of the piece in a way conditioned by this genre. The genre is not situated solely either in the composer's deeds or the listener's responses; rather the interaction of the two yields this significant framework for the communication of musical meaning. The interpretation of a genre, as Laurence Dreyfus observes, depends largely on the people who use it, which helps explain the emphasis given to affect and values in early nineteenth-century descriptions of genres.[12] And the way in which a genre was used also reveals much about contemporary attitudes toward the past and the present: the genre embodied tradition and experience, and sometimes the rejection of the same. Hence references to form in the sense of genre often reveal much about the ideological functions that a particular kind served in its societies.

Structural Form

In considering the meanings of structural or morphological form in Chopin's day, we need to distinguish among the groups who used the concept. For something quite akin to our modern structural sense of form (and in many cases, for example the sonata and the concerto, serving as the basis of it) was in common employ during the eighteenth and the first part of the nineteenth centuries. But it has been insufficiently stressed in the modern literature that form in this sense appeared almost exclusively in contexts intended primarily for composers, which is to say in composition manuals.[13] Throughout the eighteenth and early nineteenth centuries, in other words, structural form was primarily considered part of the technical arsenal that a composer presumably mastered, along with such skills as counterpoint and harmony. Like all facets of technique, and in particular like the precepts of rhetoric from which it was derived, composers deployed structural form in order to produce expressive reactions; it was not necessarily understood as an expressive feature in itself. And like other technical features, listeners tended to consider it secondary to such aspects as genre and expression.

Yet the matter is not quite so simple. For we can date precisely to Chopin's lifetime the tentative beginnings of the modern attitude that grants to structural form a leading role in the musical understanding of both composer and listener. The *Berliner allgemeine musikalische Zeitung,* a new and liberal music periodical, ran in the mid- and late 1820s several articles and reviews that touted the benefits for listeners of grasping structural form. (Many of them were by the editor, A. B. Marx, who would later become the central figure in the establishment of the doctrine of structural forms.) Robert Schumann's famous 1835 review of Berlioz's *Symphonie fantastique* apologetically demonstrates the comprehensibility and symmetry of the first movement by comparison to the "traditional model" for symphonic first movements.[14] In the following excerpt, from an 1842 review by the French critic Maurice Bourges, we can see an example of such early formal analysis applied to Chopin's Nocturnes, op. 48 (I cite only the discussion of the first Nocturne of the set, in C minor):

> Here in a few words is the outline [*coupe*] of the thirteenth nocturne. A first period, in C minor, is distinguished by the character of predominant melody [*mélodie dominante*]. The second, in C major, begins pianissimo; it belongs to the complex form that has been very nicely dubbed melodic harmony [*harmonie-mélodique*]. Then it is ended by the reproduction of the first theme, accompanied this time by throbbing chords [*d'accords battus*] that give a new warmth to the general rhythm . . .
>
> I might have feared your reproach, madame, about this exactitude in analyzing the outline of these pieces, if I had not known that you are among those who attach a great interest in the intelligence of the plan. It is the sole means of giving the performance a character of indispensable unity. Without this, how would one render sensible the distinction of essential and accessory ideas? To make one's playing a kind of painting, to give it perspective, profundity, one absolutely must master the material plan of the work, even if it is a question of a simple prelude where the arrangement hides beneath an apparent disorder.[15]

The last, rationalizing paragraph as well as the general tone of Bourges's review suggests that structural form—*plan* or *coupe* in his vocabulary borrowed from the theorist Antoine Reicha—had in 1842 something of the quality of a new-found toy that one might place at the disposal of an amateur pianist or listener.[16] And Bourges's simplistic attempt at the description or analysis of structural form remained very much the exception in criticism—French criticism, at least—for the remainder of Chopin's life. Far more common, as I remarked above, were references to "form" in its aesthetic or generic aspects.

The structural sense of form really began to catch hold firmly in Germany in the 1840s. To a large degree, this resulted from the widespread influence of Hegel's ideas on aesthetics, particularly as promulgated by such musical apologists and followers as Eduard Krüger and A. B. Marx.[17] In the pages of the *Neue Zeitschrift für Musik,* Krüger in 1842 undertook an extensive critique of Hegel's aesthetics as they applied to music. The new attitude toward the concept of form emerges clearly when we compare the earlier accounts of aesthetic form with Krüger's discussion of Hegelian "musical form" in terms of "fundamental binary and ternary structure[s]."[18] Form was no longer identified amorphously with all that constructively contributes to the perception of beauty in a musical work. Rather, for Hegel (as interpreted by Krüger), it was something more structural, more architectonic. And Marx carried this sense of architectonic form even further when he codified a doctrine of structural forms (his *Formenlehre*) in a variety of theoretical works (including the *Allgemeine Musiklehre* of 1839 and the famous *Lehre von der musikalischen Composition* of 1842). While Marx's theories were intended primarily to inform the activities of composers, their influence spread generally in the musical culture of the time, in part because of the primacy Marx gave to form in the remarkably lucid pedagogical layout of his volumes (Marx taught at the University of Berlin). As Dreyfus has noted, Marx's *Formenlehre* began to reverse the perceptual hierarchy of previous generations in its grossly anachronistic assertion that structural form determines musical genre. The comparatively incidental quality of genre in Marx's scheme, as well as the powerful influence of his *Formenlehre* for nearly a century after its inscription, together dealt the concept of musical genre a blow from which it has only recently begun to recover.

The relative novelty of structural form for listeners (as opposed to composers) and its greater prominence in German circles than in French or Polish suggest that it would not have figured very centrally in contemporary perceptions of Chopin's works. For a few progressive amateurs and for his professional cohorts, it may have been another story, but for the majority of his audience, form remained primarily a generic concept, and to some degree an aesthetic one.

Smallness: The Status of the Miniature

Unlike the concept of form, more richly inflected in the 1830s and 1840s than today, the resonances of the adjective *small*—especially the negative ones—were, when applied to artworks, not so much different from those we encounter today. It is nonetheless useful to remind ourselves that our own often covert evaluations of small forms have rather more overt historical roots.

In particular, the notion that smaller types rank lower hierarchically than larger kinds has remained ingrained since Chopin's time. An extended controversy developed in France over the perceived assault on the hierarchy of genres by Romantic artists such as Géricault.[19] Something similar followed in musical circles, according to an article from 1835 by August Kahlert, "Genre Painting in Modern Music" *(Die Genrebilder in der modernen Musik).*[20] As I noted in Chapter 2, Kahlert saw the recent glut of short instrumental compositions and the decline of larger kinds as a parallel phenomenon to the displacement of historical subjects in favor of genre painting:

> Genre painting has also become visible in music. It is characteristic that enthusiasm for the great, the far-reaching, the deep must make way for a multitude of small designs, accomplished forms for the graceful, charming, coquettish. The lowest and most popular music genre, dance music even, must have recourse to the most expensive finery in order to corrupt the meaning. Dramatic music is with the greatest of pleasure composed of nothing but small forms (Romances, Couplets, Lieder, etc.). The catalogues swarm with Sketches, Eclogues, Impromptus, Bagatelles, Rhapsodies, Etudes, etc. One wants as much variety as is possible, however nothing but the small. Because however the newer art works are too weak to represent themselves, a content is therefore *pressed upon* them, and thus arise instrumental pieces with *literary titles [Ueberschriften].*[21]

Kahlert laid bare a typical complaint against small forms, namely that the various eclogues and etudes, with their inscriptions that attempted weakly to compensate for their lack of genuine musical con-

tent, had displaced attention away from the more deserving and accomplished monumental kinds (in which category he presumably
included symphonies and sonatas). And recall, too, from Chapter 2
that Kahlert's descriptive language reveals the role of gender in the
formulation of his evaluative stance. Kahlert (and many others) de-
valued small forms in part because they were perceived as being "feminine" music.

Even among progressives, smaller kinds could seem suspect when
they were pursued to the exclusion of larger genres. Critics most often
raised this concern in connection with Chopin when considering the
limited instrumental sphere within which the composer worked.
Hence while Schumann, one of Chopin's earliest and most staunch
advocates, generally praised his achievements, he nonetheless found
himself wondering if the Pole would ever take the next step in his
artistic development:

> Ever new and inventive in the external qualities [*im Äußerlichen*], in
> the construction [*Gestaltung*] of his compositions, in special instru-
> mental effects, in the internal qualities [*im Innerlichen*] however he
> remains the same, so that we would fear that he will not rise any
> higher than he has already risen. And although this is high enough
> to render his name immortal in the history of modern art, his effec-
> tiveness is limited to the narrow sphere of piano music, whereas with
> his powers he might climb to far greater heights, and gain an influ-
> ence on the general development of our art.[22]

Schumann went on to urge contentment with Chopin's output as it
stood; nonetheless, the familiar comparison with the "greater heights"
to be achieved in what we can safely interpret to be the larger genres
remains a significant feature of Schumann's view of Chopin.[23] As we
will see, the same comparison still lurks silently—and invidiously, I
would say—even among the most well meaning of contemporary performers and critics.

Small Forms: The Preludes, Op. 28

How can the preceding analysis of both halves of the term *small form*
affect our practices as pianists and listeners? I would hope it might
expand our awareness of its historical possibilities, and in turn suggest

some alternative (and perhaps more historically appropriate) modes of understanding than those delimited by our customary notion of structural form. As just one instance of the fascinating and productive ways in which this historical orientation might affect our interpretation of Chopin, I would like to consider his smallest forms, the Preludes, op. 28. I am particularly concerned with their supposed status as a cycle to be performed integrally by pianists (one seldom hears it any other way these days) and analyzed as a unified or organic set by critics.

The assertion that the twenty-four pieces of op. 28 constitute an integral set grew in large part from lingering insecurity over the meaning of Chopin's title, "Preludes." The issue troubled commentators from the very start, as witness these famous reactions by Schumann (in a curt review of the entire set) and Liszt (in an account of Chopin's 1841 Parisian recital):

> I would term the Preludes remarkable [*merkwürdig,* which also carries the connotation "strange"]. I confess I imagined them differently, and designed in the grandest style, like his Etudes. Almost the opposite: they are sketches, beginnings of Etudes, or, so to speak, ruins, individual eagle pinions, all disorder and wild confusion.[24]

> Chopin's Preludes are compositions of an order entirely apart. They are not only, as the title might make one think, pieces destined to be played in the guise of introductions to other pieces; they are poetic preludes, analogous to those of a great contemporary poet, who cradles the soul in golden dreams, and elevates it to the regions of the ideal.[25]

Neither Schumann nor Liszt found what he expected in the Preludes. Schumann was trumped and mildly disturbed by their brevity and apparent disorder; Liszt was impressively struck by the disparity between the function suggested by their title and what he perceived as their more exalted artistic purpose.[26] A century later, André Gide concisely summed up this last line of thought when he wrote: "I admit that I do not understand well the title that Chopin liked to give to these short pieces: *Preludes.* Preludes to what?"[27] At stake for these observers is precisely the status of Chopin's Preludes when viewed against the tradition of the genre—or form, as Chopin's cohorts would likely have said—to which they evidently belong.

The preludes known to Chopin's contemporaries (and Gide's too) functioned in just the way their title would suggest: as brief, often improvisatory introductions to other, larger works. At the most utilitarian level, these pieces allowed the performer to test the feel of the keyboard before launching into a longer work, and gave the listener a chance gradually to settle into the musical experience. Czerny stated this directly in 1836:

> It is akin to a crown of distinction for a keyboardist, particularly in private circles at the performance of solo works, if he does not begin directly with the composition itself but is capable by means of a suitable prelude of preparing the listeners, setting the mood, and also thereby ascertaining the qualities of the pianoforte, perhaps unfamiliar to him, in an appropriate fashion.[28]

More engagingly, preludes tested either the pianist's improvisational mettle (when actually conceived in performance) or the composer's skill at conveying the impression of impromptu display (when notated). Composers frequently deployed block chords, rapid scalar or arpeggiated figuration, and sudden deflections toward other keys (though ordinarily without tonicizing them) to produce this sensation. They normally avoided lending much prominence to themes (preludes were ordinarily monothematic or, better, "monomotivic"), nor did they typically develop their themes or motives. Since the practice of the day demanded that the prelude conclude (though not necessarily begin) in the same key as the work that it preceded, composers published examples of preludes in all the major and minor keys: the amateur pianist who could not manage to improvise a prelude could thereby find published examples suitable to any tonal circumstance. Czerny mentioned one other interesting harmonic permutation: longer and more elaborate preludes attached to works for which the composer provided no introduction should end on the dominant-seventh chord, so as to lead directly into the theme.[29] (The possibility of open-ended conclusions has provocative ramifications for our understanding of Chopin's essays in the genre.) The Preludes by Chaulieu and Czerny shown in Example 5.1 typify the genre as it was understood in the first half of the nineteenth century.

"Utilitarian" is a word that rarely escapes the lips of a Chopin critic. It would hardly do for the "Raphael" or "Ariel" of pianists to be allied

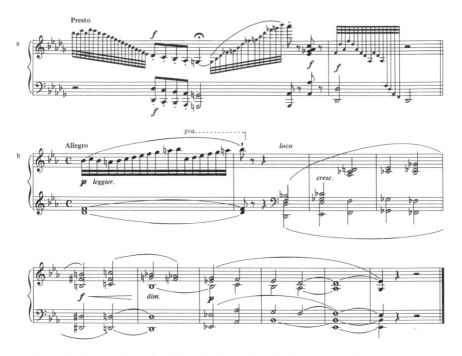

Example 5.1   (a) Charles Chaulieu, Prelude in D-flat Major (from *Vingt-quatre petits préludes,* op. 9, ca. 1820–25). (b) Carl Czerny, Prelude in E-flat Major (from *Systematische Anleitung zum Fantasieren auf dem Pianoforte,* 1836).

with the functional or even the more aesthetically appealing aspects of the prelude described above; instead critics sought more poetic or analytically ambitious explanations for Chopin's efforts in the genre. Hence Schumann's stunning and romantically charged metaphors, hence Liszt's veiled analogy with the poet Lamartine, hence Gide's musings over the title, and hence—I believe—the tendency to conceive of op. 28 as an integral, organic set.

Proponents of the grand unity of the Preludes often quite explicitly reject the "prosaic" tradition of the genre. Indeed, such rejection would seem to be a necessary step for arguments in favor of the artistic wholeness of op. 28. Jean-Jacques Eigeldinger, for example, prefaces his otherwise subtly conceived comments on the motivic unity of the set as a whole with this remark:

Clearly the collection no longer fulfills any of the functions to which its title had laid claim hitherto. To take out some of the Preludes and couple them with other Chopin pieces in the same key might be an interesting experiment at best, but could hardly be termed necessary.[30]

Having found the tradition of the prelude wanting in explanatory power, Eigeldinger goes on to construct a case for the unity of the entire set. He argues that this unity derives from the apparent omnipresence of a motivic cell characterized by a rising sixth falling back to the fifth, a cell that he contends is generated by the dictates of the temperament of Chopin's piano. Apart from this ingenious claim about the correspondence between the motivic cell and the tuning process, Eigeldinger's stance typifies those who would assert a larger meaning for op. 28.[31] In essence, critics locate the highest artistic achievement not so much in the individual preludes themselves (though they seldom deny the quality of these works) as in the nuanced motivic relationships that may be teased out of all twenty-four of the preludes working together. And concert pianists would seem to echo this position by seldom performing the Preludes as anything but a complete set of twenty-four.[32]

Two intertwined problems weaken the force of these arguments. First, they confuse levels of form, privileging a type of extended structural form (and more precisely, a later nineteenth- and twentieth-century type of structural form), and devaluing or ignoring what Chopin and his contemporaries would have understood to be the generic—formal—resonances of the prelude. Said another way, they take a willfully anachronistic viewpoint of the formal organization of the Preludes. Second, these arguments endorse—unwittingly, perhaps—the view that smallness of form works to the aesthetic detriment of a musical work. In contending that op. 28 represents a unified whole, they essentially claim that "large forms" (as an integral op. 28 must surely be considered) were a desideratum for Chopin and all his audiences. While this was certainly true of the conservative wing (represented above by August Kahlert) of the 1830s and 1840s, and occasionally even of more progressive types like Schumann, it cannot be maintained as a generally accepted attitude of the time. More worrisome still, to argue for the worth of op. 28 on the basis of its supposed function as a sublime "large form" rather than on the basis of its individual small numbers would seem at once to perpetuate some of the gender-based aesthetic justifications of the nineteenth century and to accept the premises of the old canard that Chopin was not a master of large forms even as it attempts to refute them. The attitude betrays a continuing distrust of the small, a refusal to accept Chopin's Preludes at face value.

André Gide to the contrary, then, we have no reason to worry the title to op. 28. Chopin and his contemporaries understood perfectly the genre of the prelude; what is more, they valued it on its own terms. Even in the remarks of Schumann and Liszt, we can detect their awareness of the traditional generic functions served by Chopin's Preludes. Schumann's reference to "individual eagle pinions" [*einzelne Adlerfittige*] shows that Schumann entertained no thought that op. 28 might constitute a unified set; indeed, the solitary pinions were "all disorder and wild confusion."[33] And when Liszt wrote that "they are not only . . . pieces destined to be played in the guise of introductions to other pieces," the key word is "only": Liszt at once admitted the traditional function of the genre while he praised the poetic ways in which Chopin's contributions exceeded this tradition.[34]

In Chopin's own practice as both a performer and a composer we find further confirmation that the Preludes drew on the tradition of the genre for at least some of their comprehensibility. First, in Léon Escudier's critique of Chopin's 1841 Parisian recital (which Liszt also reviewed), we read testimony of his skills at preluding:

> One may say that Chopin is the creator of a school of piano and a school of composition. In truth, nothing equals the lightness, the sweetness with which the composer preludes on the piano; moreover nothing may be compared to his works, full of originality, distinction and grace.[35]

Escudier may well have referred to preludes that the composer improvised (the verb *préluder* generally signified the improvisatory practice) as opposed to those that he composed and published (later in the review, he commented separately on the four published preludes performed at the recital). Nonetheless, by underscoring Chopin's skills in this area, he identified one of the traditional formal models against which Chopin's op. 28 would have been judged.[36]

Second, we have a hint that Chopin in performance coupled a Pre-

lude "in the guise of an introduction" (as Liszt would say) to another
of his works. A surviving printed program from his recital in Glasgow
on 27 September 1848 lists as the first item to be performed an "Andante et Impromptu." Beneath the printed line, someone entered in
ink (presumably contemporaneously) "No. 8 & 36."[37] The last
penned number conclusively places the Impromptu as the F-sharp Major, op. 36. The identity of the first work is more problematic. While
sometimes taken to allude to the *Andante spianato* in G major that
precedes the *Grand Polonaise,* op. 22 (a work that Chopin liked to
detach from the *Polonaise*), I would suggest instead that the "No. 8"
refers to the Eighth Prelude of op. 28, in F-sharp minor. Of course,
Chopin left a tempo marking for this Prelude of "Molto agitato," not
"Andante." But the parallel tonalities of the Prelude and the Impromptu (Example 5.2 reproduces the first measures of each piece)

Example 5.2   (a) Prelude in F-sharp Minor, op. 28, no. 8, mm. 1–2. (b) Impromptu in F-sharp Major, op. 36.

make a more logical join (one further facilitated by the turn to F♯ major toward the end of the Prelude, measures 29–31; see Example 5.3 below) than would follow from a linking of the *Andante spianato* and the Impromptu.[38]

More commonly, Chopin performed the preludes as separate pieces, often in groups with other preludes. (A typical program listing, this from his 1842 Parisian recital, was "Suite de Nocturne, Préludes, et Etudes.")[39] In this routine we can detect an expansion in the functional possibilities of the genre, such that preludes might also serve as separate concert pieces. Chopin appears to have been largely responsible for this functional expansion. In promoting these "concert" preludes, he essentially followed his practice in the etude, where his contributions to the genre served equally as didactic and as concert works. Chopin's last published Prelude, the C-sharp Minor op. 45, an extended work that plainly was meant to stand alone in performance, clarifies that he was moving in the direction of the "concert prelude" in op. 28. Moreover, this sort of expansion of the possibilities of the genre occurs throughout Chopin's *oeuvre* (indeed, it counts among the chief reasons we celebrate him as a composer). It would be a mistake to presume that "expansion" of the genre meant "negation" of its tradition. Far from it: the expansion in meaning could not have taken place without a deep understanding of and complicity in the tradition from which it partially departs.

As to evidence of the force of formal tradition in the musical construction of the Preludes, an adequate discussion of this issue would overwhelm the boundaries of this chapter. In any event, a number of studies have chronicled quite nicely (if not always explicitly in terms of the tradition of the genre) many of the ways in which the formal qualities of brevity, monothematicism, openness, fractured syntax, and stylized improvisation reveal themselves in various individual preludes.[40] For the purposes of this essay, I wish to draw attention to only one compositional aspect of the Preludes, closure.[41] The endings are one of the most striking features of the preludes, and have much to reveal once we expand our sense of form beyond the structural into the generic.

The endings to the Preludes seldom give comfort. By this I mean that the endings often seem to stand somewhat apart from the body of the prelude; their gestures at closure sound unrelated to what has

passed before. In some instances, this difference can be understood as
a consequence of the monothematic tendency of the genre: when the
musical figure unfolded throughout the body of the prelude seemed
unsuitable as a closing idea, Chopin evidently imported some other
kind of notion to serve as the ending. The stark final cadences of the
A-Minor, D-Major, and F-sharp-Minor Preludes (Example 5.3) produce an arresting textural contrast to the disjointed (in the case of the
A-minor work) and exuberant (in the other two instances) figuration
that precedes them. Other times, though, the dissimilar close arrives
despite the capability of the principal motive to support a similar cadence. The endings to the E-Minor, C-Minor, and G-Minor Preludes
fall into this category (Example 5.4). On still other occasions, Chopin
separated perceptually a cadence that otherwise continued to reproduce the principal motive of the piece. The blurring caused by the open
pedal in the B-Minor Prelude and the *ritenuto* in the last two measures

Example 5.3   (a) Prelude in A Minor, op. 28, no. 2. (b) Prelude in D Major,
op. 28, no. 5. (c) Prelude in F-sharp Minor, op. 28, no. 8.

Example 5.4   (a) Prelude in E Minor, op. 28, no. 4. (b) Prelude in C Minor, op. 28, no. 20. (c) Prelude in G Minor, op. 28, no. 22.

of the D-flat-Major Prelude effectively isolate the cadential gestures from what precedes them (Example 5.5). And finally, there are those cadences that flow smoothly from the body of the prelude but nonetheless simply undermine full closure in one way or another. The imperfect cadence of the B-Major Prelude provides a mild example, and the famous e♭″ that colors the end of the F-Major Prelude a more radical one (Example 5.6).

Now plainly the structural qualities of these "irregular" endings contributed to the "poetic" ethos of the Preludes as constructed by the likes of Liszt and Schumann. It is not difficult, for example, to perceive a connection between the nature of closure in op. 28 and Schumann's characterization of the individual pieces as "ruins." But the generic resonances of these endings cast even more fascinating light on Chopin's strategy. For the frequent deflections of closure in op. 28

Example 5.5 (a) Prelude in B Minor, op. 28, no. 6. (b) Prelude in D-flat Major, op. 28, no. 15.

Example 5.6 (a) Prelude in B Major, op. 28, no. 11. (b) Prelude in F Major, op. 28, no. 23.

at once evoke and transform a particular strand of the generic tradition: the conclusions of improvised, longer preludes, which Czerny described as ending on dominant-seventh chords. The evocation is nowhere more charged than in the F-Major Prelude (Example 5.6b), the E♭-tinged ending of which has been the subject of many elaborate, and not entirely adequate, "structural" explanations. But the final measures make most sense when heard in generic terms as an ironic commentary on this tradition of the open-ended prelude. The e♭" of measure 21 recalls the similar gesture of measure 12, where the added seventh helped push the harmony to the subdominant in the following measure. While the harmony of the ending of the Prelude cannot really be heard as an applied dominant (Agawu observes that "the identity of the F♭^{7} is . . . transferrable [from measure 12], but not its syntactical property"),[42] the memory of its earlier function is enough to call to mind the tradition of dominant-seventh cadences. And this tradition leads us, if ever so fleetingly and skeptically, to consider whether the F-Major Prelude should quirkily serve as an introduction to a larger work in B♭ major.

Chopin evoked this quality of open-endedness in order to transform the nature of closure in the short, notated prelude, where previously (and indeed still, in several of the preludes of Chopin's op. 28) full closure had prevailed. As we have seen, Chopin ordinarily transformed the closural tendencies of the genre less radically than in the F-Major Prelude: rather than challenge the very idea of closure, Chopin normally preferred simply to leave matters somewhat undone at the ends of preludes. And curiously enough, one reason he may have been prompted to transform the genre in this way was to facilitate one of its traditional generic functions. For when a prelude lacks full closure, it more effortlessly serves "in the guise of an introduction" to another work. In other words, by ending preludes abruptly and incompletely, Chopin allowed for an ensuing longer work to fulfill the closural promise left hanging in the introductory prelude. The memory of this possibility for fuller closure would have animated the "concert" prelude too, with closure deferred from prelude to prelude (if they were performed in groups together) or even into the next gathering of pieces. Perhaps actual full closure might arrive; perhaps it might not: the ambiguity or insecurity thus embodied in the unfolding recital would have had a strong appeal to the aesthetic sensibilities in Chopin's time.[43] The most common kind of accolade that befell Chopin after his recitals in the 1840s—he was constantly dubbed the "poet," "Ariel," or "sylph" of the piano, as we saw in Chapter 3—probably had something to do with the play of ambiguity created by his "concert" preludes. Indeed, this ambiguity might well have influenced Liszt's roundabout description of the genre as acting in the *guise* of an introduction.

Chopin issued a kind of challenge to his audiences in publishing the Preludes, a challenge we have by and large not met. By asking listeners and performers to accept a transformed genre whereby individual preludes might serve both as introductions to other works and as self-standing concert pieces, he challenged the conservative notion that small forms were artistically suspect or negligible. But in considering just the endings of preludes, we have seen how the modern practice of interpreting form primarily as a structural attribute has led on the one hand to a blinkered view of the possibilities of the genre, and on the other, to a problematic conception of the Preludes as a unified set. An examination of other attributes of op. 28 would only magnify these conclusions.

Perhaps it is time to accept Chopin's challenge. Rather than continue to schedule performances of the complete op. 28 and to con-

Example 5.7   Prelude in A Major, op. 28, no. 7.

struct analytical monuments to its "unity," we need to perform and study the preludes individually. We need to stop reading the title "Prelude" as an obfuscating irritant, and instead to see it as a highly significant clue that can lead to powerful interpretive insights. Understood in this way, Chopin's historical challenge proves to be a good deal more provocative than the anachronistic performing and analytical practices of today, for it would ask audiences to accept the possibility of a work like the A-Major Prelude (Example 5.7) standing alone in performance. In short, it would demand that we finally remove the veil of aesthetic suspicion from smallness.

III

The Musical Work as Social Process

⸘ 6 ⸘

Chopin in the Marketplace

Multiple editions of Chopin's works and the variants found in them have perplexed many an editor and critic. Why did the composer release his works in more than one country, and why more or less contemporaneously? Who was responsible for the alterations in the editions: composer, copyist, publisher, or engraver? If Chopin, why would he allow different versions of the same passage to appear in print? If not the composer, under what authority were readings changed? Each of these questions bears centrally on the study of Chopin's music, and behind each query lurks the institution of music publishing. Before we can weigh the musical import of the variants (I will tackle this issue in the next chapter), we must grasp the mechanics of the international music publishing industry, for it was within the framework created by this industry that the variants occurred.

Two facets of music publishing are relevant here. The first—the principal subject of this chapter—is individual: how Chopin dealt with his publishers in France, the German-speaking states, and England, and what his machinations tell us about the kinds of sources that formed the basis of the editions of his music and the amount of control he had over the text ultimately printed in them. The second is more general: what the possibilities and constraints of music publishing on the Continent and in England were in Chopin's time, and how the nature of this business affected the way Chopin released his music. A full treatment of this second, general area of inquiry is beyond the scope of this chapter, but a few words on the subject will help us better understand Chopin's relations with his publishers.[1]

International commerce in music publishing in the first half of the nineteenth century derived much of its character from the evolution of copyright laws in the individual countries and states. Though several important international copyright agreements were signed during Chopin's lifetime, none of them involved France, the composer's residence, and hence did not benefit him. Instead, what copyright protection he did receive derived from a combination of internal statutes, liberal legal interpretations of the rights of foreigners under these statutes, and financial pressure by publishers on associates in countries where statutes and legal decisions were less clear on the rights of foreigners. When legal interpretations were handed down, the decisions often hinged on the date of publication of the work in question: if it had been released abroad prior to its publication at home, then normally claims of piracy could not be brought in the home country. The date of publication was usually taken to be that listed in the copyright registers of the countries in question, though in fact this date of registration did not always correspond to the actual date when the work was released for sale.

Publishers might have logically deduced that to ensure copyright in their own country was a straightforward matter: simply register the work at home before it was registered abroad. But the disadvantages of anticipating the date of registration abroad must have also been apparent, particularly to the composer, who wished to preserve copyright in all the countries where he or she published: earlier publication in one country weakened his or her status in the other.[2] If, however, the work was registered on the same day in the various countries, then none of the publications would have priority, and presumably, copyright could be retained wherever the work was registered. Common sense, on the part of composers, publishers, and any legal counsel they might have retained, must have played a major role in the evolution of this means of registering works, for even though simultaneous publication was already a well-known and often-used means of disseminating musical works by the second decade of the nineteenth century, the notion that registration on the same day at home and abroad could guarantee copyright in all of the countries did not receive its first legal affirmation until 1848.[3]

For Chopin, the importance of international publication was two-fold: first, by selling the same work to three different publishers he could increase his income from that work over what he would have obtained from a single sale of it, and second, by publishing the work legally in three countries he could presumably avoid the piracies that would remove his control over the texts of his printed music. The second benefit could crumble, however, if the dates of registration did not correspond in the various countries; consequently Chopin spent much time urging his publishers to agree upon the dates of publication of his works.

What a surprise, then, to discover that the machinery of the system went awry for Chopin. A glance at the known dates of registration (which, it needs stressing, may not necessarily coincide with the dates of publication) for the composer's works in France and England (the deposit records for the German-speaking states are lost) reveals that none of his publications can definitely be shown to have been released on the same day.[4]

The English courts were more insistent that publication in England precede or coincide with that on the Continent, but in fact both the English and French publishers risked loss of copyright by not holding to the letter of the law. However, only if challenged in court could copyright be endangered, and no assault on the ownership of copyright in a work by Chopin ever took place. The publishers must have sensed the unlikelihood of anyone ever pirating a Chopin composition (to my knowledge, no pirate edition of a piece by Chopin has ever surfaced in France, and only for Chopin's last three publications, opp. 63–65, might there exist English piracies), else they surely would have been more exacting in the registration of his works.[5] At any rate, "simultaneous publication" is a misnomer when applied to multiple editions of Chopin's music; nevertheless, because the editions were at least intended to appear simultaneously, and because Chopin labored to ensure their simultaneity, I will continue to use the term to refer to those editions that appeared in different countries within a few months of one another.

Chopin's Methods of Publication

Publishing was, for Chopin, fraught with frustration. Various publishers had to be contacted, prices negotiated, dates of release set, manuscripts prepared for the engraver, and proofs corrected. Plans seldom came off with ease, and until a work reached the public (and even at times after it was released), publishers were the target of Chopin's worst invective.[6] It is these splenetic outbursts in the composer's business correspondence that have drawn the most attention from commentators, while the discussions of publishing practice have been passed over.[7] Yet the nuts-and-bolts details found in these letters and in documents from publishers' archives contain valuable information for the study of Chopin's music, evidence that helps sort out the tangle of how Chopin published his works, what kinds of sources he and his publishers used to prepare given editions, and how much control Chopin had over the published text.

When Chopin entered the international market in 1832, the methods and options for dealing with music publishers in France and abroad were firmly established. Rights to publication in foreign countries could be sold directly to the foreign publisher by the composer; they could be offered to a subject of the foreign country, who would then find a publisher; or they could be tendered to a publisher in France, who would sell them in turn to an associate abroad. Monetary rewards were mostly limited to what could be garnered from initial outright sale of rights; escalation clauses, commission arrangements, division of profits, short leases of copyright, and royalty payments, though all possibilities in contracts between authors and publishers in the nineteenth century, were not common in the music world of Chopin's time.[8] Dates of publication were generally established by negotiation; the lead in making arrangements could be taken by either the composer or the publisher. Four types of sources could be sent to foreign publishers: manuscripts in the composer's hand, manuscripts in one or more copyists' hands, printed proof sheets from the French edition (which might or might not be corrected by the composer or copyist before being sent), or, perhaps, plates from the French edition.[9] Thus Chopin's ire arose not from attempting to forge new pathways in international music publishing, but from trying to coordinate the diverse options of the existing framework so that he obtained the maximum benefit. His struggles will emerge clearly when we examine his negotiations and publishing practices in France, the German-speaking states, and England.

France

Shortly after Chopin's debut before Parisian audiences in 1832, he was approached by Aristide Farrenc, who promptly contracted to become the composer's French publisher and representative in the international market.[10] Chopin's first experience with a Parisian publisher reveals much, both about the basic mechanics of publishing a work in Paris and about the composer's tumultuous personal relationships with his publishers. Farrenc never did issue a work by Chopin; their agreement dissolved among accusations by the publisher that the composer was "very lazy and eccentric," and that the passagework in some of his pieces was so difficult as to make them disadvantageous for a publisher to release.[11] (Chopin had, in the meantime, taken up with Maurice Schlesinger, who was to become his primary publisher in Paris.)[12] A close look at Chopin's fledgling efforts to publish in France will set the stage for his later dealings.

When Farrenc called on Chopin the day after his first concert in Pleyel's salon (25 February 1832), the publisher asked to see the contents of the composer's portfolio, and acquired by written deed the copyright to five works: the Concerto in E Minor (op. 11), "pour Piano, avec acc. d'orch. ou Quatour exécuté par Mr. Chopin à son concert," the Trio in G Minor (op. 8), the Krakowiak (op. 14), the Fantasy on Polish Airs (op. 13), and the Concerto in F Minor (op. 21), the last three works all described, like the E-Minor Concerto, as being accompanied by orchestra or quartet.[13] For several weeks Farrenc mulled over his options in marketing the music of his latest acquisition, and because Chopin had earlier been contacted by Heinrich Albert Probst concerning the publication of his works in Germany, the Frenchman decided to offer Probst's successor, Friedrich Kistner, the German rights to Chopin's compositions.

Three letters from Farrenc to Kistner (dated respectively 17 April, 4 May, and 21 December 1832) detail similarly the mechanics of manuscript transmission.[14] Chopin delivers to Farrenc the autograph manuscripts of the five works, after correcting them scrupulously and adding descriptive tempo indications, metronome marks, and rehearsal letters. Farrenc, with the help of his wife, first makes exact copies of these manuscripts, and then has Chopin verify the copies against the originals. The French publisher then sends the copies to Leipzig, evidently keeping the originals for his own edition. However, in his last letter, written after the rupture with the Polish composer, Farrenc claimed that many of Chopin's manuscripts were inadequate in their original state, so that it was necessary for Chopin first to recopy his own manuscript before Farrenc could make a copy in turn to forward to Kistner.

Letters from Schlesinger to Kistner following Chopin's break with Farrenc paint a somewhat different picture. First, Schlesinger found the idea of publishing two concertos in close succession to be unsound fiscally, so he chose to drop one from Chopin's portfolio.[15] At the same time, he was able to acquire the rights to four other works. Thus the package he offered to Kistner contained the Fantasy, op. 13, the Krakowiak, op. 14, the E-Minor Concerto, op. 11, the Trio, op. 8—all of which had been previously owned by Farrenc—and the new works, the Nocturnes, op. 9, the Mazurkas, opp. 6 and 7, and the Etudes, op. 10.[16] Second, Schlesinger proposed a different method of sending Chopin's music to Leipzig. After Chopin delivers the autograph manuscripts for these works to Schlesinger, the Parisian will have them engraved and, after the composer has corrected the proofs, will ship Kistner copies of them for the use of the German in the preparation of his own edition.[17]

Both Farrenc and Schlesinger, then, portrayed a system wherein Chopin delivers an autograph manuscript to his Parisian publisher, who in turn uses it as the basis for the French edition, either as is, or after the composer makes a clean manuscript copy of it (although Farrenc may simply have been trying to discredit Chopin further in the eyes of Kistner by denigrating the utility of his manuscripts). Each of the publishers had control over the choice of foreign countries in which to publish, the selling prices of the works, and the dates of publication. Thus at the start of his career, Chopin signed with his Parisian publishers an agreement that delivered him from any responsibility in the publication of his works beyond what was required to produce the French edition, that is, polishing his manuscript score and correcting the proofs. In his later years, when more of the burden of negotiating arrangements with publishers at home and abroad fell on him, he must have fondly recalled the halcyon days of his first years in Paris.

Although Chopin's entrepreneurial duties escalated as his career blossomed, his part in the preparation of *Stichvorlagen* (manuscripts used for engraving) for his Parisian editions remained essentially the same. Far and away the majority of the French editions were engraved from autograph manuscripts. Occasionally, in the years when Chopin had available to him copyists whom he considered reliable (roughly 1835–1841), one of their manuscripts would be delivered to the Parisian publisher (see, for example, the Fontana copies of the Mazurkas, op. 33 [number 4 of which is in the Library of Congress], the Tarantella, op. 43 [Paris, Bibliothèque Nationale, fonds du Conservatoire], and the Allegro de Concert, op. 46 [New York, Pierpont Morgan Library]).[18] But it may be safely assumed that the French editions of Chopin's music were invariably prepared from manuscript versions that were usually, but not always, in the composer's hand.[19]

Evidence and conclusions about Chopin as a proofreader are less clear-cut. From Schlesinger's letters to Kistner there emerges a strong portrait of Chopin as a meticulous corrector of proofs at the beginning of his Parisian career:

> Chopin is not only a man of talent but he is anxious to maintain his reputation, so he always still polishes his works after they are long since finished; all that he sold us is done, I have had it many times in my hands, but there is a difference with him between *finished* and *delivered* . . . I think that we publishers cannot be angry that an author is so precise, that is always good, for the works will thereby always be better than [those] from the scribblers of whom there are only too many, and who quickly write themselves out; I hope that will not be the case with Chopin.
> . . . only today I received from Chopin the first proofs of the first six Etudes, filled with mistakes; he is so anxious that it is difficult to receive something from him.[20]

That Schlesinger's description is correct is borne out by a comparison of the extant autograph sources for the works being discussed (opp. 6–11, 13, 14) with the French first editions. Numerous alterations of phrasing and articulation marks, pedalings, fingerings, dynamics, accidentals, and pitch could only have come at the proof stage. Direct evidence of these sorts of changes survives in a set of proofs for the Etude, op. 10, no. 2 (Paris, Bibliothèque de l'Opéra). These corrected sheets reveal that, in the early works, Chopin must have made further changes after he read the proofs, for readings appear in the first edition that are not found in the proofs.[21] How these later additions were made is not clear: Schlesinger could have printed another set of proofs after Chopin returned the first, heavily corrected exemplars (although this would be unlikely given the added printing costs that Schlesinger would have to absorb), or Chopin could have communicated the changes verbally or in a now-lost letter. That Chopin would continue to alter his text after returning a first set of proof sheets demonstrates that, when Chopin began preparing texts for his editions in France, he was if anything overeager in his efforts to submit maximally refined versions of his works.

Some of this zeal must have waned, though, as he grew older. In his middle years in Paris, when the services of Fontana and other faithful copyists were available, phrases in letters testify that Chopin allowed them to correct proofs:

> Pleyel wrote to me that you were very *obligeant*, that you corrected the Preludes.[22]

> I am sending you two Nocturnes . . . Perhaps there lack still flats or sharps.[23]

> You may recollect that through the many years after my arrival in Paris, as many times as he [Chopin] published something, he asked me about looking over first the manuscripts, because he almost never wanted to take time over such minutiae himself, next about proofs.[24]

Not all of these quotations, of course, refer to proofs: the second clearly discusses the manuscripts of the two Nocturnes, op. 48, and the first could apply to the manuscript(s) of the Preludes, although this seems less likely than proofs, since the manuscripts for op. 28 had been mailed some seven months before the letter. But the sense of the three excerpts taken together is that, for a period in his life, Chopin was perfectly happy to dump the drudgery of proofreading into the hands of an assistant.

Yet the composer never stopped reading proofs altogether. Chopin at times would review a copyist's manuscript before sending it to a publisher (on 29 July 1841 the composer wrote to Schuberth of Hamburg to alert the publisher to two errors in Fontana's copy).[25] If he checked manuscript copies, there is equal reason to believe that he might read over copyist-corrected proofs as well. Moreover, the composer would still at times have been likely to do all the proofreading himself, even if Fontana or someone else was around to assist. Jan Ekier, general editor of the new Polish complete edition of Chopin's works, finds evidence that the composer corrected the proofs for the Ballade, op. 38, and a close look at the printed sources for the Nocturnes, op. 37 reveals another case.[26]

For many years, scholars believed that the sole surviving example of the proof stage in a work by Chopin was that for the Etude, op. 10, no. 2.[27] But two exemplars of the Troupenas edition of the Nocturnes, op. 37 (and perhaps also the Mazurkas, op. 41) conserved in the Bibliothèque Nationale and originally deposited in accordance with copyright law (the one copy in June 1840, the other in July 1840) preserve what must be at least a late stage of the proofreading process. Physically and musically, the two copies differ greatly. Looking first at physical characteristics, the two exemplars are printed on different paper and have slightly different title pages (the earlier copy lacks the opus number and price, as well as the Troupenas control stamp found on the later copy).

Musical differences are equally numerous. The earlier copy lacks pedal signs and phrase marks altogether. Written performance indications are at odds in the two editions: the later exemplar prints a *sostenuto* in the opening upbeat measure of the first Nocturne that is not found in the earlier exemplar, while the earlier copy offers a curious *presto* in measure 11 of the same work, an indication that disappears in the later version. The earlier copy prints, in measure 15 of op. 37, no. 1, grace notes without beams (that is, as quarter notes); in the later copy, they are printed as eighth-note graces.[28] The crescendo (mm. 119–122) and *ppp* (m. 138) present in the later copy of op. 37, no. 2 are lacking in the earlier copy. Clearly the earlier exemplar represents a musically incomplete version, one that Troupenas never released to the public, as the absence of a price and control stamp on the title page suggests.

But why would Troupenas have deposited an unfinished version of a work? A clue comes from across the Channel. Wessel's firm registered op. 37 at Stationers' Hall on 19 June 1840, which must have been approximately the date for international publication agreed upon by Troupenas, Wessel, and Breitkopf & Härtel.[29] Now what would happen if, as this date arrived, Troupenas saw that his engraving was not complete? To fail to deposit the work would be to jeopardize his copyright in France (although, as I mentioned above, prior publication abroad did not necessarily mean that copyright would be lost in France). Safer then to deliver to the authorities a copy of the engraved work as it stood in June, without the "final" musical alterations. Troupenas then made a second deposit in July, after the engraving was complete and the work was ready to place on sale. This deposit would ensure copyright protection for the precise text released to the public, where previously only the deficient earlier version had been covered.

Having determined that part of the proofreading state is preserved in some printed copies of op. 37, can one be certain that Chopin was the proofreader? That the pedal marks and phrasing indications are totally lacking in the earlier exemplar of the first Nocturne could simply indicate that the engraver, following some preset order of working, had yet to enter these signs onto the plates when it came time to run off copies for the copyright authorities. The Troupenas *Stichvorlage* for op. 37 does not survive; however, some help in determining what kind of text the French engraver worked from may be obtained from the copyist's manuscript of the same works used by the Breitkopf engravers (Warsaw, Biblioteka Narodowa). In this copy, all of the pedal signs and many of the phrase marks are in the hand of the composer, as is the indication *sostenuto* at the opening of the work (although in the Breitkopf copy the word appears above the upbeat measure rather than between the staves, as is the case in the later Troupenas version). If Chopin, according to his normal practice, gave Troupenas his own manuscript for engraving purposes, and if this autograph manuscript was the same one that served as the basis for the scribal copy (which seems likely, as Chopin was not in the habit of making extra clean copies of a work when one would do), then the autograph used by Troupenas's engraver likely also lacked pedal marks and phrasing.[30] Although Chopin ordinarily included such signs in his autograph manuscript, some external deadline (perhaps imposed by the copyist or by Troupenas) could have forced the composer to relinquish his manuscript earlier than he would have liked, but with the knowledge that he could make whatever emendations needed after the scribe finished the copy, or after the proofs were printed. That the composer was responsible for the alterations and additions in the manuscript copy used by Breitkopf & Härtel weighs strongly in favor of his role in making changes in the Troupenas proofs as well.[31]

Chopin for the most part ceased in 1841 to depend on copyists for help in the preparation of manuscripts and editions. With one or two exceptions, the composer alone copied and proofread compositions from the Mazurkas, op. 50 onward.[32] Add to these duties the need to negotiate prices and arrange dates of publication with publishers, and it becomes easy to understand why his correspondence during times when he was readying works for press took on a harried tone. A prime example of the kinds of problems that beset Chopin before he could publish a work comes in two letters concerning the eventual release of the Nocturnes, op. 55 and the Mazurkas, op. 56.[33]

Prior to the first letter, the composer had contracted with Breitkopf & Härtel and Wessel for the publication of the two works, and had arranged the proposed dates of release with them (20 August 1844 is the date mentioned by Chopin, although the two works were registered with the Dépôt légal on 21 August). All was going well until suddenly Chopin, who according to his custom was passing the summer at Nohant at George Sand's chateau, received word that Schlesinger in Paris wanted to delay the date of publication. Chopin was frantic, for a change in the date meant not only numerous letters to Leipzig, London, and Paris trying to set up a new date, but also the risk of disturbing carefully planned production schedules of the German and British houses. A sudden change of plans so late in the game could hurt the composer in future dealings with the two firms. Hence Chopin was quick to dash off a letter to Auguste Franchomme in Paris:

> [31 July 1844]
> Chateau de Nohant near *La Châtre. Indre*
> Dearest. I send you Schlesinger's letter and another for him. Read them—he wants to delay publication and I cannot. If he says *no;* give my manuscripts to *Maho* in order that he take them to Mr. Meissonnier for the same price 600 fr.—I think he will accept.— However I would rather that Schlesinger engrave them.—[crossed out: If *Meysonnier* does not want them, give them to whom you want. It ap(pears)] It should appear the 20th but you know that it is necessary only to register the title that day.—I beg your pardon [illegible cross out] for all this business. I love you and address you

like my brother.—Embrace your children. My respects to Mme Franchomme.

Your devoted friend

F. Chopin

A thousand compliments from Mme Sand.

Upon receipt of this letter, Franchomme acted quickly and managed to settle the affair successfully with Schlesinger. The cellist wrote back to Chopin on the same day he received the composer's letter (2 August), but in the meantime, Chopin had had second thoughts on the best way to rearrange the matter if Schlesinger remained obstinate. Thus his second letter in as many days to Franchomme:

[Nohant, 1 August 1844]

Dearest, I was in a great hurry yesterday when I wrote you to approach Meissonnier through Maho *if Schlesinger refuses* my compositions. I forgot that Henri Lemoine bought for a high price my Etudes from Schlesinger—and that I would rather that it was Lemoine rather than Meissonnier who engraves my manuscripts. I am giving you plenty of trouble, dear friend—but I send you here a letter for H. Lemoine. Read it and settle it with him. It is necessary that he publish or register the title the 20th of this month (August)— Only ask him 300 fr. apiece—that makes 600 fr. for both. Tell him that he only need pay me on my return to Paris, if he wants.—Even give him both for 500 fr. if you believe it necessary—I still would rather [do that] than give them to Meissonnier for 600 fr. as I wrote yesterday without reflecting.—If you have however already arranged something with Meissonnier—that is different—If *not,* do not let them go for less than 1000 fr. Because *Maho,* who is the agent of Haertel (who pays me well), could, knowing that I sell so cheaply in Paris, make me lower my price in Germany.—I torment you much with my business. It is only in the case that Schlesinger persists in not wanting to publish this month.—If you think that Lemoine would give 800 fr. for the two works, ask it—I did not write him *the price* to leave you complete liberty.—I have no time to lose before the departure of the courier. I embrace you dear brother—write me a word.

Yours truly,

Chopin

My respects to Madame.—A thousand kisses to the children.

Ch[ateau] de Nohant near *La Châtre. Indre*

To Franchomme went the actual task of hammering out an agreement with the French publisher, but he acted only on instructions from the composer. Chopin's letters give an idea of how he would operate were he in Paris to carry on the bartering himself. What is clear is that he was able to exert a certain amount of leverage at this stage in his career: if one publisher did not hold to an established bargain, others could be counted on to step in and take over. Thus both Meissonnier and Lemoine could be dangled in front of Schlesinger's eyes as competitors who would gladly publish the two collections if Schlesinger continued to dawdle. Of the two, Lemoine was preferable because he paid higher prices, and because such a deal would avoid the risk that Maho, who was the agent of both Meissonnier in Paris and Breitkopf in Leipzig, might tell the German firm that Chopin was selling his works for less in Paris than he was getting from Germany (as shown in Table 6.1 later in this chapter, Chopin had sold the rights for opp. 55 and 56 to Breitkopf for 1200 francs—twice what he eventually received from Schlesinger).[34] The composer would thus risk losing future revenue from sales to this house.

Despite his bargaining power, however, Chopin does not appear very forceful in these letters. His vacillations on which publisher to choose and on what price to demand reflect his desire to remain with Schlesinger. It is unlikely that this wish arose out of any altruistic feelings of loyalty and friendship—Chopin was all too willing to heap insults on Schlesinger in his letters—rather, it likely came from a respect for the relative marketing power of Schlesinger's firm. Not only was Schlesinger's one of the largest houses in Paris, which implied a well-established clientele and means of diffusion, but he sat at the helm of the *Revue et Gazette musicale de Paris* as well. By publishing with Schlesinger, Chopin could count on the ready-made audience that frequented the publisher's shop at 97, rue Richelieu, and on all the good publicity that one of the two most prominent music journals in Paris could manufacture (the other journal, *La France musicale,* was owned by Schlesinger's bitter competitor Léon Escudier, and was thus less likely to print a kind word about one of his rival's composers). Chopin was undoubtedly relieved upon reading that Franchomme had successfully arranged the matter with Schlesinger.

Chopin's prominent position in the Parisian music world is reflected in another publishing practice, one alluded to in the letter of 1 August

1844 to Franchomme: the resale to a new publisher of works released earlier by a different one. The first known instance of the resale of works by Chopin occurred as early as 1834, when Schlesinger purchased the plates of the Rondo, op. 16 and the Mazurkas, op. 17 from the assets of Ignace Pleyel & Cie, but the practice did not begin in earnest until Chopin's name was well-established in the 1840s.[35] Lemoine, mentioned in the letter to Franchomme as having bought some etudes from Schlesinger at a high price, purchased a number of works in 1844, including the Etudes, opp. 10 and 25, the Variations, op. 12, and the Waltz, op. 18. Chopin, having signed over the rights to his works with his original sale, had no control over the resale of his works, but in theory could have been called upon to make revisions by the new publisher (who would presumably pay the composer for this labor) in order to increase the commercial value of the work. Such may have been Brandus's ploy when he announced a forthcoming publication: "We have just acquired the property rights to the PRELUDES of CHOPIN of which we are preparing a new edition."[36] Grabowski observes that the Catelin edition exists in two slightly different states, and that the second state already bears the control stamp of Brandus (which would indicate that it dates from no earlier than 1846).[37] We do not know who was responsible for the changes in this "new edition." But, in general, the input of the composer cannot automatically be discounted in those "second editions" that were released during his lifetime, for numerous examples are known where he altered material that was already in print (although the cases known involve only the original publisher, and not one who purchased plates from the original—well-known examples include the cancelled two measures in the last movement of the Sonata, op. 35 between the first and second states of the Troupenas edition, or the revised final cadence in the Schlesinger edition of the A-flat Etude from the *Trois Nouvelles Etudes*).

To summarize Chopin's publishing practices in France: throughout his career, he ordinarily gave an autograph manuscript to the French publisher for use in engraving the edition; in a few instances, he sent them copyists' manuscripts. In his early and late years in Paris, he undertook responsibility for proofreading his works himself, often going over them more than once before allowing the work to be published. In his middle years (roughly 1835–1841), he allowed copyists to read over proofs, and at least some of the time Chopin would check over these copyist-corrected proofs before submitting them to the publisher. But during these years Chopin did not entirely relinquish proofreading, so that the critic faces the sometimes difficult decision as to who made changes between the *Stichvorlage* and the first edition of a given work. As his star rose in the Parisian music world, Chopin was able to assert himself to a greater extent in his negotiations with music publishers, safe in the knowledge that if one did not meet his demands, another would likely take the place of his competitor. Resale of earlier works to different publishers became more common in the 1840s, and the possibility exists that the composer made alterations in some works before they were released by the new publisher. Characteristic of Chopin's publishing practices in France, then, is a great degree of authorial control over all stages of the preparation and release of the musical text.

The German-speaking States

Leipzig was the center of the German music publishing world, so it is not surprising that a Leipzig firm was the German partner in Chopin's first simultaneous publication venture,[38] or that the majority of the rest of his works were issued by a Saxon house. Other cities occasionally lured Chopin away, so that a sprinkling of works came out in Vienna, Berlin, Mainz, and Hamburg. But for the most part, Chopin's relations with German publishers were confined to Leipzig.

Chopin's first Leipzig publisher was Friedrich Kistner. The actual choice of this house, as shown above, seems to have been made by Farrenc, though at the composer's suggestion, for Chopin had been contacted by Kistner's predecessor, Heinrich Albert Probst, as early as 18 July 1831.[39] After Chopin broke with Farrenc and signed with Schlesinger, the latter chose to honor the existing arrangement with Kistner. The correspondence between Farrenc and Kistner on the one hand and Schlesinger and Kistner on the other, which I have already drawn upon for a picture of Chopin's early publishing practices in Paris, also depicts clearly the pathways used in Germany at the start of the composer's career.

This correspondence describes two possible modes of manuscript transmission. According to Farrenc, Chopin should give an autograph manuscript to the French publisher, who would make a copy of it by hand to send to the German publisher, having first allowed Chopin to "verify" the copy. Ideally, the French edition would be engraved from the autograph and the German edition from the copy, though Farrenc indicates that Chopin's autograph was not always satisfactory for engraving purposes, so another copy might be involved. Chopin apparently made his final corrections on the autograph manuscript itself (hence part of the reason for the difficulties with Farrenc): no proof stage is indicated. Figure 6.1 presents a stemma of this scheme (a bidirectional arrow indicates that either one route or the other might be employed).

Schlesinger offered another tableau. Chopin would present an autograph to the French publisher, who would engrave a set of proof sheets to be corrected by the composer. After laboriously completing this task, Chopin would return the corrected proofs to Schlesinger, who would send a copy of them to the German publisher. From the correspondence, it is not clear whether Schlesinger engraved the corrections onto the existing plates to send to Germany, or whether Chopin marked multiple sets of proofs, which could then be sent to foreign publishers. Another alternative would have Chopin mark one set of proofs, and the French publisher would transfer the corrections by hand to a different set of proofs that would be sent to Germany. If Chopin marked multiple proofs (or if the French publisher transferred readings by hand to another set of proofs), each edition would be

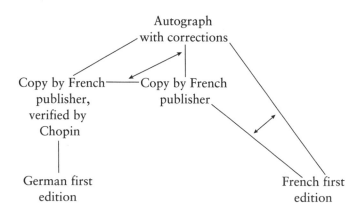

Figure 6.1   Farrenc publishing scenario.

derived from them. If the corrections were added to the plates, then each edition would be derived from this same source. These three related procedures are shown in Figure 6.2.

In all schemes, the French publisher would receive an autograph manuscript, but after this the routes diverge. In Schlesinger's plan,

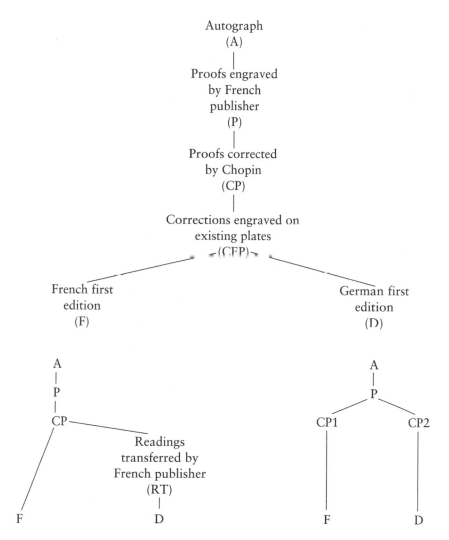

Figure 6.2   Schlesinger publishing alternatives.

Chopin's hand appears with certainty later in the process. How Chopin was to "verify" the copy made by Farrenc and intended for Germany is not clear: the "verification" could have been as rigorous as a corrected proof, or it could have been merely a hurried and cursory check. But under all three plans, the German publisher would prepare his edition from a non-autograph source. Farrenc's manuscript copies may be of only hypothetical significance, for he ultimately was replaced as a publisher by Schlesinger. But the method described by Farrenc cannot necessarily be discarded altogether, for Chopin released works with other French publishers (Pleyel and Prillip) in his early years, and the possibility exists that Farrenc's scheme was used by them to forward the composer's music abroad.

Schlesinger's shipment of proofs to Kistner resulted in closely related editions, as, for example, in the Etudes, op. 10. Both editions exhibit very similar physical layouts; the number of measures per system usually agrees, and often the number of systems per page does as well (although this occurs less often because Kistner's smaller typeface often admitted six systems to a page compared to Schlesinger's normal five). Similarity in physical layout characterized the Kistner and Schlesinger editions of opp. 6–11 and 13–14; in later works where two manuscripts are known definitely to have served as *Stichvorlagen*, the disposition of measures and systems usually differs, for the two engravers in the two countries were likely to have cast off their respective manuscripts separately. Most details agree in the two editions of op. 10 also; when variants occur, Kistner usually has omitted something.

In the early French editions, we found evidence for an additional proof stage not mentioned by Schlesinger in his letters to Kistner. Someone also communicated these later changes to Leipzig, for in the Etude, op. 10, no. 2, the same readings that are present in the Schlesinger edition but missing in the corrected proof sheets also appear in the Kistner edition. This in turn suggests that Schlesinger either engraved Chopin's additional corrections onto the existing plates before sending them to Kistner, or copied them onto another copy of the proofs by hand. Had Chopin made multiple copies of the corrected proofs, one would expect more variants between the French and German editions: he would have been tempted to "compose" while supposedly adding notations and while copying from one set of proofs to the other. In other words, one of the possibilities for the transmission of Chopin's text that could be derived from the Schlesinger-Kistner correspondence may now be dismissed, and the other two may be combined. The resulting stemma appears in Figure 6.3. A more detailed conception of the publication process in these early works results, one that includes compositional additions until the very moment the post took the work out of Chopin's hands. It thus demonstrates that the drive for ultimate refinement that so characterized the composer at the zenith of his career was already present when he was a fledgling pianist fresh in town.

After completing the transaction for opp. 6–11 and 13–14, and mailing all proof sheets, Chopin and his French publishers never again dealt with Kistner. For the release of his next works, the Introduction and Variations Brillantes on the Rondeau "Je vends des Scapulaires" from Hérold and Halévy's *Ludovic,* op. 12, and the Nocturnes, op. 15, the composer contracted with Breitkopf & Härtel, which was to become his principal publisher across the Rhine.

Assessing the nature of Chopin's transactions with Breitkopf can be tricky. A large body of manuscripts used by the Leipzig firm as *Stich-vorlagen* have come down to us; once in the Leipzig archives of Breitkopf, they now form the basis of the Chopin collection at the Bibli-

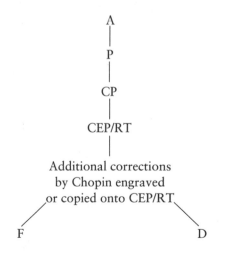

Figure 6.3 Schlesinger publishing scenario: 1.

oteka Narodowa in Warsaw. But the earliest of these manuscripts that can securely be shown to have been used by a Breitkopf engraver is that for the Mazurkas, op. 24 (Warsaw, Biblioteka Narodowa).[40] What of the earlier works published by Breitkopf? Did the system employed by Schlesinger with Kistner continue to be used with the hometown competitor of the Saxon, or did the participants initiate some other method of forwarding Chopin's music? A collection of correspondence from Heinrich Albert Probst, Breitkopf & Härtel's representative in Paris, to his employers in Leipzig describes vividly the nature of Chopin's relationship with Breitkopf at the beginning of his career and during the years 1837–1840.[41] The documents contain numerous insights into how Chopin functioned as an entrepreneur and how his works were received in Paris.

Probst's very first letter to Breitkopf describes the acquisition of two new works by Chopin, and adds a note about the popularity of the already purchased Nocturnes, op. 15:

> [Paris, 31.X.1833] You will however still receive through me from Chopin 3 Mazurkas and a beautiful Rondo. The Nocturnes Op. 15 are divine and the amiable Chopin comes more into fashion daily, even the great man K[alkbrenner] let a student, Dlle Lambert, play his first concerto in public.[42]

Did the Mazurkas, op. 17, originally number three rather than four? Probst's next letter also refers to only three:

> [Paris, 23.XI.1833] Around New Year you will receive from Chopin 3 Mazurkas and a beautiful Rondo, probably at a price similar to Op. 13 and 14. Here the little one is more and more epoch-making, even if not everyone can play him.[43]

Although the contract that Chopin signed with his English publisher also mentions just "Trois Mazurkas" (see Table 6.2 later in this chapter), it is likely that Probst was simply in error, since the German receipt for op. 17, written four days after the above lines, states clearly "Quatre Mazurkas."

The first clue as to the form in which Chopin's music was being forwarded to the Breitkopf firm comes in the next letter:

> [Paris, 21.XI.1833] The 2nd proofs of the Chopin Nocturnes follow, the changes and metronome added. I have bought from him 4 Ma-

zurkas Op. 17 [and] a Rondo Op. 16.—Do you make a good profit with Chopin?[44]

Not only, then, did Breitkopf set its edition from Schlesinger proofs, it received two sets of them. This suggests that some sort of agreement must have existed between the publishers to cover cases when the composer made substantial changes or additions, such as Probst mentions, after the initial proof stage. The forwarding of a second set of proofs could also account for how Kistner's edition of op. 10, no. 2 came to include readings not present in the extant set of French proofs for the work. Probst's passing comment thus requires one last refinement of the stemma for the early publication process (Figure 6.4).

Probst continued to ply Chopin with requests for new works; while he was able to report to Leipzig on the likelihood of obtaining rights to the Waltz, op. 18, he added a note that echoes to a degree the sentiments expressed earlier by Farrenc:

[Paris, 30.I.1834] It is a difficult job to put Chopin, this true bonbon of the local musical ladies, in some kind of order. The Mazurkas are very beautiful and easy and I think these little works will pay for themselves. I also still intend to separate a volume of Waltzes from

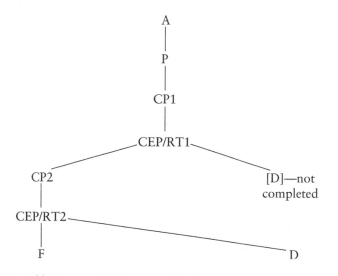

Figure 6.4 Schlesinger publishing scenario: 2.

him. That would for the time being be enough for you from Chopin. Or what do you think of it?[45]

Any new artist on the Parisian musical scene would be distracted from his work, but Chopin's lack of attention to his business affairs continued to frustrate his publishers. Three months later Probst had still to receive the works in question, and remarked in his report to the home office:

[Paris, 20.III.1834] Chopin is so negligent in everything that only with trouble can one get the missing items from him . . . From Chopin, I get what I want.[46]

Finally, in May, Probst could report that the Waltz would soon be sent, and added that the result, akin in his mind to one of Carl Maria von Weber's most popular works, was worth the wait:

[Paris, 16.V.1834] Next week Chopin Op. 18 and *Le Pianiste* No. 6 and 7 will go off to you. The Waltz has ca. 10 plates, but is exquisite and will create a furor there as here; it is an Invitation to the Dance although styled completely different. It pleases me to have secured this little pearl for you.[47]

The Breitkopf firm, when it began issuing the works of a composer, wished to be his or her sole representative in Germany. If another publisher released a work by the composer, Breitkopf worried both that potential profits were going to the other house from the sale of the work and that the other house might woo the composer away from the Breitkopf fold. Thus Probst, knowing that brows in the Breitkopf house would be furrowed when they read Peters's announcement of the publication of Chopin's Bolero, op. 19, hastened to send Leipzig the following news:

[Paris, 15.IX.1834] Through Keller, Peters has purchased for 500 francs Chopin's newest work, a Bolero. The thing seemed not important enough for me to bid still more for it . . . Chopin will return to us next time; I have put a stop to Keller's activities, also Peters will not be too pleased to have paid 500 francs.[48]

Probst was correct to reassure his employer, as Härtel's swift response indicates:

[Leipzig, 24.IX.1834] Your news of the activities there of composers has relieved me from the disquiet caused by Peters's announcement of the publication of a work by Chopin. Inasmuch as you earlier wrote with so much certainty that something from Chopin could not escape you so easily, that announcement by Peters came very unexpectedly to us and indeed we almost imagined seeing the scarcely-begun association with Chopin broken again.[49]

Probst's reaction was to demonstrate that he still had Chopin's ear by describing the composer's latest works that were for sale:

[Paris, 2.X.1834] Would you like to engrave the 2nd and 3rd Concertos by Chopin? It would cost 800—1000 francs, maybe also only 600. Tell me your opinion, I only have a hand in the affair, can take it or leave it.[50]

The second concerto was, of course, the F minor, published eventually as op. 21. References to a third concerto crop up as early as 1830, when Chopin mentioned he was at work on a concerto for two pianos, and the composer's father asked twice around the time of Probst's note if his son had completed his third concerto.[51] Most scholars have assumed that the work was never completed and that the first movement only later surfaced as the Allegro de Concert, op. 46 (published in 1841), although no documentary evidence to support this notion has ever been cited. That Probst boasted he could obtain the work in 1834 might belie the notion that the concerto was never completed; at the very least, it suggests that the composition had developed to a point beyond that previously thought.

Before Probst's letter reached Leipzig, Härtel sent another missive to Paris, urging that his representative buy whatever he could from Chopin to stave off the bad effects of the Chopin-Peters association:

[Leipzig, 8.X.1834] What's doing with Chopin? I would very much like soon to follow Peters's announcement of Op. 19 with one from us. Ought he to have nothing finished in his head? And even if it is only the smallest trifle, you must bring forward a new opus.[52]

Probst, in his next letter, tried to ease his employer's anxiety by remarking that the Bolero was far too costly and that Chopin was sure to resume his relations with Breitkopf:

[Paris, 15.X.1834] I am glad that the distance between us is not causing you to be misled, that you are persuaded of the truth that I am devoted to your interests. So the work Op. 19 by Chopin caused you alarm. Check it and say that the old hand Probst is right. It cost

> Peters 500 francs . . . He has no reserves, Chopin must give me some-
> thing, I am glad that he is coming along to your satisfaction.[53]

Härtel must have been reassured, and, in fact, Probst was correct:
Chopin returned to the Breitkopf firm to publish not only his next
works, but the majority of the pieces he was to issue during the remainder of his career as well.

Before leaving these negotiations, however, I should note Härtel's
response to the offer of two piano concertos:

> [Leipzig, 16.X.1834] You speak of the Chopin concertos nos. 2 and
> 3. We are inclined to engrave one of them, if you can get it away for
> 5–600 francs. You know both well and can make the choice; I would
> not like both at once, at all events the 3rd not till winter.[54]

Härtel's reasoning was precisely that of Schlesinger when he was faced
with the option of publishing both the E-minor and F-minor concertos.
Two concertos by the same composer issued simultaneously would
simply undermine each other's sales: at least several months must separate their appearance.

A gap in the correspondence occurs here, and the next surviving
note from Probst to Leipzig dates from April 1837. I will return to
this later batch of letters shortly; first I want to consider other types
of evidence concerning publication methods in the early works. Probst
cites only one set of works, the Nocturnes, op. 15, as having been set
from proofs. But other works from the period surely also derived from
proofs. When we compare Breitkopf-Schlesinger pairs of editions to
see if they share similar physical formats, as did the Kistner-Schles-
inger editions, we generally find that the texts and physical layouts
match closely. (I examined the first of the works issued in tandem by
Breitkopf and Schlesinger, the Variations, op. 12, as well as the Waltz,
op. 18, and the *Grande Polonaise Brillante précédée d'un Andante
spianato,* op. 22: the last of these displayed a remarkably high degree
of correspondence between the two editions.) And similar findings
result when we compare editions released by other publishers in the
early years (for example, the Bolero, op. 19, issued by Prillip in France
and Peters in Leipzig).

Bibliographical evidence, then, would lead us to believe that for all
of Chopin's works through op. 22, the method of publication for German works was something very like that used by Schlesinger and Kist-

ner, for the physical pictures of the Breitkopf-Schlesinger editions (and the Prillip-Peters duo) resemble what was found in the composer's first foray into simultaneous publication. But still other documents exist that contain further hints at what kinds of sources Breitkopf (and by implication the other German publishers) employed to produce editions of Chopin's works.

The archives of the Chopin Society in Warsaw contain a number of photographs of receipts for the sale of the composer's music to Breitkopf & Härtel. Although these photographs have been in the collection of the Chopin Society for some time, they have been virtually ignored by Chopin scholars.[55] The receipts hardly provide exciting reading; it is easy to understand their neglect. However, a careful perusal of the information in them reveals much about the kinds of arrangements Chopin made with the Saxon firm, including what kinds of sources the composer sent eastward. Table 6.1 distills the salient features of the notes.

Of immediate interest is the central block of works whose receipts record the sale of a *manuscrit*. Covering almost every piece Chopin published with Breitkopf from late 1835 to early 1840 (lacking only the Mazurkas, op. 24 and the Waltzes, op. 34), these receipts are flanked above and below by other ones that sell *ouvrages* of a composition. What does this change in terminology tell us about the forms in which Chopin's music was sent to Leipzig? About the meaning of *manuscrit* there can be little doubt: although it is not always clear whether the term describes an autograph or a copyist's manuscript, *manuscrit* can only refer to a handwritten source of some kind.[56] Do *ouvrages* and *composition* by analogy indicate only printed sources? Obviously not: manuscripts used by Breitkopf as *Stichvorlagen* are extant for compositions included in the later group of receipts using this terminology. But for the earlier group of receipts, we know of no Breitkopf *Stichvorlagen* (with the possible exception of the manuscript of the Concerto in F Minor, op. 21—see note 40), hence the change in wording from *ouvrages* to *manuscrit* likely signifies a change in publishing practice as well. That *ouvrages* could at once mean "manuscripts of works" in the late compositions and exclude the use of manuscripts in the earlier works does not necessarily create a paradox, for the two groups of receipts were prepared by different agents of Breitkopf. For the works through op. 41, Probst acted as the inter-

Table 6.1 Provisions of Breitkopf & Härtel Receipts

Receipt Date	Works	Copyright Domain	Type of Document Sold	Amount Paid (Francs)	Comments
28.X.33	12, 15	D	Ouvrages		Written on Schlesinger stationery
18.XI.33	12, 15	D		300	Paid to Schlesinger, who signed receipt. Verso has handwritten version of title page, and note "Publier le 4 Decbr."
27.XI.33	16,17	D+ ≠ F, GB	Ouvrages	200	
13.V.34	18	D+ ≠ F, GB	Composition	200	In German
3.VII.35	20, 21	D+ ≠ F, GB	Ouvrages	1000	
14.XI.35	27	D+ ≠ F, GB	Manuscrit	300	
26.XI.35	22	D+ ≠ F, GB	Manuscrit	500	
9.I.36	23	D+ ≠ F, GB	Manuscrit	400	
29.I.36	26	D+ ≠ F, GB	Manuscrit	300	
9.IV.36	27	D+ ≠ F, GB	Manuscrit	300	"Duplicat"
28.II.37	25	D+ ≠ F, GB	Manuscrit	1000	
11.IX.37	39, 30, 31	D+ ≠ F, GB	Trois Manuscrits	1000	"Trois" written over "Un"
21.VI.38	33	D+ ≠ F, GB	Manuscrit	300	
22.I.39	28	D		1000	Addressed to Probst
15.I.40	35–41	D+ ≠ F, GB	Sept Manuscrits	2500	Opus numbers jumbled
31.X.43	52–54	All countries ≠ F, GB	Compositionen		In German

Date	Opus	Countries	Type	Amount	Notes
16.XII.43	12, 15, 16–18, 20–31, 33–42, 46–49, 52–54	All countries ≠ F, GB	Ouvrages		"Quittance spéciale" listed for honorarium
16.VII.44	55, 56	All countries ≠ F, GB	Ouvrages		"Quittance spéciale" listed for honorarium
16.VII.44	55, 56	D		1200	The "Quittance spéciale" for the above receipt
21.XII.44	57, 58	All countries ≠ F, GB	Ouvrages		"Quittance spéciale" listed for honorarium. Opus numbers reversed by Chopin.
19.XI.46	60–62	All countries including Russia ≠ F, GB	Ouvrages		"Quittance spéciale" listed for honorarium
30.VI.47	63–65	All countries ≠ F, GB	Ouvrages		"Quittance spéciale" listed for honorarium

Key: D = Germany; D+ = Germany and all countries; F = France; GB = Great Britain; ≠ = excluding.

mediary between Chopin and Breitkopf. Sometime after April 1840, Probst's role as middleman was taken over by J. Maho, who was responsible for the remainder of the receipts. Thus one man, Probst, changed *ouvrages* to *manuscrit* in the earlier receipts. That he never returned to the earlier usage after making the alteration can only mean that he was compelled to do so by a shift in the kinds of materials he was forwarding to Leipzig.

The possibility exists also that Chopin himself was responsible for the change in practice, for he visited Leipzig in late September 1835, that is, two months after the last Probst receipt to use *ouvrages* (for opp. 20–21) and six weeks before the first receipt to employ *manuscrit*. Chopin did take advantage of his trips abroad to call on publishers and deliver manuscripts—we will encounter another instance in the section on England—and he may well have initiated the practice of providing the German publishers of his works with manuscripts on his 1835 journey.

If Probst's change in terminology mirrors a switch in the publication method for Germany, another dilemma arises. Recall that I singled out the Breitkopf edition of op. 22 as being similar in both physical layout and musical text to the French issue, and thereby deduced that the two editions were set from a common engraved source. But the receipt for op. 22 states resolutely that a manuscript was sold to the Leipzig house. Either the supposition that physical characteristics provide firm evidence about the nature of a *Stichvorlage* for a given edition is incorrect here, or the receipt errs in using the work *manuscrit*. To refute the evidence of the physical picture of the editions one would have to posit a remarkable coincidence of events, whereby two engravers, working in different cities at different times with separate manuscripts, first cast off the measures on their respective manuscripts exactly alike, and then struck onto their respective plates in exactly the same location such things as accents, slurs, fingerings, and pedal marks. Such a coincidence approaches the impossible, particularly when stretched over twenty-plus plates. Yet it must be added that the evidence drawn from the editions may not be totally reliable; the Schlesinger edition I consulted (housed at the University of Chicago) is a later issue that employs the original Schlesinger plates, but was released sometime between 1851 and 1854, and the Breitkopf edition (also housed at the University of Chicago) could also be of later vintage. But even if there had been some alteration of the plates of either edition prior to their issue, it is still unlikely that the two would independently reach their nearly identical states.

Probst's use of *manuscrit* cannot be taken at face value for op. 22. Possibly the composer had delivered proofs for the work during his visit to Leipzig in September, and merely neglected to inform Probst of the fact upon signing the receipt in Paris. Another possibility is that Chopin delivered no music of any kind for op. 22 during the Leipzig journey, the composer instead promising the eventual shipment of a manuscript score. Upon return to Paris, he signed a receipt on this information, but ultimately sent proofs in place of a manuscript. Such an account, which presumes that something did not go according to plan in the preparation of the score, might explain why nearly three-quarters of a year passed before Breitkopf published the work (the firm did not release it until August 1836), and seems more likely than the composer giving an inaccurate picture of what he proffered in Leipzig.

With the exception of the quirky op. 22, then, the evidence of the sales slips confirms the story pieced together from bibliographical clues and Probst's testimony. Until mid-1835, Chopin's German publishers engraved his editions from printed proofs originating in France. From late 1835 through the remainder of his career, Chopin as a rule sent manuscripts eastward. As was the case with his French publishers, Chopin provided German firms copyists' manuscripts along with autographs from 1835 to 1841; in fact, German houses used most of the extant scribal *Stichvorlagen* (see, for example, the Fontana copy of the Scherzo, op. 31 [Warsaw, Biblioteka Narodowa], the copy of the Sonata, op. 35, tentatively ascribed to Adolf Gutmann [Warsaw, Biblioteka Narodowa], and that of the Nocturnes, op. 37, in the hand of an unknown scribe [Warsaw, Biblioteka Narodowa]). Chopin reviewed most of the manuscripts prior to forwarding them to Leipzig, adding such things as pedal markings, slurs, tempo and character indications, and dynamics. The steady flow of scribal copies toward Germany and Austria stopped with the Fontana manuscripts of op. 48 in late 1841. Although Chopin did once send another non-autograph copy of a work to Leipzig (for the publication of the Berceuse, op. 57), commencing in 1842 he mostly sent manuscripts in his own hand to German publishers.

For a closer look at how Chopin's relationship with Breitkopf & Härtel developed from 1837 to 1840, we turn once again to the Probst-Härtel correspondence. By 1837 Chopin had become a fixture on the Parisian musical scene. But as Probst reported about the Etudes, op. 25, publishers, not immune to pathological images of the sort we encountered in Chapter 3, still regarded the composer's production as being hampered by the disorderly conduct that marked his early years in town:

> [Paris, 12.IV.1837] Chopin consumptive in bed, have however reminded him by letter of his Etudes and think the sickness will make him work and bring order into his life.[57]

Probst's concern over the whereabouts of the Etudes was understandable: the receipt for op. 25 was signed and payment made in February (see Table 6.1). Breitkopf evidently also worried that Chopin's way of life might lead to financial risks for them, for in the next letter to mention Chopin, Probst hastened to reassure his employers otherwise, though at the same time admitting that the composer was in debt to him:

> [Paris, 16.VI.1837] Chopin cannot be pushed, his great talent always insures your costs. I myself would like to put this in order with him, since he already got an advance of 600 francs from me 7 months ago.[58]

Only in July did Chopin deliver the manuscript, at the same time offering Probst the German rights to opp. 29–31. Chopin found that his latest works were in high demand by several publishers, and thus felt justified in increasing the honorarium requested from Breitkopf. The composer's strong bargaining position clearly irked Probst:

> [Paris, 9.VII.1837] Enclosed Chopin Etudes and Thompson's *clichés*. Chopin has another 3 works finished, however each will be more expensive, since German publishers beg him on all sides for manuscripts. I have however bought Impromptu Op. 29, Scherzo op. 30 [*sic*], 4 Mazurkas Op. 31 [*sic*] for—don't be alarmed—1000 francs. He pressed me and I did not exactly want to chance it. He demanded firm and strong 1200 francs. Now tell me frankly furthermore if you want to continue to purchase on such exorbitant terms, or if you want to see him in other hands for a while. I almost advise it . . .

Send on my account to the Pleyel & Co. house 1500 francs, because
Chopin will need money. Pleyel is about to go with him to London.[59]

Chopin's demands, "exorbitant" or not, must have given Breitkopf
pause, for four months passed before he paid the composer (see Table
6.1).

Further testimony to the intense competition among German publishers for Chopin's works comes in Probst's next report to Leipzig:

[Paris, 26.X.1837] Dear friends, your system of buying everything
from one author leads to nothing, with the current competition and
inflation [*Hinaufschrauberei*] of which you have no idea . . . Schlesinger in Berlin published (since you publish none) an album and the
son here furnishes him the manuscripts. With his newspaper influence he snapped away from me a good work Polonaise Op. 141 by
Kalkbrenner and 2 Nocturnes by Chopin Op. 53 [*sic*], what can I
do. The authors say: *"car tel est notre plaisir."*[60]

Roughly six months passed before Probst could send to Leipzig any
substantial news about Chopin (he did note in passing on 9 January
1838 that "Chopin's Etudes are making quite a stir").[61] When Probst
did report to Breitkopf, it was with a major deal still in the making:

[Paris, 21.IV.1838] From Chopin I should receive manuscripts at the
beginning of July for ca. 2000 francs, and since I have already given
somewhat of an advance, I ask for ca. 3000 francs remittance when
you have the opportunity.[62]

His next letter clarifies the nature of the proposed bargain:

[Paris, 2.V.1838] Chopin's 24 Preludes 1000 francs, Second Ballade
500 francs, 4 Mazurkas 300 francs can be regarded as settled. On
Chopin I have quite favorable opinions that he will long shine as a
new genius.[63]

Two of the three works Chopin was offering for sale would not be
completed for some time: the Preludes and the Ballade (see the dates
of the sales receipts in Table 6.1). The Mazurkas, op. 33, on the other
hand, were nearly ready, Breitkopf intending them for publication in
an album:

[Paris, 31.V.1838] Before my departure you will receive from Chopin
and Meyerbeer the contributions to the album.[64]

Chopin in fact delivered the manuscript in June:

> [Paris, 11.VI.1838] Chopin will certainly deliver by the end of this month.[65]

> [Paris, 27.VI.1838] I received from Chopin 4 Mazurkas Op. 33.[66]

It was November before Probst returned to the subject of the Preludes, only to report that they were still to be completed. But he added word of another purchase, once more calling to Breitkopf's attention the diseased status of their composer:

> [Paris, 3.XI.1838] Chopin has gone quite ailing to Spain with his beloved—Mad. la Baronne Dudevant (Georges [sic] Sand) wholly to seek refuge in the sand. He will complete his Preludes there. In the meantime I have 3 Waltzes, which Schlesinger enticed away [from Chopin], in the manner of the first in E-flat, for 1000 francs all 3 and you will shortly receive the proofs.[67]

Despite ordinarily transmitting his music to Germany though manuscripts after late 1835, Chopin saw the system of his early days in Paris employed once again for these three Waltzes, op. 34.[68] When Probst did receive the proofs for op. 34, he found them overpriced:

> [Paris, 9.XI.1838] Today I mailed via Schlesinger 1 packet, included the unfortunately very expensive, frightfully extended 3 Waltzes by Chopin that he scribbled only for travel money & Burgmüllers Op. 22, 23, 24 . . . Chopin has gone to Palma on the island Majorca.[69]

Probst was still grumbling at the end of the month about the price paid for the Waltzes:

> [Paris, 27.XI.1838] Schlesinger gave you property rights to an album of 12 Romances by Panseron to compensate you for the high cost of Chopin. Would you rather see the Waltzes in the hands of Schlesinger in Berlin? There was nothing else to do but bite the bullet, since Chopin is a man without all consideration. I hope the Preludes will compensate you.[70]

Chopin's increasingly higher prices troubled Probst more and more, and began to affect his views on the quality of the composer's output. We see this clearly in his letter to Härtel announcing the shipment of the manuscript of the Preludes:

[Paris, 10.III.1839] The Cracovienne is causing a furor here through Elssler. Janet mailed to you by coach 500 copies, enclosed Chopin Preludes manuscript. With receipt for 1000 francs, furthermore documents from Panofka, Osborne and bills from Deleuil, Pertheaux, Laurent and de Berny. I christened the Preludes by Chopin Op. 28 (in your earlier contract with him it was intended for a four-hand Sonata that maybe will not come about at all). Chopin wants to have nothing more to do with Schlesinger and Camille Pleyel, who besides still has not enough to do, meddles out of love for Chopin in the publication of his works. I naturally much prefer this very affable Pleyel to Schlesinger. Now however Chopin, by way of thanks to Pleyel, will be still more exorbitant and demands prices beyond the bounds of reason à la Herz. I flatly refused the like, pretended that I must seek counsel, and now put the question to you how much you want to pay for the 3rd Scherzo (8–10 plates), a Pilgrim's Ballade [*eine Ballade des Pèlerins*] (12 plates) and 2 Polonaises (14 plates). I acted as if you could and would give at the highest 1000 francs for everything together, but did not commit myself. Here Chopin's music has fallen somewhat into the background owing to Thalberg, Henselt, Schubert, Bertini, Liszt. One plays it rarely, in concerts no more at all, since it is not effective. I think Chopin jumps out of the frying pan into the fire [*kommt aus dem Regen in die Traufe*].[71]

Only ten months earlier, Probst had written about the same composer: "On Chopin I have quite favorable opinions that he will long shine as a new genius" (letter of 2 May 1838, quoted earlier). Geniuses evidently did not demand the kinds of prices Chopin did.

Many interesting details pepper the above letter. We have long known that the opus number of the Preludes was assigned out of sequence; more recently scholars have uncovered and discussed Chopin's offer of a four-hand sonata "op. 28."[72] Now we know securely that Probst appropriated the old number for use with the Preludes (the fact that Probst was responsible might explain why no opus number appeared on the first French edition). Still more tantalizing is Probst's passing reference to op. 38 as "eine Ballade des Pèlerins." Many writers have attempted to associate Chopin's ballades with ballades by the Polish poet and dramatist Adam Mickiewicz, but none have drawn on any evidence from the composer. Nor, for that matter, do any of the poems suggested have anything to do with pilgrims. What can Probst's description mean? Did it derive from Chopin himself? In September 1838, Félicien Mallefille published an open letter to Chopin lauding a performance of the composer's "Ballade polonaise."[73] Could this be our "Ballade des Pèlerins?" In any event, the title resonates with a significant image among the Polish émigré community in Paris in the 1830s. One of their newspapers bore the name *Pielgrzyma Polskiego* [The Polish Pilgrim], and the editor of the newspaper, Mickiewicz, returned to the motif often, most prominently in his prose pamphlet *Księgi narodu polskiego i pielgrzymstwa polskiego* [The Books of the Polish Nation and of the Polish Pilgrims]. If my argument from Chapter 1 about the nationalist sentiments embedded in the generically mixed Nocturne in G Minor, op. 15, no. 3, is valid, it would not be at all surprising to discover further that Chopin wished to contribute musically to the laments expressed by his fellow émigrés through his "Pilgrim's Ballade."

In his next letter to Leipzig, Probst urged speed in the engraving of op. 28, and corrected a detail in the dedication:

> [Paris, 15.III.1839] You should have Chopin's Préludes engraved immediately, because Wessel in London wants to publish already in May, although he only paid 300 francs for them, he nevertheless presses like mad. The dedication should not be to Kessler but rather should say: 24 Préludes pour le Piano dédiés à Mr. Camille Pleyel par son ami Fred. Chopin.[74]

Breitkopf never did alter the dedication, and it appeared in Germany with Kessler's name on the title page. Wessel's plans to issue the work in May ran afoul; the firm did not enter the work in Stationer's Hall until 30 August. (Probst later stated that the Preludes would be released on 30 June in Paris; this too proved premature—see his letter of 25 April 1839).[75]

Chopin's prices continued to trouble Probst in his communiqués to Härtel:

> [Paris, 24.III.1839] Chopin is in Marseilles, I await with pain your answer regarding his new works. The Ballade and 2 Polonaises are already here, but all publishers are obliged to refuse the new, frightful demands. Even Pleyel withdrew, because after all he plainly does not want to lose his money.[76]
>
> [Paris, 29.IV.1839] Chopin will probably come here soon and sell his works himself. *Vedremo.*[77]

Probst finally met with Chopin in December, and the encounter triggered a long outburst to Härtel:

[Paris, 2.XII.1839] Yesterday I finally had a rendezvous with Chopin, he has 7 manuscripts finished, namely Grand sonata, Second Ballade, 2 Nocturnes, Third Scherzo, Four Mazurkas, Two Polonaises, One Impromptu and demands 3500 francs in return. My complaint that he makes acceptance impossible through such frightful prices was in vain, I should only write you, he would moreover do it himself, he is certain you will take the works at any price. According to my calculation based on the prevailing high rates the works would come to around 2500 francs at the highest, thus one could ask in accordance with your instructions up to 2000 francs, only I have not done this. He was too arrogant, said he was sick, indeed looked terrible, since he could give no lessons his works must therefore give him support. That sounds very good, if only the buying public takes it into consideration. The works themselves, from which he has played me quite a bit, are still gloomier than the earlier ones and will meet with still less approval, since they are not grateful to play. The sonata is clever, but dreary and baroque throughout. The remaining works are scribbled-down morsels of the well-known type, such as you already have better. My advice is to let him go, without losing careful sight of him, for he after all has much imagination and value. He will not so easily find a publisher who makes things as easy for him as you. Also he said he must have money immediately, the Manichaeans were all on hand, he needs it badly. I proposed he demand only 3000 francs. No, he said, 3500 francs or nothing. Since he will now be cultivated by many publishers from Germany, without the people knowing what *he* costs, it is therefore absolutely necessary to leave him to his fate for a while, otherwise next time he demands still more exorbitantly. If he has something good or marketable, I will already earlier lay a hand on it before another will be aware, for Chopin has the habit of playing his works for years ahead of time before he writes them down. Wessel pays him a guinea for 4 pages and Schlesinger also very badly. Pleyel is fed up to his eyes with the Préludes and has no more dealings with him.[78]

This letter presents a fascinating collision of perceptions about market forces and aesthetic value. For among the many judgments that opp. 35–41 have received, surely Probst's "gloomy" and "scribbled-down morsels of the well-known type, such as you already have better" most suggest an aesthetic vision thoroughly under the sway of Chopin's high prices. Probst refused to pay the 3500 francs demanded, and suggested that Breitkopf turn Chopin loose on the market so that the publishers who continued to hound the composer for manuscripts would discover the costs and time involved (Probst's comment that Chopin was in the habit of playing works for years before writing them down is a telling, if rather exaggerated, one for a study of his compositional procedures), and presumably stop competing for his works. Probst still felt that Breitkopf paid too handsomely for Chopin's music; we saw earlier, in Chopin's letters to Franchomme concerning opp. 55 and 56, that the composer was very aware of the high honorariums he was able to command from Breitkopf. The Leipzig firm must have enjoyed brisk sales of Chopin's works in order to continue to pay the composer more than he received from his publishers in France and England.[79]

Probst's portrait of the haggard, arrogant, yet desperate Chopin demanding an extraordinary fee for opp. 35–41 might offer a clue about why the French editions of these works are so problematic. Recall that all of the Troupenas editions exist in multiple states, with the composer almost surely responsible for the changes in the later states. Perhaps the financial embarrassment in which Chopin found himself in the winter of 1839–1840 somehow disrupted the normal procedures he followed when ushering works into print. Troupenas might have been able to lure Chopin away from his regular French publisher, Schlesinger, with promises of ready cash. And Chopin, generally harried and working with a new publisher with different personnel and procedures, may have overlooked many errors in the first states of the Troupenas edition that under ordinary circumstances he would have noticed.

Probst, with Breitkopf's permission, continued to refuse to yield to Chopin's prices, and the composer demanded to write directly to Leipzig:

[Paris, 20.XII.1839] Still before the receipt of your letter of the 12th current Chopin was at my place and pressed for a decision. I held to your orders and told him that you would on no account accept the new prices of his works. He wished however not to break with your house (on account of the prompt payment) and has written you directly. Yesterday I shared with him your decision of the 12th current, without however also stating the sum. He awaits your answer and so I ask you to make your offer to him, Rue Tronchet No. 5.[80]

Chopin's letter to Breitkopf & Härtel, dated 14 December 1839, survives, and in it he stated that the price of 500 francs for each of the 7 manuscripts was one below which he would never go.[81] But as both the next letter and Table 6.1 show, he did come down 1000 francs when the deal was finally concluded:

> [Paris, 10.I.1840] Chopin was today at my place and finally consented to 2500 francs, which I must pay him immediately. The 7 manuscripts follow by coach . . .[82]

The last letter from Probst to Leipzig to mention Chopin makes the comment:

> [Paris, 25.III.1840] Chopin sold the 7 works to Troupenas for 2100 francs.[83]

In other words, Troupenas bought the works for 400 francs less than Breitkopf: Probst once again implied that his employers paid too dearly for Chopin's music.

What these letters from Probst to Härtel reveal most strongly is Chopin's strong position as a commodity in the music publishing world. We witnessed earlier his bargaining power with respect to the sale of French rights to opp. 55 and 56 in 1844, but already in 1837–1840 Chopin could command and receive high prices (although not always as high as he would like). For Chopin, it was definitely a seller's market, and Probst readily confirmed that if Breitkopf would not buy the composer's works, another German publisher gladly would.

Returning to the mechanics of the publication of Chopin's works: while the composer in his early years and once or twice later sent proofs of his music to Germany to serve as engraver's copy, I know of no case where he corrected proof sheets engraved by one of his German publishers.[84] Once his music in whatever form—proof, scribal copy, or autograph—left his hands for Leipzig, Vienna, or another German publishing center, Chopin ceased to oversee the musical text. This then marks the main difference in Chopin's publishing methods in Germany and France, for in Paris, he normally could emend his text until the moment of publication, and ofttimes after, as we have seen with respect to some of the later issues of his French editions.

That the composer did not correct proofs for his German publishers does not mean, however, that the published edition unfailingly reproduces what was found in the manuscript. Engravers did, of course, misinterpret or omit readings, but more important, they occasionally also revised passages to bring Chopin's notation into accord with what must have been Breitkopf's "house policy." Most of these changes are on the order of reversing the direction of a series of stems in a melodic line. But occasionally the emendations made by the Breitkopf "editor" were in some fashion interpretive, particularly where accidentals were added to "clarify" pitches that seemed vague in the manuscript.[85] Traces of the "editor" (who may be synonymous with the engraver) turn up in the manuscripts in the form of additions made in light lead or red pencil.

German publishers did rerelease works issued earlier in Chopin's career, as did their French counterparts, but there is no indication that Chopin played any part in the preparation of them. Often these later states retain the plate number of the original edition, but print radically different texts. A telling example occurs in the Waltz, op. 34, no. 2. The Breitkopf edition, plate number 6033, first appeared in December 1838; the later issue, bearing the same plate number, was released sometime after 1 January 1841.[86] Comparison of the two shows differences in phrasing, pedal marks, articulation, and, occasionally, pitch. The variants in the later state typically regularize what was asymmetrical in the early print. One of the hallmarks of Chopin's style is that written-out repetitions of musical passages almost never appear in exactly the same guise as their predecessors (when he wanted an exact repetition, he usually notated it with repeat signs or, in his manuscript, with numbers marking off the measures to be played over). That the changes in the later state contradict this trait suggests the culpability of a foreign hand.

The information in Table 6.1 discloses something of the kinds of agreements Chopin was signing with Breitkopf, business arrangements that were particularly significant for the distribution of the composer's music throughout those parts of Europe not inhabited by the three partners in simultaneous publication. Nearly all of the receipts contain a clause stating that Chopin would cede his rights for Germany and all other countries, with the exception of France and England. Breitkopf & Härtel likely attached special importance to this clause, for, as one of the largest music publishers in Europe, they had a firmly established network of sales associates throughout the continent, reaching such far-flung locales as Milan, Stockholm, and Moscow.[87] Letters from Chopin's family testify to the availability of his works in Warsaw; these were probably shipped from Leipzig for sale in one of the Warsaw music shops.[88] For distribution in Italy, another scheme may have been used. A large number of contemporary Italian editions of Chopin's music are known, but in only one case (for the Tarantella, op. 43) can one demonstrate that the edition was released at roughly the same time as those in France, Germany, and England.[89] All of the others must have been either pirated from one of the three authorized publishers, or purchased from a firm that had been assigned the legal right to Chopin's music in Italy. Breitkopf is the most likely candidate to have sold rights to Italy, given its connections in Milan (most of the Italian editions emanated from Milanese firms like Lucca or Ricordi). Schlesinger (or another Parisian house) is another possibility, since some of the composer's agreements with French firms also provided rights for "tous les pays."[90] But because Breitkopf's operation was more extensive than Schlesinger's, and because trade routes were more accessible to the Saxon than to the Frenchman (Milan being at the time part of the Austrian monarchy), the Leipzig firm probably was more influential in the production of Chopin's music in Italy. The same may be said for the rest of Europe and Russia. Whatever music of Chopin that was played outside of France and England during the composer's lifetime largely stemmed either directly or indirectly from a German edition.

Chopin's relationships with his German publishers, then, take on great importance for the distribution and reception of his works throughout Europe. In his early years, Chopin provided his German publishers with proof sheets from the French edition; in late 1835, shortly after the composer's visit to Leipzig, he switched to sending manuscripts, a practice he maintained almost without interruption for the remainder of his career. Until 1842, many of these manuscripts sent across the Rhine were in the hands of copyists; afterwards, they were mostly written out by the composer himself. Whereas the composer often carefully checked over and emended the proofs and copyists' manuscripts before posting them, after a work left his hands Chopin had no more control over what was printed in Germany. Thus

Chopin probably never saw the minor "editorial" touch-ups added by someone at the Breitkopf house, nor was he aware of the wholesale changes that sometimes occurred in later states of his German editions. But in assigning Breitkopf wide latitude in the distribution of his music, Chopin took his most important step in assuring the spread of his music throughout the western world.

England

Just how Chopin published his works in England has been one of the major puzzles plaguing those who study the composer's music. For years researchers have drawn a blank on Chopin's dealings with Christian Rudolph Wessel, who published almost all of the composer's music that appeared in England. Documentation on this aspect of the dissemination of Chopin's music has been woefully lacking: Maurice J. E. Brown, in a 1958 article on the subject, relied mainly on what little information he could garner from advertisements in periodicals and journals and from the title pages of the Wessel editions in the British Library. In the second edition of his *Index,* he managed to add some (but not all) dates of publication that were entered in the Stationers' Hall registers.[91] The first known letter from Chopin to Wessel surfaced only in 1978, and we still cannot locate any manuscripts that Wessel might have used to engrave his editions.[92] It is not surprising that until recently editors and critics generally passed over the English editions of Chopin's music.

The discovery of a number of documents in the archives of Wessel's modern-day successor, Edwin Ashdown Limited, is thus of no small import, for much of the structure of Chopin's business relations with Wessel may now be fleshed out.[93] Forming the bulk of this cache are Chopin's contracts with the English publisher, but key information is also provided by letters from contemporaries of Chopin. Most of what can be learned about the composer's dealings across the Channel comes from these new papers; some clues may be sifted from a close reading of published correspondence with family, friends, and publishers. It is to this latter source that we turn for the first signs that Chopin had contracted with an English publisher.

In the autumn of 1832, Nicholas Chopin received a letter from his son in which he depicted his entry into the world of Parisian musical culture. Nicholas, in his response, remarked about Fryderyk's fledgling publication ventures:

> The decision you have made to publish your works is very necessary, because many people hear tell of you without being able to know your compositions and, to tell the truth, they should precede your arrival wherever you would go. Moreover, the proceeds that you would obtain would make you a small fund, which might realize your project to go next spring to England, where your works would already have reached.[94]

The elder Chopin's words in the last sentence may be read in two ways. Either he was making a general comment on the advisability of publishing one's works—a major benefit being that they could act as a sort of calling card when one traveled to a different country—or he was referring to a specific comment by his son that arrangements had been made to issue his compositions in England. Now if the latter were the case, the date of the letter would correspond with other known events in the composer's life, for it was just at this time that Chopin successfully negotiated his first agreement with a Parisian publisher, who in turn was contacting possible partners in Germany. If Nicholas was alluding to a *fait accompli*, then we may presume that at the same time when Schlesinger was looking eastward for a publishing arrangement, he was also inquiring in England. Arguing against such an interpretation of Nicholas's lines, however, is the absence of contracts between Fryderyk and Wessel for the earliest of the works issued in tandem with France and Leipzig (opp. 6–11; see Table 6.2), the lack of an entry for a work by Chopin in Stationers' Hall prior to that for op. 13 (15 April 1834), and the absence of Wessel's name on the list of publishing partners printed on Schlesinger's title pages for opp. 6–11. Yet the dates of publication for these works in England as listed by Brown in the *Index* (where they were probably derived from contemporary advertisements) are very close to the dates of publication on the Continent. Moreover, the contracts for opp. 6–11 could simply be lost, or may never have existed: a ledger of copyright assignments maintained by the Wessel firm contains no mention of any agreement prior to that for opp. 13–17. Nicholas's letter is equivocal, then, as to whether by the autumn of 1832 Chopin was already in contact with Wessel. But even if this date is premature, the actual date when the two signed a business agreement for the first time could not have fallen much later.

By late 1833, if not sooner, Chopin was firmly entrenched with Wessel. Confirmation of this comes not only from the earliest contracts (which, although filled out in 1836, are backdated to November 1833) and advertisements in journals, but also from a letter from Johann Nepomuk Hummel to Wessel. This letter is only the second known missive from Hummel to an English publisher.[95] Here is a summary, with a translation of the relevant portions:[96]

> Weimar, 3 Dec. 1833
> [Hummel discusses the publication date for his Rondo. The January date proposed by Wessel is unacceptable, because the other publishers cannot meet this deadline. He goes on to discuss his fee, which Wessel feels is too high, and his terms for payment, which Wessel wishes to alter, but which Hummel as a matter of principle will not. Hummel will only deliver his works for ready cash.]
>
> Messrs. Chopin & Pixis can submit to a different agreement and later payment, and certainly wish it also; only *I* cannot accept this.— All that I can do is: that you pay 5 guineas for it, which I will collect from you upon sale of the manuscript, payable one month after the date, which will fall around the end of January 1824 [*sic*].
>
> [Hummel closes with a few more details on the sale, and asks that the property deed be sent to him through his brother-in-law in London.]

Hummel is discussing his Rondo for Piano and Orchestra, op. 127, the sole work that he published with Wessel.[97] But more relevant than the Kapellmeister's machinations over the publication date and the payment for his Rondo is the revelation that, by November 1833, Chopin was sufficiently established with Wessel to be held up as an example to Hummel of how another Continental composer received payment from London. Hummel found delayed payment unacceptable, but Chopin evidently had no firm objections to it, for, as we will see, he continued to receive his honorarium in deferred installments from Wessel at various times throughout his career.

What of the transmission of Chopin's music to England? From the composer himself, the earliest inkling as to what kinds of materials he was forwarding to England comes in a letter to Fontana of 20 or 27 June 1841, in which the composer told his factotum to prepare a copy of the Tarantella, op. 43 for Wessel's use.[98] Two years later, on 15 October 1843, Chopin sent a letter to Auguste Léo and included "my manuscripts for London."[99] After this date, there is little doubt that Chopin continued to ship manuscripts to England, for three more letters, two to Léo (who acted as Chopin's intermediary with London) and one to Franchomme, allude to manuscripts for Wessel.[100] And from the last letter, to Franchomme, one can ascertain that Chopin sent manuscripts in his own hand, for, in reference to possible delays by the French and German parties in the publication of opp. 60–62, he wrote: "I would not like for this matter to drag out, having sent my copy to London at the same time as [the ones I sent] to you."[101]

Before June 1841, however, Chopin had published more than thirty opuses with Wessel, and the main body of evidence for the composer's methods of publication in these works survives not in his correspondence, but in eighteen contracts between the Wessel firm and Chopin. Only one of these contracts, for opp. 60–62, was previously known to musicologists,[102] its seventeen companions having passed an untold number of years behind a file cabinet in the Edwin Ashdown offices, where they evidently sustained the water damage that now mars them. According to Mr. S. E. Ashdown, the contracts were only recovered when he was overseeing the redistribution of some furniture in the office. Fortuity thus allows the overview of the contracts found in Table 6.2.[103]

Immediately catching the eye are the three contracts dated 20 July 1837, whose works (opp. 25, 29–32) are all described as being in "M.S." More direct testimony as to what was used by Wessel as *Stichvorlagen* for these works could not be desired, but accepting the information sketched into the printed contracts at once raises questions about the particular circumstances of their signing and whether what is written in them reflects in any way on what is present (or better, not present) in the contracts on either side of the ones in question.

Special events did attend the drawing up of the contracts for opp. 25 and 29–32: Chopin, on his first journey to England between 10 and 25 July 1837, signed them in person. Traveling with Chopin was Camille Pleyel, who witnessed the signing. In only two other instances did the signers leave unchanged the printed "London" indications on the receipt portions of the contracts (rather than replacing them by a handwritten "Paris"); as we shall see, these contracts also herald un-

Table 6.2 An overview of the Wessel contracts

Receipt Date and Place	Contract Date	Works	Copyright Domain	Amount Paid (Pounds)	Witness	Comments
5.IV.36 Paris	5.IV.36	26, 27	GB	8	Fontana	
6.IV.36 Paris	XI.33	13–17	GB	20	Fontana	Op. 17: "Trois [sic] Mazurkas." Receipt date written over "Nov 1833"
6.IV.36 Paris	XI.33	18–24	GB	28	Fontana	
20.VII.37 London	20.VII.37	25	GB	16	C. Pleyel	Ops. 21 and 24 originally reversed. Described as "(M.S.) compositions." To be published on 14.X.37. Blank dedication
20.VII.37 London	20.VII.37	[29], 30	GB	10	C. Pleyel	Both in "M.S." Op. 29 called "Op. 28," to be published 14.(15 in a second listing).X.37. Dedicated to D'Agoult. Op. 30 with blank date of publication
20.VII.37 London	20.VII.37	31, 32	GB	10	C. Pleyel	Both in "M.S." and both with blank date of publication. Op. 31 with changes in dedication and title

4.IV.38 Paris	4.IV.38	29, 33, 34	GB, Ireland	15	Stapleton	With correct number for op. 29
1.VIII.39 Paris	1.VIII.39	28	GB, Ireland	15	Léo	Receipt "received by bill £24 at 3 months date."
31.X.39 Paris	31.X.39	38–40	GB, Ireland	24	Ludlow	
III.40 Paris	III.40	41, 42	GB, Ireland	16	Ludlow	Incipits in contract
V.40 Paris	V.40	35–37	GB, Ireland	24	Ludlow	
1.VIII.41 London	1.VIII.41	43	GB, Ireland	6	Schlesinger	
14.I.42 London	14.I.42	44–50	GB, Ireland	36	Schlesinger	
VIII.43 Paris	—	52–56	GB, Ireland	19:19:–	Léo	Incipits in contract
16.V.45 Paris	2.V.45	57, 58	GB, Ireland	20	Léo	Incipits in contract
VI.45 Paris	—	43–47	GB, Ireland	?	Léo, Brandus	Incipits in contract. "July 1842" in left margin of receipt. Amount paid entered variously as £47, £40, £40:7:–, and £47
VIII.45 Paris	VIII.45	59	GB, Ireland	10	Léo, Brandus	Incipit of no. 1 in contract
20.IX.46 Paris	13.VIII.46	60–62	GB, Ireland	30	Léo, Brandus	Incipits in contract

usual circumstances. Not a great deal is known about the itinerary of
Chopin's first London sojourn; he evidently wished to maintain a low
profile.[104] Planning ahead in Paris, however, Chopin must have
counted on transacting business, for in his luggage he included manuscripts for five works, which he delivered into Wessel's hands when
he called on his shop on 20 July. Just as we saw with his German
receipts, the first mention of a manuscript in connection with the English firm was linked to a personal visit by the composer.

In the Breitkopf & Härtel receipts, the absence of the word *manuscrit* prior to late 1835 is evidence that those works published before
this date were in fact done so without employing manuscripts. Does
the lack of "M.S." in the Wessel contracts signed either before or after
20 July 1837 provide clues in the search for *Stichvorlagen?* We need
to ponder two different groups of engraver's sources: those for the
early set of works, or opp. 13–24 and 26–27, and those immediately
following the 1837 contracts, or opp. 28 and 33–42 (I will account
below for opp. 44–50 by a different type of documentary evidence).

Considering the later group first, the fact that the contracts fail to
note whether works were in "M.S." cannot by itself demonstrate what
was used to engrave the editions. In other (late) works, as we have
seen, Chopin testified himself that autographs or copyist's manuscripts
were sent to London, and in none of the contracts for these works
does there appear the notation of "in M.S." Conversely, we cannot
automatically assume that the visit of July 1837 triggered a flow of
manuscripts toward England that went unmentioned in the contracts.
For example, Chopin wrote to Fontana concerning opp. 35–41:

> I am sending you a letter from Wessel, certainly about my old busi-
> ness. Troupenas purchased my 7 compositions and will conduct
> business directly with Wessel, so you do not have to trouble your-
> self.[105]

By "conduct business" did Chopin mean that Troupenas would also
forward the music for the works (in proofs?) to London, or was the
composer referring only to the negotiation of prices and dates of publication? If the former, then the texts printed by Wessel should bear a
familial resemblance to those issued by Troupenas; in fact Ekier finds
just such a relationship in his examination of the extant sources for
the Ballade, op. 38.[106] The English and French editions share readings

not found in the German sources and sometimes not present in the French *Stichvorlage,* which indicates that the French and English editions were set from a common set of engraved and corrected proof sheets. Thus both manuscripts and proofs of Chopin's music must have crossed the Channel after the appearance of "M.S." in the contracts.

The three contracts that predate the ones signed in London pose their own set of problems. One of the three, for opp. 13–17, clearly was drawn up well after the works were published, and the first three works in the contract for opp. 18–24 had also been released more than a year before the date of the receipt. For these works there is little doubt that proof sheets served as the basis for the English editions; not only had Chopin still to commence employing copyists, but his French publishers were also forwarding proofs to Germany. That proofs were mailed to England as well is borne out by comparison of the Parisian and London editions of the time. In the Bolero, op. 19, for example, a few pages of the Prillip and Wessel editions have slightly different layouts, but by and large the two agree precisely. Readings match throughout; on occasion Wessel will print fingerings not present in Prillip, but in cases where Prillip does have fingerings, Wessel always reproduces exactly those printed by his Parisian cohort.

With the remaining works in the early contracts (opp. 21–24 and 26–27), we enter the period in Chopin's career during which he made frequent use of copyists; it is with these same compositions that he began to send manuscripts to Germany. Here again, the common characteristics of the editions published in England and France suggest that Chopin must still not have been sending manuscripts to London. In the Nocturnes, op. 27, a pattern of variants develops that is very similar to that found in op. 19: readings are in the main alike, and where they differ, the French version simply lacks what is present in the English. Each edition, it should be noted, is laid out in exactly the same fashion.

Bibliographical data would seem to support the notion that the absence of "M.S." in the early contracts accurately reflects the fashion in which the works were readied for publication. To be certain, however, we should compare the English and French editions for the works in the contracts signed in London to see if substantially different patterns of variants obtain. A look at the Schlesinger and Wessel editions of the Impromptu, op. 29, reveals a majority of variants of the sort we have seen in earlier works (for example, signs present in Wessel but absent in Schlesinger). However, a different type of variant (where the two editions contain divergent readings that cannot be explained by "editorial" touching up in England) occurs often enough to paint a different picture from what we have encountered in earlier works. The case for two different (but related) manuscripts being used to set the two editions seems airtight.[107]

Gaps still remain in the survey of the types of source materials Chopin sent to England, particularly for some works published after the July 1837 contracts. To comprehend fully Chopin's actions in this period, one must realize that his opinion of the Wessel firm declined seriously sometime after the London contracts were signed. By 1839, Chopin had chosen to employ an intermediary in dealing with England, and in fact sold his English rights to the Preludes, op. 28 to Camille Pleyel, who, as the following receipt from the Wessel archive confirms, sold them in turn to Wessel:[108]

> [1 August 1839]
> The undersigned recognizes having ceded to Messrs Wessel & Co., music publishers in London, the exclusive right to engrave, publish and sell in England, Ireland and Scotland a work by Mr. Frédéric Chopin entitled: twenty-four preludes for Pianoforte dedicated to his friend Camille Pleyel, and for which Mr. Frédéric Chopin has transmitted to me the property rights for France and England—Said assignment to Messrs Wessel & Co. is made at the cost of the sum of Three hundred francs which they have settled with me and by which receipt for sale in Paris the 1st of August 1839.
>   Camille Pleyel
>   rue de rochechouart
>   No 20—
> The above sale approved
>   Frédéric Chopin

In his letters to acquaintances in 1839, Chopin never stated firmly what led him to want to break with Wessel, though in later years, it becomes clear that one reason was his unhappiness with the descriptive titles the London publisher added to most of Chopin's works.[109] Chopin's reticence on the subject may have stemmed from vacillating feelings about rupturing his business relationship with Wessel. Pondering such a break would have troubled him on three counts: the potential loss of revenue from the sale of his works in England, the difficulty of reaching a new agreement with a different English publisher, and the possibility that, lacking a solid relationship with a London house, his works would become easy prey for English pirates. By late 1839, Chopin had evidently decided that he would be risking too much, for in a letter of 25 September to Fontana, he asked his amanuensis to inform Wessel that he had several works (opp. 35–41) for sale at 300 francs apiece.[110] But again he evidently changed his mind, for as we saw in the excerpt from the letter of 23 April 1840, Troupenas ultimately handled the negotiations with Wessel for these works.

The underlying causes of Chopin's dissatisfaction with Wessel remained, even though he kept to a minimum direct contact with the firm. Hence trouble was bound to arise. In March 1841, Chopin sent to Wessel the following letter concerning his two most recently published works, the Mazurkas, op. 41, and the Waltz, op. 42:[111]

[Paris, 16 March 1841]

Sir

My last two compositions appeared two-and-a-half months ago—and I have not seen Mr. Ludlow—Have the kindness to send me the amount as soon as possible.—and write me if you want to continue to publish me. Many compliments to all your House.

F. Chopin

Although Ludlow (an associate of Wessel) did arrive in Paris soon after this letter (see the contract of III.40 in Table 6.2), Chopin again began to entertain serious thoughts of severing contact with Wessel.

Matters quickly fell apart when the composer was trying to market the rights for opp. 44–49. In September 1841, Chopin received a letter from Wessel that aroused his ire. Once again the titles added by Wessel were immediately responsible, but there must have been some residual frustration over his earlier problems in receiving payment as well. As in 1839, Chopin expressed his dismay by not selling his English rights directly to Wessel. He instead offered them to Schlesinger along with the French rights, and at a very low rate (only 100 francs for op. 45), explaining that he wished to have no more to do with Wessel.[112] But he tried yet again to patch things up with the English house, for he asked Fontana in a letter of 6–7 October if he had heard from Wessel yet.[113] Fontana had, and what was in the Wessel response touched off a heated outburst from Chopin:

> Now concerning Wessel, he is an ass and a cheater. Do what you want, answer, but say I have *no thought of ceding* my rights to the Tarantella because he did not *send it back* in time, and that if has lost on my compositions, it is doubtless due to the *stupid titles* he has given them in spite of my prohibition and in spite of my *repeated railings* at Mr. Stapleton; that if I listened to the voice of my soul, I would never have sent him anything more after *those titles*. Rant, as only you may.[114]

The descriptive titles rankled the composer severely, and combined with the English firm's shoddy business habits, stretched Chopin's patience to the limit. But in asking Fontana to respond to Wessel, Chopin allowed the firm a last chance, and on 18 October he was still awaiting word from London before deciding how to market his compositions in England.[115] What response Chopin received could not have pleased him, for in acknowledging the payment made by Breitkopf & Härtel for opp. 46–49, the composer wrote: "I am not sending you the London address, because I was forced to abandon Wessel and have not yet made definite arrangements with anyone—."[116] Chopin ultimately sold the English rights to Schlesinger, who in turn vended them to Wessel—a deal in which the French publisher probably came out ahead, for the composer had let him have the English rights at a bargain rate, and he received in return some 900 francs (at roughly £1 = 25 FF) from London.

Schlesinger cemented the deal personally in London in January 1842, the date of the contract for opp. 44–50.[117] Some details about the business end of this trip and a surprising revelation about a facet of the publication practice in England come in an unpublished letter from Ignaz Moscheles to his friend and publisher Maurice Schlesinger:[118]

London 2 Nov. 1842

[Moscheles begins by bringing to Schlesinger's attention a new apparatus for developing finger strength and agility developed by Casimir Martin. He goes on to request that Schlesinger send to Moscheles's daughter Emily a number of Chopin editions, listing opp. 1–9, 11, 15–17, 19, 24, 26–27, 29–30, 37–41, and adding at the end "from here, all the following."]

I would myself have turned here to Wessel & Co. about the Chopin items but I have long had nothing to do with him because of his shabbiness in business, and what is more Chopin's last items are the reason why I have completely broken with him.

You will recall that the 6 works by Chopin that you brought to London and sold to Wessel would be corrected by me in advance with the stipulation that W[essel] should give me 6 exemplars for each. You told me this demand was granted. When I thereupon asked W[essel] he told me impudently he was not liable to me for that, *you* had used my corrections, and he only sent additional corrected proofs to the engraver. Is it so?

[Moscheles closes by saying that a report in Schlesinger's *Revue et Gazette musicale* has greatly exaggerated his position in London, and asks him to correct it.]

Here then is direct testimony of nonauthorial revisions in Chopin's English publications. Moreover, Moscheles's "corrections," as opposed to those of others who proofread the composer's music, could not have been made with the prior permission of Chopin. Moscheles and Chopin were more than casual acquaintances—the two had played a four-hand recital before Louis-Philippe in 1839, and were kept abreast of each other's fortunes through their common friend Auguste Léo—but Moscheles did not number among the Pole's close friends. It is inconceivable that Chopin would consent to "corrections" by someone who was not an intimate without insisting that he see them before they were handed over to the publisher. Schlesinger alone was responsible for pressing Moscheles into service to proofread opp. 44–49.

But did Moscheles's labors actually show in the English edition? When he went to Wessel's shop to claim his six copies of the works he had proofread, Wessel "impudently" told him that in fact Schlesinger had used the "corrections," and that Wessel instead gave his engraver corrected proofs that the French publisher sent him. Schlesinger's response to Moscheles's query is lost, but as curious as Wessel's statement sounds, he could well have been telling the truth. In several instances in the works concerned, the French and English editions show telltale signs of deriving from a common printed source.[119] Thus Jan Ekier reports that the Wessel edition of op. 47 repeats all of the variants of the Schlesinger edition, and he is able to find only two minor instances where the English text deviates from the French.[120] If Wessel had used Chopin's text with Moscheles's additions, such a close agreement would not likely have occurred. Corrected proofs sent by Schlesinger must have formed the basis of the Wessel edition.

What then became of Moscheles's emendations? The surviving sources for the *Allegro de Concert,* op. 46, may offer a clue. Ernst Herttrich, in his critical report to the Henle edition, offers readings from two different states of the French first edition.[121] The first state, housed in the Bibliothèque Nationale, differs in many respects from the second, which is part of the collection of the Chopin Society in Warsaw (the second state also includes autograph entries in Chopin's hand—Herttrich does not say, but presumably this copy of the edition derives from the scores once owned by Ludwika Jędrzejewicz). Comparing the Wessel edition of op. 46 to these two states of the French edition, we discover that in every instance where the Wessel edition disagrees with the first state of the French edition, it agrees with the second state. (A particularly telling example occurs in m. 95, where only the Wessel edition and the second state of the French edition show the grace-note figure before the third beat.) Obviously then, the Wessel edition and the second state of the French edition must derive from a common source.

Now the French editions of opp. 44–49 had already been published, in November and December 1841, before Schlesinger traveled to London in January 1842 to sell Wessel these works. Presumably, then, it was these published versions that Schlesinger brought with him by way of exemplars. And therefore what Moscheles must have "corrected" was something akin to the first states of these editions (and it would not have been surprising if his corrections made the first state resemble, if not duplicate, the second state, for, as Krzysztof Grabowski notes, most of the flaws in the first state are simple grammatical errors).[122] But Wessel did not use these states to set his edition. For before Wessel went to press, he received from Schlesinger newly corrected proofs, equivalent to the second state. (Why did Schlesinger prepare a second state? Chopin may have demanded that Schlesinger reissue the editions in order to correct the grammatical errors in the first state. And, if he remained true to habit, he probably did not refrain from making additional "compositional" changes, such as the ornament added to m. 95.) Upon receiving these new proofs, Wessel probably returned to Schlesinger Moscheles's "corrected" proofs: in telling Moscheles that Schlesinger had used his corrections, Wessel probably only guessed at the fate of Moscheles's proofs once they were back in Schlesinger's hands. More likely is that Schlesinger simply discarded Moscheles's interventions upon receiving them from Wessel.

As was the case with German publishers, once a work reached the London engraver's hands, Chopin ceased to have any control over the text printed. He seems to have been somewhat more aware of what was appearing before the public in England than in Germany, but only in regard to the titles that Wessel persisted in adding. And this information likely came to Chopin not through the printed editions themselves, but from what was entered into his contracts with the London publisher.

Later issues of Chopin's music did appear in London during the composer's lifetime. These are easy to spot, since from late 1841 Wessel issued Chopin's editions using a passe-partout title page containing a running list of the composer's works published to that date. Thus, if the title page of an edition of the Waltz, op. 18 lists Chopin compositions through op. 55, then that edition was released in the latter part of 1845 or the early part of 1846. The textual significance of these later issues may be minimal, for in the cases where I have compared early and later issues of Wessel editions, no differences emerged.

In the course of his career, Chopin's methods of publication in England followed a zigzagging path. After mid-1843, autograph manuscripts likely served as the basis for all Wessel editions, but before, Chopin and his French publishers shipped proofs, copyists' manuscripts, and autographs across the Channel. Through mid-1837, he transmitted his music westward solely by means of proofs. When he traveled to London in July 1837 he included manuscripts in his baggage, but these manuscripts did not herald a total change in publishing method, for upon his return he continued to send proofs to London. By 1841, Chopin's opinion of Wessel's aesthetic sense and business habits was as low as it could be, and for a short time he evidently broke off relations with the London house. Still, the composer took great pains to ensure that, as much as possible, his English editions reflected accurately what he had written, even when he was not in direct contact with London.

From this survey of Chopin's methods of publication emerges a picture of a small corner of Parisian cultural and economic life in the 1830s and 1840s. We gain a glimpse of a composer's business relations with his publishers at home and abroad, and witness the twistings and turnings necessary to cement deals. Reading carefully through the hurly-burly of negotiations and the maze of provisions and options, we learn what kinds of sources Chopin and his publishers used to prepare given editions and the amount of control the author had over the music eventually published in them. The bargaining was not always gentlemanly: accusations and threats flew from both composer and publisher. Yet out of the atmosphere of mutual distrust came publications of signal importance for the history of music.

≀ 7 ≀

The Chopin "Problem":
Simultaneous Variants and
Alternate Versions

Twentieth-century critics have stumbled repeatedly upon encountering the welter of variants in the sources for Chopin's music. Often the same phrase might differ in all the surviving sources, which may include multiple autograph manuscripts, copyists' manuscripts, three first editions, later states of editions, and a handful of copies of these editions formerly owned by pupils of Chopin and annotated by him in lessons. So endemic and troubling was the situation that it became reified as "the Chopin problem," one to which a variety of largely anachronistic and entirely unreconcilable "solutions" were devised. What has been mostly lacking is a sense of the historical contexts in which these variants were produced. In this chapter I want first to explore some of these contexts, and then to suggest that these variants are essential to the aesthetic mode of existence of Chopin's music, as understood both by Chopin and by his audiences in the 1830s and 1840s. As we will see, this suggestion has significant consequences for the study of Chopin's music in general, and its editing in particular. For when we conceive of variants as something basic to the existence of the work of art, they become less a "problem" and more a necessary part of our informed understanding.

To grasp the circumstances by which variants have become a "problem" for editors, we need first to understand something of the publishing system within which Chopin worked, for it was this system that permitted the proliferation of variant readings. As we saw in the previous chapter, Chopin's compositions ordinarily appeared in print at roughly the same time in three different countries—France, England, and one of the German-speaking states—and with three different publishers. (We still refer to this as "simultaneous" publication, even though examination of copyright deposit records in the respective countries reveals that none of the editions were truly simultaneous.) Chopin opted for this complex method of international publication for two reasons: first, by selling the work to three different publishers, he increased his income from it; and second, by publishing the work legally in three countries, he could hope to avoid the piracies that would remove his control over the texts of his printed music.

Chopin could supply copy to the three publishers in a variety of ways, but matters really get interesting when he prepared separate engraver's manuscripts for each of the publishers. For what in the hands of most composers would have been a simple copying operation was for Chopin anything but. He was constitutionally unable simply to copy; for him, "copying" always occasioned further composing. We will see some graphic evidence of this shortly. Indeed, he seldom could stifle this compositional impulse: when reading copyists' manuscripts or proof sheets, when writing out manuscripts to give as gifts, and when teaching students from printed editions, he was likely to jot down "revisions" of one sort or another. Composition for Chopin was an open-ended process, unbound by the nature and physical restrictions of the source or the limits of publication. And because it was so, and particularly because Chopin was willing to allow different readings of a work to appear in print at the same time, variants have achieved the status of a "problem" for modern editors and critics.

Faced with this "problem," and—it must be said—usually not well informed about the historical particulars of the production of Chopin's music, most editors have sought to "solve" it by establishing a text that, in their reconstruction, most nearly approximates the intentions of the composer. It is with such solutions that we encounter the specter of anachronism. For the case of Chopin provides compelling evidence in support of Jerome McGann's argument against invoking the notion of a composer's intentions to resolve conflicting variants.[1] Like McGann, I feel that to appeal to "composer's intentions" is to apply ideological rather than historical standards to the music, and to assume that the creative artist worked autonomously, uninfluenced by a public or by institutions such as publishing houses or concert halls. The idea of the "autonomous artist" took hold in the Romantic era, when it formed an essential part of the ideology of the creative artist. But what makes the application of this ideology to editing problematic is that it often had more to do with some composers' self-images than with their documentable creative actions. The ideology bolstered their personal mythology.

Hence, when Chopin's editors choose between variants on the basis of "composer's intentions" and try to reduce the amount of "contamination" introduced by sources that cannot securely be linked to the composer, they in effect tacitly accept this ideological (and fictional) view of the relations between the composer, his works, his institutional affiliations, and his audience. At the same time, by attempting to place the user of an edition in unmediated contact with the wishes of the composer, they silently ignore the set of circumstances that actually attended the production of musical texts in the nineteenth century. In this way, editions executed according to the guidelines of "composer's intentions" distort an essential feature of the music they are trying to preserve.

From what basis should editors of Chopin's music proceed, if not from the intentions of the composer? Again I cast my lot with McGann in viewing musical compositions as social rather than purely personal products. Compositions attain their artistic form of being when they engage a social "institution" or a public of some sort. When music is perceived in this way, text-critical authority likewise becomes a social rather than a personal phenomenon. Authority resides in the structure of the explicit or implicit agreements between the composer and his "institution," in the collaboration between the composer and his publisher, opera house, symphony orchestra, or gift recipient.[2] The fully "authoritative" text is likely to be that which reflects its social production.

In an editorial method that recognizes the social status of a work of art, the criterion of "composer's intentions," whether original or final, diminishes in value: such intentions form only part of a broader context that needs to be considered. Equally suspect, then, is the idea of a "definitive" text or texts, which may not correspond to any concept embraced or understood in the nineteenth century. The social circumstances may reveal that more than one authoritative version exists.

The sources preserving Chopin's music reveal clearly the problematic nature of the notion of "composer's intentions" in general, and "final intentions" in particular. This emerges forcefully in four examples of variants dating from Chopin's later years.

First, I want to consider a well-known passage from the middle section of the Nocturne in B Major, op. 62, no. 1. Nearly all of the sources of this section that can definitely be traced to Chopin survive. We can consult the sketch, the *Stichvorlagen* (the manuscripts used for engraving) for the French edition of Brandus and the German edition of Breitkopf & Härtel, and the French, German, and English first editions. And from all of these sources emerges a dizzying array of variants for measures 53–55 (Ex. 7.1 presents these variants in my reconstruction of the order in which they were conceived by Chopin). We can be reasonably certain that Chopin made all of these changes himself. We know that he read proofs for the Brandus edition, which accounts for the differences between the Brandus autograph *Stichvorlage* and the actual Brandus edition produced from this *Stichvorlage*.[3] We can also be certain that at some time Chopin had before him on his music desk all three *Stichvorlagen* for the three editions (the Wessel autograph is now lost), for we can determine from his correspondence that he sent off all three autographs on the same day.[4] In other words, we may assume that Chopin knew he was mailing different versions of measures 53–55, but chose not to bring them into agreement.

Why would he have let the variants stand? It is possible that he was prevented because of lack of space in the Brandus *Stichvorlage* from bringing it into agreement with the Breitkopf manuscript. Knowing that he was going to read proof for the Brandus edition, he may have decided to postpone the alteration until the proof stage. But this meant making the alteration by memory; from evidence throughout his career, it seems clear that Chopin usually read proof either against his sketches or simply against his memory. In either instance, he would not have had a copy of the revised version as represented in the German and English autographs before him when he corrected the French proofs.

If this reconstruction of events is correct, how do we make a modern

Example 7.1   Nocturne in B Major, op. 62, no. 1, mm. 53–55.

edition of these measures? The Brandus edition clearly represents the chronologically "final" version, which might suggest that it should serve as the basis for a modern edition. But it does not quite agree with the German or English editions; Chopin's memory while making the changes in the French proofs may have been faulty. That is, when Chopin shipped off the German and English autographs, he presumably also thought of these as "final" versions. So we are left with at least two "final" versions of this passage, one represented by the German and English sources, and one by the French edition. Even if we depend solely on the concept of "composer's intentions" to solve editorial problems, we would still be confounded in this instance. Where do we locate Chopin's "final" intentions?

Different modern editors have opted for different solutions: some have followed the German sources, some the French edition, some the French autograph,[5] and some have conflated more than one source. All, however, print in the body of their edition only *one* version of the passage. Here is where the socially determined model of textual criticism I have proposed would lead to a different result. For if we assume that the production of musical texts in the nineteenth century was a collaborative process and that textual authority arises from the nature of the agreements between the composer and the institutions that printed his music, then both the German and French editions emerge as fully "authoritative" versions of the Nocturne in B Major. To publish only one of them would be to deny the validity of the arrangements that yielded the other. A single text would thus do injustice to the historical and aesthetic circumstances surrounding the work. The modern edition that would print two versions would come closest to achieving "authority" as it was understood in the nineteenth century (and, as I think will soon become clear, as it was understood by Chopin himself).[6]

The second example I want to consider is a passage from the Waltz in D-flat Major, op. 64, no. 1. Here the editor confronts an even more bewildering array of sources, for not only was the Waltz published, it was presented as a gift in manuscript form by Chopin several times. Fortunately, in the phrase I will discuss, measures 21–28, the editions are consistent; we need only discuss the manuscripts (Ex. 7.2). Small consolation, this, for three types of autograph manuscripts exist: the sketch, the Brandus *Stichvorlage,* and three presentation manuscripts (one found in Bonn, one given to Juliette von Caraman, and the other from the Rothschild collection).[7]

Example 7.2 shows a pattern of variants all too familiar when there exist multiple presentation manuscripts of the same work.[8] Looking only at the left hand, we can see that none of the three presentation manuscripts agrees precisely with either version of the passage contained in the sketch, nor does any agree with the Brandus autograph (which in turn does not match the sketch). In other words, the five autographs display five different versions of the accompaniment in measures 21–28.

How does an editor make informed decisions in this situation? Even an editor aware of the social dimensions of textual authority might be tempted to omit the presentation manuscripts from consideration. These manuscripts, the argument might go, did not enter into a social relationship in the same way that a *Stichvorlage* did—Chopin offered them as gifts, he did not give them to an engraver. Moreover, since all of the presentation manuscripts opt for the octave transposition which Chopin in his sketch marked *łatwiej* ("easier"), he might have specifically tailored the presentation manuscripts for less skilled pianists. If Chopin had to compromise his higher vision for these pianists in the presentation manuscripts, then these sources should not have much worth to the editor. In effect, the editor's judgment in this instance would be that the presentation autographs may be ignored in a modern critical edition because they do not display the same level of quality, the same careful compositional concern, as the *Stichvorlage*.

Now presentation manuscripts are one of the least understood categories of Chopin's autographs. We do not really know what the musical functions of these autographs were—whether their recipients simply valued them as treasured keepsakes, or whether they actively performed from them. Only a detailed study of the role of presentation manuscripts in nineteenth-century musical culture can provide answers (and such a study would be very welcome indeed). Nevertheless, we do know enough about Chopin's gift-giving habits with respect to waltzes to know that the text-critical reasoning I just described is false. Chopin favored no genre for presentation more than the waltz.[9] In other words, individual recipients were just as much part of the "normal" audience for waltzes as was the general music-buying public.

Example 7.2   Waltz in D-flat Major, op. 64, no. 1.

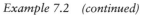

Example 7.2 (continued)

As far as the waltzes are concerned, then, the argument that Chopin's technical adjustments lessen the value of the presentation manuscripts paradoxically misreads the composer's intentions even as it invests all textual authority in them. The argument fails to consider the social nexus of the work of art. Surely Chopin's readings had meaning to the recipients of the gift. This meaning deserves to be communicated to the user of the critical edition, if for no other reason than that it may inform us about an ornamental or variational tradition significant to the genre of the waltz. Just as in the case of the Nocturne in B Major, the standard of "composer's intentions" provides no unequivocal guidance to the editor. The variants in the autograph sources reflect an essential aspect of the nature of op. 64, no. 1, and only a critical edition that prints multiple versions can successfully transmit this idea.

My third example comes from the Etude in E Major, op. 10, no. 3. Again we might consider the problems of multiple autographs and editions, but I am particularly interested in some changes Chopin made in the middle section of Jane Stirling's copy of the piece some dozen or so years after he wrote it. The sketch of the piece, from 1832, shows that Chopin labored especially hard over the middle section and retransition. His solution as published seems so convincing, with its gradual dissolution of a lyrical thematic style and its gradual introduction of virtuosic athematic diminished seventh chords, that his alteration of it in the Stirling edition comes as a shock. Example 7.3 shows the result of Chopin's trimming—so much for diminished seventh chords, and so much for the introduction of a contrasting thematic style into the Etude.[10] Yet, taken by themselves, the changes yield a viable, if blander, version of the middle section.

What does this revision portend for an editor? It is demonstrably the last change Chopin made in the Etude; does the result represent his final intention, "die Fassung letzter Hand," for the piece?[11] The answer might hinge on whether the revision was didactically motivated, intended only for a particular student who could not manage rapid diminished seventh chords, or whether it was compositionally motivated, intended as a radical rethinking of the overall shape of the Etude. The didactic explanation seems to me most likely—other alterations in the Stirling exemplars clearly seem to be facilitations—yet the compositional motivation cannot be ruled out: the Stirling edi-

Example 7.3   Middle section of the Etude in E Major, op. 10, no. 3, as revised by Chopin in Jane Stirling's copy of the French first edition.

tions also contain clear examples of this type of change (for example, a cut of twenty-four measures in the B-Minor Mazurka, op. 33, no. 4).[12] Even when the issue is phrased in didactic versus compositional terms, we do not really lessen its burden on the textual critic. Who is to say that a didactic change has no aesthetic meaning? Certainly it had some to the student for whom the change was made. Chopin made the revision as part of his "agreement" or "arrangement" with Jane Stirling, and having done so, he brought the change into public view. A concern for the social nature of music would suggest that a critical edition take at least some notice of the revision in the text it presents to the modern public.

Not wishing to leave readers with an exaggerated impression of the complexity of the variants facing Chopin's editors, I offer as my last example a more commonplace (but for the discriminating pianist, just as vexing) sort of difficulty. For the Nocturne in F Minor, op. 55, no. 1, the seven extant sources of measures 18–20 yield five different versions of the right hand (Ex. 7.4).[13] All of these versions derive from

Example 7.4   Nocturne in F Minor, op. 55, no. 1, mm. 18–20.

or were approved by Chopin. They reveal two main issues: how to slur the measures, and whether the third beat of measure 19 should be performed in even or dotted rhythm.

The first two versions rightfully belong to the prehistory of the published work. The first forms part of a complete presentation manuscript of an early conception of the work, in a different key and entitled simply "Andante." Properly speaking, therefore, it is not a "version" of the Nocturne at all, for the Nocturne as such did not yet exist. And the second reading occurs in an autograph that Chopin explicitly rejected for public ("public" here meaning editorial) consumption, and hence it never engaged any "social" institution of any sort. These two versions should not be ignored in the modern edition, however: surely they must be clearly represented in the critical commentary. Providing documentation of the genesis allows students of the score to grasp more fully the compositional context within which the public shape of the work emerged. And it permits musicians to exercise their own critical judgment as to whether Chopin revised effectively or not, and to opt for a "private" reading if they so desire. In making editions, we do not want to foreclose the possibility that unpublished versions might be more interesting to today's musicians than the published ones.[14]

But the three remaining variants did indeed enter into the social contract, and thus each needs to be represented in the main text of a properly conceived edition. (At this point, readers will not be surprised to learn that no existing edition even goes so far as to list the variants in its apparatus.) The gain for the user of such an edition is significant: the pianist, rather than being offered a precise prescription for performance, is presented with a range of options for the articulation of the phrase (the implication being that other possibilities falling within this range but not explicitly notated by Chopin would also be acceptable). The edition would thus capture something of the fluidity and variability that Chopin himself brought to the performance of his music.

What I hope emerges from these four examples of variants in Chopin is the sense that their status as "problems" results at least in part from anachronistic views of the nature of musical composition and the nature of the musical work in the nineteenth century.[15] When editors opt for one particular reading on the grounds that it embodies the composer's "final intention" or his "definitive version," they in effect interpret the act of composition and the composition itself in ways that simplify history. Composers in the nineteenth century were not autonomous figures, and their scores did not necessarily represent unique, invariable forms of their music.

But I do not want to give the impression that editors and critics should abandon their concern for Chopin's intentions. Far from it: exploring and explaining his intentions, as best we can reconstruct them, will always be central to our understanding of his work. Rather, I want to suggest that we need to take a broader, historically grounded view of these intentions, one that recognizes both their social dimension and the more fluid view of the work of art current in Chopin's day than in ours. For one of the clearest messages of the variants in Chopin's music, whether viewed from the standpoint of his "intentions" or from his collaboration with public "institutions,"is that composition was an ongoing *process* for Chopin. We can and certainly must distinguish stages in this process: at some points Chopin chose not to place the work before his public, and at some points he did. Editors particularly need to respect the first stage. But faced with versions that did attain a social status, editors should not cite a misguided notion of "final intentions" and refuse to publish all but the last version Chopin released. If Chopin allowed multiple versions of a piece to appear before the public, then this reflects something essential to the constitution of a work of art in the 1830s and 1840s. Our editions should reflect this fluidity; we do Chopin, his music, and his era a disservice by fixing in print only one view of a given artwork.

Hence we should conceive of variants not as a "problem" to be solved but as a reflection of one of the essences of Chopin's art. Chopin saw composition as an ongoing process, and in holding this view he mirrored the thoughts of his public. For Chopin and for listeners in the nineteenth century, music was a fluid, not fixed, concept. This explains why, in nearly every source he touched, he continued to compose, to revise, to cut. In so embracing variants, we take an important step toward restoring to Chopin's works the status they held in their own time.

Notes
Credits
Index

Notes

1. The Rhetoric of Genre

1. Robert Schumann, *Gesammelte Schriften über Musik und Musiker,* ed. Martin Kreisig, Fünfte Auflage, 2 vols. (Leipzig, 1914), vol. 1, p. 111. Paul Rosenfeld's standard English translation of Schumann's writings (it has appeared under several publishers; I cite from Robert Schumann, *On Music and Musicians,* ed. Konrad Wolff [New York, 1969], p. 120) follows the quotation I have given with the clause "in which I detect the most terrific declaration of war to the entire past," which in English might indicate that this remark applies to the Chopin Nocturne. But Schumann's "in ihr" ("in which") would seem to refer to "*die* Leonoren-Ouvertüre," not to "*das* Chopinsche Notturno." Unless otherwise indicated, all translations in this book are my own.

2. Most previous positions on the meanings of the concept of genre in music have been formulated by German scholars. The most interesting, extensive, and carefully articulated of these were proposed by Carl Dahlhaus. In his *Esthetics of Music*—published in Germany in 1967—and in his *Foundations of Music History,* trans. J. B. Robinson (Cambridge, 1983)—the German original of which appeared in 1977—he touched on the topic many times. And he devoted several essays entirely to the subject. These include "Zur Problematik der musikalischen Gattungen im 19. Jahrhundert," in *Gattungen der Musik in Einzeldarstellungen: Gedenkschrift Leo Schrade,* ed. Wulf Arlt, Ernst Lichtenhahn, and Hans Oesch (Bern, 1973), pp. 840–895; "Die neue Musik und das Problem der musikalischen Gattungen," *Gestaltungsgeschichte und Gesellschaftsgeschichte: literatur-, kunst- und musikwissenschaftliche Studien,* ed. Helmut Kreuzer (Stuttgart, 1969), pp. 516–528 (reprinted as "New Music and the Problem of Musical Genre," in Dahlhaus, *Schoenberg and the New Music* [Cambridge, 1987], pp. 32–44); "Traditionszerfall im 19. und 20. Jahrhundert," *Studien zur Tradition in der Musik. Kurt von Fischer zum 60. Geburtstag,* ed. Hans Heinrich Eggebrecht and Max Lütolf (Munich, 1973), pp. 177–190; "Was ist eine musikalische Gattung?," *Neue Zeitschrift für Musik* 135 (1974): 620–625; "Mendelssohn und die musikalischen Gattungstraditionen," *Das Problem Mendelssohn,* ed. Dahlhaus, Stu-

dien zur Musikgeschichte des 19. Jahrhunderts, vol. 41 (Regensburg, 1974), pp. 55–60; "Formenlehre und Gattungstheorie bei A.B. Marx," *Heinrich Sievers zum 60. Geburtstag,* ed. Günter Katzenberger (Tutzing, 1978), pp. 29–35; "Gattungsgeschichte und Werkinterpretation: Die Historie als Oper," in *Gattung und Werk in der Musikgeschichte Norddeutschlands und Skandinaviens: Referate der Kieler Tagung 1980,* ed. Friedhelm Krummacher and Heinrich W. Schwab, Kieler Schriften zur Musikwissenschaft, vol. 26 (Kassel, 1982), pp. 20–29; and *Systematische Musikwissenschaft,* ed. Dahlhaus and Helga de la Motte Haber, Neues Handbuch der Musikwissenschaft, vol. 10 (Wiesbaden, 1982), pp. 109–124. See also his article "Gattung" in the *Brockhaus Riemann Musiklexikon,* ed. Dahlhaus and Hans Heinrich Eggebrecht, 2 vols. (Wiesbaden, 1978), vol. 1, p. 452.

Other notable German theorists of musical genre include Walter Wiora, "Die historische und die systematische Betrachtung der musikalischen Gattungen," in his *Historische und systematische Musikwissenschaft,* ed. Helmut Kühn et al. (Tutzing, 1972), pp. 448–476; Wiora, "Zu einigen Grundfragen der Gattungsgeschichte," *Die Musikforschung* 30 (1977): 185–188; Wulf Arlt, "Aspekte der Gattungsbegriffs in der Musikgeschichtsschreibung," in *Gattungen der Musik,* pp. 11–93; Arlt, "Gattung—Probleme mit einem Interpretationsmodell der Musikgeschichtsschreibung," *Gattung und Werk in der Musikgeschichte Norddeutschlands,* pp. 10–19; and Stefan Kunze, "Überlegungen zum Begriff der 'Gattung' in der Musik," *Gattung und Werk in der Musikgeschichte Norddeutschlands,* pp. 5–9.

In English, formal accounts of the concept are scarce. The term "genre" is seldom even listed in dictionaries and encyclopedias of music; symptomatically, it is absent from *The New Grove.* Two recent exceptions to this trend are James A. Hepokoski, "Genre and Content in Mid-Century Verdi: 'Addio, del passato' (*La traviata,* Act III)," *Cambridge Opera Journal* 1 (1989): 249–276; and Vera Micznik, "Mahler and 'The Power of Genre,' " *Journal of Musicology* 12 (1994): 117–151.

3. Alastair Fowler, *Kinds of Literature: An Introduction to the Theory of Genres and Modes* (Cambridge, Mass., 1982), p. 37.

4. I have been alerted to the problems inherent in definitions by John M. Ellis, *The Theory of Literary Criticism: A Logical Analysis* (Berkeley and Los Angeles, 1974), pp. 31–35.

5. The main exposition of Wittgenstein's theory of meaning is in *Philosophical Investigations,* trans. G. E. M. Anscombe, 3rd ed. (New York, 1968). Ellis, *The Theory of Literary Criticism,* explicitly applies Wittgenstein's concepts to the study of literature.

6. Adena Rosmarin, in *The Power of Genre* (Minneapolis, 1986), similarly argues against equating "genre" with "class" (p. 46). Rosmarin's theory of

genre as a pragmatic, heuristic tool meant to serve a critic's explanatory needs (pp. 3–51) properly stresses the communicative properties of the concept. However, her explicit denials of a role for history in this critical process are discomforting. Ann E. Imbrie, "Defining Nonfiction Genres," *Renaissance Genres: Essays on Theory, History, and Interpretation,* ed. Barbara Kiefer Lewalksi, Harvard English Studies 14 (Cambridge, Mass., 1986), pp. 45–69, and Fowler, *Kinds of Literature,* pp. 37–53, both lobby against purely taxonomic applications for genre.

7. See Ellis, *The Theory of Literary Criticism,* pp. 31–35. Barbara Herrnstein Smith makes a similar point about the interpretation of verbal structures in *On the Margins of Discourse: The Relation of Literature to Language* (Chicago, 1978), p. 119.

8. I use the term "rhetoric" in its wider sense of referring to the whole complex network of relationships that may connect a writer (composer) with an audience. See Wayne C. Booth's *The Rhetoric of Fiction* (Chicago, 1961).

Peter J. Rabinowitz has explored in interesting ways the roles of readers and listeners in the apprehension of popular literary genres and of music in general. See *Before Reading: Narrative Conventions and the Politics of Interpretation* (Ithaca and London, 1987); "The Turn of the Glass Key: Popular Fiction as Reading Strategy," *Critical Inquiry* 11 (1985): 418–431; "Assuming the Obvious: A Reply to Derek Longhurst," *Critical Inquiry* 12 (1986): 601–604; and "Musical Analysis and Theories of Reading," *Mosaic* 18 (1985): 159–173.

9. See E. D. Hirsch, Jr., *Validity in Interpretation* (New Haven, 1967), p. 93; and Hans Robert Jauss, *Toward an Aesthetic of Reception,* trans. Timothy Bahti (Minneapolis, 1982), pp. 3–45, 76–109. Wulf Arlt, "Gattung—Probleme mit einem Interpretationsmodell der Musikgeschichtsschreibung," p. 18, invokes Jauss while touching on the issue of genre as a communicative concept.

10. On the notion of "generic contracts" see Philippe Lejeune, *Le pacte autobiographique* (Paris, 1975), and Heather Dubrow, *Genre,* The Critical Idiom, vol. 42 (London and New York, 1982), pp. 31–37.

11. See Dubrow, *Genre,* pp. 106–107.

12. This topic is amplified in Judith Becker and Alton Becker, "A Grammar of the Musical Genre *Srepegan,*" *Journal of Music Theory* 23 (1979): 1–43; Becker and Becker, "A Reconsideration in the Form of a Dialogue," *Asian Music* 14 (1983): 9–16; and Dubrow, *Genre,* p. 32.

13. See *Literature as System: Essays Toward the Theory of Literary History* (Princeton, 1971), pp. 107–134.

14. See the *Allgemeine musikalische Zeitung* 15 (1813), col. 68–70; Zenck, "Entwurf einer Soziologie," pp. 270–272, also discusses this review.

15. Eugene K. Wolf's *The Symphonies of Johann Stamitz: A Study in the Formation of the Classic Style* (Utrecht, 1981), and Neal Zaslaw's "Mozart, Haydn, and the *Sinfonia da Chiesa*," *Journal of Musicology* 1 (1982): 95–121, are exemplary of the work in this field.

16. See Gary Saul Morson, *The Boundaries of Genre: Dostoevsky's "Diary of a Writer" and the Traditions of Literary Utopia* (Austin, 1981), p. 75. I have found Morson's book particularly valuable in formulating my thoughts on genre.

17. Nino Pirrotta cautions against indiscriminately applying criteria derived from music of later periods to works of the early seventeenth century. See Chapter 6, "Early Opera and Aria," in Pirrotta and Elena Povoledo, *Music and Theatre from Poliziano to Monteverdi*, trans. Karen Eales (Cambridge, 1982), pp. 237–280.

18. See Morson, *The Boundaries of Genre*, p. 52; and Ellis, *The Theory of Literary Criticism*, p. 35.

19. On such hierarchies see Dahlhaus, "Zur Problematik der musikalischen Gattungen im 19. Jahrhundert," pp. 851–858.

20. Writers of dictionaries often articulated the common bond between the two genres. None was more direct than R. Hippolyte Colet: "The Nocturne is a Romance sung by two, three, or four voices"; *La panharmonie musicale, ou cours complet de composition théorique et pratique* (Paris, 1837), p. 302.

21. In particular, see the comments by Charles Rosen, *The Classical Style: Haydn, Mozart, Beethoven* (New York, 1972), pp. 439–440; and by Leo Treitler, "History, Criticism, and Beethoven's Ninth Symphony," *19th-Century Music* 3 (1980): 193–210.

22. On this point see Wolfgang Iser, *The Implied Reader: Patterns of Communication in Prose Fiction from Bunyan to Beckett* (Baltimore, 1974), pp. 57–80.

For a particularly fine analysis of generic mixture in a work by Bach, see Laurence Dreyfus, "J. S. Bach and the Status of Genre: Problems of Style in the G-Minor Sonata BWV 1029," *Journal of Musicology* 5 (1987): 55–78.

23. See Chapter 4.

24. See Piero Weiss, "Verdi and the Fusion of Genres," *Journal of the American Musicological Society* 35 (1982): 138–156.

25. *Literature as System*, pp. 73–106, 135–158.

26. Dahlhaus makes this same point in "Zur Problematik der musikalischen Gattungen im 19. Jahrhundert," p. 854.

27. This point is not universally accepted by literary theorists, particularly those who interpret genre according to structuralist precepts. The failure to address the idea of generic change can weaken the positions of otherwise convincing critics. For example, the stance of Jonathan Culler (*Structuralist*

Poetics: Structuralism, Linguistics, and the Study of Literature [Ithaca, 1975], pp. 136–140, 145–148) may be faulted for its too rigid notion of genre.

28. *Neue Zeitschrift für Musik*, 31 July 1835, p. 33. As with my initial quotation from Schumann, this one has been mistranslated by Rosenfeld (or more accurately, only partially translated).

29. *Le pianiste* 1 (1834): 78–79. *Genre* has numerous meanings in French. In the review, its sense is clearly "fashion" rather than the larger concept that is the concern of this chapter.

30. *Le pianiste* 1 (1834): 103.

31. My statistics on its usage are derived from Jean-Jacques Eigeldinger, *Chopin: Pianist and Teacher as Seen by His Pupils,* trans. Naomi Shohet, Krysia Osostowicz, and Roy Howat, ed. Roy Howat (Cambridge, 1986), pp. 121–122; and from Bertrand Jaeger, "Quelques nouveaux noms d'élèves de Chopin," *Revue de musicologie* 64 (1978): 85.

32. In this light, it is interesting that someone—perhaps Chopin—crossed out these words in Jane Stirling's copy of the French edition. See Frédéric Chopin, *Oeuvres pour piano: Fac-similé de l'exemplaire de Jane W. Stirling avec annotations et corrections de l'auteur,* introduction by Jean-Jacques Eigeldinger, preface by Jean-Michel Nectoux (Paris, 1982), p. 73.

33. Associations with Polish folk culture are not uncommon among writers who discuss this Nocturne. The great Polish man-of-letters Jarosław Iwasz-kiewicz, in his *Chopin,* trans. Georges Lisowski (Paris, 1966), pp. 117–119, devotes space to what he calls the "Ukrainian" cast of the opening of the Nocturne. Similar comments are made by Eigeldinger, *Chopin: Pianist and Teacher,* p. 153. Viktor Cukkerman mentions in passing the resemblance of the opening to the mazurka. See "De l'emploi des genres et des formes dans l'oeuvre de Chopin," in *The Book of the First International Musicological Congress Devoted to the Works of Frederick Chopin,* ed. Zofia Lissa (War-saw, 1963), p. 115. Also Ludmila Moskalenko, "Elementy taneczne w nok-turnach Chopina," *Rocznik Chopinowski* 13 (1981): 37–47, and especially pp. 43–45, discusses the dancelike elements of the piece. Moskalenko's article is hampered by a dependence on the overly deterministic and function-ridden generic theories of Arnold Sochor.

34. It is probably fortuitous that the opening of Chopin's *religioso* melody nearly duplicates the beginning of the Credo III, a seventeenth-century chant (*Liber usualis,* p. 68). Although he did incorporate a melody from Rossini's *La gazza ladra* into the trio of his early Polonaise in B-flat Minor, Chopin was not in the habit of quoting known tunes in his compositions—the sup-posed and often cited quotation of the Polish Christmas carol "Lulajże Je-zuniu" in the trio of the B-Minor Scherzo, op. 20, dissolves when one com-pares the whole tune in the trio with contemporary transcriptions of the entire

Christmas melody (there are similarities only in the first three measures of each). For the original tune, see Michał Mioduszewski, *Pastorałki i kolędy z melodyjami* (Cracow, 1843), p. 92.

35. The vast majority of Polish church chorales collected by Mioduszewski are notated in F major; see *Pastorałki i kolędy,* passim. Sieghard Brandenburg's "The Historical Background to the 'Heiliger Dankgesang' in Beethoven's A-minor Quartet Op. 132," *Beethoven Studies 3,* ed. Alan Tyson (Cambridge, 1982), pp. 161–191, is an excellent exploration of nineteenth-century perceptions of church modes.

36. Arthur Hedley, Maurice J. E. Brown, and Nicholas Temperley, "Chopin, Fryderyk Franciszek," *The New Grove Dictionary of Music and Musicians,* ed. Stanley Sadie (London, 1980), vol. 4, p. 303.

37. This is not to say that Polish composers had not previously linked ideas of national expression with religious music, only that the mazurka was not viewed as a customary place for their fusion. On Polish religious music of the nineteenth century, see Alina Nowak-Romanowicz, "Les éléments nationaux chez les compositeurs de la musique religieuse polonaise dans la première moitié du XIXe siècle," *Etat des recherches sur la musique religieuse dans la culture polonaise,* ed. J. Pikulik (Warsaw, 1973), pp. 71–86.

38. The sketch occupies one page of a bifolio. Two of the other pages of this bifolio contain a sketch for the Etude in F Minor, op. 10, no. 9; the remaining page is blank.

39. Though Chopin could have varied the reprise through ornamentation, the themes of the opening section do not respond well to elaboration. No less a composer than Schumann tried to ornament the first theme of op. 15, no. 3, in a projected and abandoned set of variations on the Chopin Nocturne. In a letter of 23 October 1836 to Stephen Heller, Schumann referred to the Nocturne as "one of my favorite pieces" (Stephen Heller, *Lettres d'un musicien romantique à Paris,* ed. Jean-Jacques Eigeldinger [Paris, 1981], p. 93), but, favorite or not, its principal theme resisted his embellishments. The unfortunate torso is published (with some errors) in Karol Musiol, "Robert Schumann und Fryderyk Chopin: ein Beitrag zur Genesis der ästhetischen Anschauungen und des poetischen Stils der Musikkritik Schumanns," *Beiträge zur Musikwissenschaft* 23 (1981): 56–58; Joachim Draheim has published a corrected and completed edition: Robert Schumann, *Variationen über ein Nocturne von Chopin (g-moll, op. 15 Nr. 3),* ed. Draheim (Wiesbaden, Leipzig, and Paris, 1992).

40. Chopin's most famous asymmetrical melody before the Nocturne is the opening tune of the E-Major Etude, op. 10, no. 3, whose eight measures are divided as 5 + 3.

41. Letter of 25 December 1831; Fryderyk Chopin, *Korespondencja Fry-deryka Chopina,* ed. Bronisław Edward Sydow, 2 vols. (Warsaw, 1955), vol. 1, p. 210.

42. Letter of 1 December 1830 to Chopin's parents; Fryderyk Chopin, *Korespondencja Fryderyka Chopina z Rodziną,* ed. Krystyna Kobylańska (Warsaw, 1972), p. 64.

43. Letter of 8 August 1835 to Józef Nowakowski in Warsaw; Chopin, *Korespondencja,* ed. Sydow, vol. 1, p. 258–259.

44. G. W. Fink, "Edouard Wolff," *Cäcilia* 21 (1842): 225–230.

45. The work (Wolff's op. 45) was issued by Maurice Schlesinger (plate number M.S. 3296); the first advertisement for it (as well as for other works of Wolff) appeared in the *Revue et Gazette musicale de Paris,* 9 May 1841, p. 268. The complete work is reproduced in Jeffrey Kallberg, ed., *Piano Music of the Parisian Virtuosos, 1810–1860,* vol. 6: *Edward Wolff (1816–1880): Selected Works* (New York and London, 1993), pp. 181–189.

46. Note also that Wolff's strategy for ending his piece imitates another G-minor work by Chopin; its last four measures match precisely the harmonic progression at the end of the Prelude in G Minor, op. 28, no. 22.

47. Wolff's *Nocturne en forme de Mazurke* was not the only nocturne written by a lesser-known Pole to mix in elements from the mazurka. The third number of Ignacy Felix Dobrzyński's *Nocturnes,* op. 21 (ca. 1833), bears the heading "Allegretto alla masovienna," a reference to a Polish folk dance closely related to the mazurka. Dobrzyński, however, did not model his piece on any nocturne by Chopin.

48. M. A. Szulc, "Zbiór wiadomości i uzupełnień dotyczących życia i utworów Fryderyka Chopina," *Echo Muzyczne* 20 (1880): 159; as given in Krystyna Kobylańska, *Rękopisy Utworów Chopina: Katalog,* Documenta Chopiniana, no. 2, 2 vols. (Cracow, 1977), vol. 1, p. 104.

49. Kobylańska, *Rękopisy,* vol. 1, p. 105.

50. See letter of 21 August 1830 to Titus Woyciechowski; Chopin, *Korespondencja,* ed. Sydow, vol. 1, p. 131.

51. Eigeldinger, *Chopin: Pianist and Teacher,* p. 153.

52. For the dates of Smithson's performances, see Hector Berlioz, *Correspondance générale,* ed. Pierre Citron, 5 vols. to date (Paris, 1972–), vol. 2 (1975), p. 55.

53. This admittedly hypothetical reading of the Nocturne in light of *Hamlet* comes from Eigeldinger, *Chopin: Pianist and Teacher,* p. 218. Giovanni Morelli, in accepting uncritically Szulc's story, also tries to interpret the Nocturne in terms of *Hamlet,* though this in itself does not invalidate the comparison he makes between the Nocturne and the second movement of Berlioz's *Harold*

in Italy. See "Après une représentation de Hamlet," in *Chopin opera omnia,* ed. Carlo de Incontrera (Venice, 1985), pp. 121–139, and especially pp. 129–136.

54. Three excellent books in English investigate Polish history and culture. For a broad survey, see the magisterial work of Norman Davies, *God's Playground: A History of Poland,* 2 vols. (New York, 1984). Czesław Miłosz's *The History of Polish Literature,* 2d ed. (Berkeley and Los Angeles, 1983), takes a more specifically cultural tack. Andrzej Walicki's *Philosophy and Romantic Nationalism: The Case of Poland* (Oxford, 1982) is a detailed exploration of the philosophical, historical, and intellectual underpinnings of Polish romantic nationalism. I have freely culled the discussion that follows from these three sources, and from others cited below.

55. A detailed account of cultural life among the émigrés in France may be found in Maria Straszewska, *Życie literackie Wielkiej Emigracji we Francji 1831–1840* (Warsaw, 1970).

56. Walicki, *Philosophy and Romantic Nationalism,* pp. 64–85, cautions that a wide variety of meanings—political, linguistic, and cultural—of the national idea were then current. On the subject of different meanings of "nationalism," Walicki notes in his Introduction (p. 5) that the term "nationalism" is employed in Poland and other eastern European countries primarily in a pejorative sense, as roughly equivalent to "chauvinism," "state expansionism," and "national egoism." In Polish eyes, the figures of the Great Emigration were not "nationalists," they were "patriots." Like Walicki, I employ the term in its more positive and variable English sense.

57. Walicki, *Philosophy and Romantic Nationalism,* p. 83.

58. Ibid., pp. 239–241.

59. Ibid., pp. 243–245. The relationship between social utopian thought and music has been treated extensively by Ralph P. Locke in *Music, Musicians, and the Saint-Simonians* (Chicago, 1986).

60. The closest he came to this subject occurred in a letter of 25 December 1831 to his friend Titus Woyciechowski in Warsaw; Chopin described the enthusiastic reception given General Ramorino (who had aided the Poles against the Russians) by anti-government demonstrators in Paris. The crowd, who cried out at one point "vive les Polonais," included among their number some Saint-Simonists, about whom Chopin knew enough to say that they were trying to form a new religion and that they had a large number of converts. See Chopin, *Korespondencja,* ed. Sydow, vol. 1, p. 208.

61. As just one example, note Witwicki's "Only may you constantly keep in mind: national character *(narodowość),* national character, and once again national character; that is a practically empty word for ordinary writers, but not for a talent such as yours." See letter of 6 July 1831 in Chopin, *Kores-*

pondencja, ed. Sydow, vol. 1, p. 179–180. On the relationship between Chopin and Witwicki, see Franciszek German, "Chopin i Witwicki," *Annales Chopin* 5 (1960): 200–222. For an interesting discussion of the suggestions that Chopin compose a Polish national opera, see Ferdynand Hoesick, *Chopin: Życie i twórczość,* 3 vols. (Warsaw, 1910–1911); rev. ed., 4 vols. (Cracow, 1962–1968), vol. 2, pp. 105–109.

62. Elsner tried at least three times to induce Chopin to write a Polish opera, once through the agency of Chopin's sister Ludwika, and twice on his own (one of these times was after the publication of op. 15). See letters of 27 November 1831, 13 November 1832, and 14 September 1834 in Chopin, *Korespondencja,* ed. Sydow, vol. 1, pp. 191–196; 220–221; 246–247.

63. See letter of 14 December 1831 to Elsner in Chopin, *Korespondencja,* ed. Sydow, vol. 1, p. 205.

64. See Walicki, *Philosophy and Romantic Nationalism,* pp. 253–291.

2. The Harmony of the Tea Table

1. "The Technology of Gender," in *Technologies of Gender* (Bloomington, 1987), p. 5.

2. For a thorough exposition of how the language of formalist criticism places barriers in the path of social and cultural history, see Rose Rosengard Subotnik, "Toward a Deconstruction of Structural Listening: A Critique of Schoenberg, Adorno, and Stravinsky," in *Explorations in Music, the Arts, and Ideas: Essays in Honor of Leonard B. Meyer,* ed. Eugene Narmour and Ruth A. Solie (Stuyvesant, N.Y., 1988), pp. 87–122.

3. I find this often to be the case in the writings of Susan McClary. Throughout her otherwise finely nuanced collection of essays (*Feminine Endings: Music, Gender, and Sexuality* [Minneapolis, 1991]) McClary appeals to "the common semiotic codes of European classical music" (p. 68) to bolster her readings of the gendered and sexualized nature of such chronologically and culturally divergent works as Monteverdi's *Orfeo,* Beethoven's Ninth Symphony, Donizetti's *Lucia di Lammermoor,* Bizet's *Carmen,* and Tchaikovsky's Fourth Symphony. She premises her discussions on the belief that "any five-year-old has sufficient experience from watching Saturday morning cartoons to verify most of the signs [she] will read" (p. 68). But this is to ground her criticism in what seems to me to be an unsupportable belief in the immutable nature of semiotic codes. Did listeners in the 1820s really hear the "unspeakable violence" and "explosive rage" that McClary finds at various moments of Beethoven's Ninth Symphony (pp. 128–130)? I think it more likely that McClary instead has documented (and documented valuably) a sexual politics that governs the hearing of some *modern* listeners; what re-

mains silent in her exposition are the voices of Beethoven's generation. More-over, the appeal to semiotic codes of any sort is worrisome, for in most critical applications these codes turn out to represent a kind of deep structural analysis once-removed, and therefore no more societally based than any other reductive theory.

4. The precariousness of this second alternative is particularly clear to me. It both tinges the first alternative with the shadow of a traditional mode of explanation, and suggests that I am unable to free myself from orthodox analytical gestures. On the other hand, at this stage (and perhaps at any stage) it would be naive to expect anything but slippery epistemological ground when trying to reconcile or confront the disciplines of feminist studies and music history. At the very least, then, my alternative models may open the way for more radical perspectives.

5. I am chagrined to admit that this basic question occurred to me only when I had nearly completed a first draft of a book on Chopin's nocturnes. In other words, for a long time I was content to formulate a model of listeners' responses to the nocturne while simply ignoring who actually made up that body. This was tantamount to asserting a "neutral" audience—but of course, from my side, "neutral" had a decidedly "male" cast. Patterns of exclusion run deep: even after I had been made aware of the social dimensions of an issue like genre, I forgot that society is a gendered construct.

6. See in particular the discussions in Janet Todd, *Feminist Literary History* (New York, 1988), p. 136, and Rita Felski, *Beyond Feminist Aesthetics: Feminist Literature and Social Change* (Cambridge, Mass., 1989), pp. 82–153.

7. Christoph von Blumröder, "Notturno/Nocturne," *Handwörterbuch der musikalischen Terminologie,* ed. Hans Heinrich Eggebrecht (Wiesbaden, 1982–1983), pp. 9–10.

8. G. W. Fink, *Allgemeine musikalische Zeitung,* 13 August 1834, col. 543.

9. *Allgemeine musikalische Zeitung,* 20 July 1836, col. 473.

10. Ferdinand Hand, *Aesthetik der Tonkunst,* 2 vols. (Jena, 1841), vol. 2, pp. 314–315.

11. Carl Kossmaly, *Allgemeine musikalische Zeitung,* 17 January 1844, col. 34.

12. Maurice Bourges, "Lettres à Mme la Baronne de * * * sur quelques morceaux de piano modernes. Quatrième Lettre," *Revue et Gazette musicale de Paris,* 17 April 1842, p. 171. The same strategy occurs in an unsigned review of three sets of nocturnes by J. C. Kessler printed in *Le pianiste* 1 (1834): 124–125.

13. Robert Schumann, *Neue Zeitschrift für Musik,* 10 August 1838, p. 56.

14. *Musical World,* 23 February 1838, p. 120.

15. Arthur Loesser, *Men, Women, and Pianos: A Social History* (New York, 1954), pp. 64–67, and pp. 379–397, passim; William Weber, *Music*

and the Middle Class: The Social Structure of Concert Life in London, Paris, and Vienna (London, 1975), pp. 35–36; Judith Tick, *American Women Composers Before 1870* (Ann Arbor, Mich., 1983), pp. 13–31; Tick, "Passed Away Is the Piano Girl: Changes in American Musical Life, 1870–1900," in *Women Making Music: The Western Art Tradition, 1150–1950,* ed. Jane Bowers and Judith Tick (Urbana, Ill., 1986), pp. 325–348.

And it was not just the pianos of the middle class that were played mostly by women: among Chopin's high-born pupils, women outnumbered men at the rate of at least 3 to 1.

16. Cited from Loesser, *Men, Women, and Pianos,* p. 382.

17. *Le pianiste* (1835): 48; cited and translated in Weber, *Music and the Middle Class,* p. 35.

18. Loesser, *Men, Women, and Pianos,* p. 386.

19. "Men, Women, and Music at Home: The Influence of Cultural Values on Musical Life in Eighteenth-Century England," *Imago Musicae* 2 (1985): 51–133. The quotation is taken from his "Music, Domestic Life, and Cultural Chauvinism: Images of British Subjects at Home in India," in *Music and Society: The Politics of Composition, Performance, and Reception,* ed. Richard Leppert and Susan McClary (Cambridge, 1987), p. 85. See also his "Sexual Identity, Death, and the Family Piano," *19th-Century Music* 16 (1992): 105–128, especially 111–115.

20. Henri Blanchard, *Revue et Gazette musicale de Paris,* 10 January 1847, p. 18.

21. There is a good discussion of night imagery in von Blumröder's "Notturno/Nocturne," pp. 7–8. And recall the anonymous review of Chopin's Nocturnes op. 27, cited above.

22. Naomi Schor, *Reading in Detail: Aesthetics and the Feminine* (New York, 1987).

23. Ernst Gombrich, *The Sense of Order: A Study in the Psychology of Decorative Art* (Ithaca, N.Y., 1979), p. 23; citation from Schor, *Reading in Detail,* p. 19.

24. Svetlana Alpers, "Art History and Its Exclusions: The Example of Dutch Art," in *Feminism and Art History: Questioning the Litany,* ed. Norma Broude and Mary D. Garrard (New York, 1982), pp. 180–199.

25. Ibid., p. 194.

26. Ibid., p. 195.

27. Schor, *Reading in Detail,* p. 20.

28. August Kahlert, "Die Genrebilder in der modernen Musik," *Neue Zeitschrift für Musik* (12 June 1835), pp. 189–191.

29. Ibid., p. 190–191.

30. Schor does document the rising interest in and greater value assigned to detail beginning with Hegel and the rise of realism and continuing to the

present day. But she also observes that the growth of realism did not lessen criticism of detail in some quarters, but instead made it more shrill. Moreover, even when the detail attained positive associations, it did not, until very recently, lose its affinity to the feminine; *Reading in Detail,* pp. 23–97.

31. In an 1834 article entitled "Über Chopin's Klavier-Kompositionen," Kahlert registered his astonishment at and admiration for Chopin's skills as a pianist. A portion of this article is printed in Jean-Jacques Eigeldinger, *Chopin: Pianist and Teacher as Seen by his Pupils,* trans. Naomi Shohet et al., ed. Roy Howat (Cambridge, 1986), pp. 289–290.

32. Cited from von Blumröder, "Notturno/Nocturne," p. 10.

33. Frederick Niecks, *Frederick Chopin as a Man and Musician,* 2 vols. (London, 1902; reprint ed., New York, 1973), vol. 2, p. 261. The 1973 reprint reproduces a later edition of the Niecks biography, which was first published in 1888.

34. Ibid., vol. 2, p. 213.

35. James Huneker, *Chopin: The Man and His Music* (New York, 1900; reprint ed., New York, 1966), p. 142.

36. Judith Fetterley, *The Resisting Reader: A Feminist Approach to American Fiction* (Bloomington, 1978), p. xx.

37. Christine Battersby, *Gender and Genius: Towards a Feminist Aesthetics* (Bloomington, 1989), pp. 103–112, provides an interesting analysis of nineteenth-century justifications of the "feminine" side of male "genius."

38. Janet Todd, *Sensibility: An Introduction* (New York, 1986). Todd has also traced the process whereby the extremely high value placed by critics on early nineteenth-century poetry written by men served to downgrade the predominant mode of didactic fiction practiced by women at the same time; *Feminist Literary History,* pp. 111–114.

39. And Charles Ives's notorious *mot* even more succinctly encapsulates this attitude about Chopin: "one just naturally thinks of him with a skirt on, but one which he made himself." See Charles Ives, *Memos,* ed. John Kirkpatrick (New York, 1972), pp. 134–135, as cited in Maynard Solomon, "Charles Ives: Some Questions of Veracity," *Journal of the American Musicological Society* 40 (1987): 452. Along these lines, I also cannot resist quoting Cesar Cui's description of Scriabin's musical style as "bits filched from the trousseau of Chopin"; cited from Judith Tick, "Charles Ives and Gender Ideology," in *Musicology and Difference,* ed. Ruth A. Solie (Berkeley and Los Angeles, 1993), p. 88.

40. Artur Rubinstein, *My Young Years* (New York, 1973), pp. 86–87.

41. Kahlert, "Die Genrebilder," p. 189.

42. Hugo Leichtentritt, *Analyse der Chopin'schen Klavierwerke,* 2 vols. (Berlin, 1921), vol. 1, pp. 1–2.

43. Cone develops his theory of personae in *The Composer's Voice* (Berkeley, 1974). For a précis of the generic background of the piano nocturne, see Jeffrey Kallberg, "Understanding Genre: A Reinterpretation of the Early Piano Nocturne," *Atti del XIV Congresso della Società Internazionale di Musicologia*, 3 vols. (Turin, 1990), vol. 3, pp. 775–779.

44. *School of Practical Composition: Complete Treatise on the Composition of All Kinds of Music, Opus 600*, trans. John Bishop, 3 vols. (London, 1848; reprint ed., New York, 1979), vol. 1, p. 97.

45. Wolfgang Krueger, tracing the iconography of depictions of serenades back to the late fifteenth century, reveals that, until the early eighteenth century, the woman was ordinarily portrayed emptying her chamber pot on the singer's head; *Das Nachtstück: Ein Beitrag zur Entwicklung des einsätzigen Pianofortestückes im 19. Jahrhundert* (Munich, 1971), pp. 11–12 and 165–167.

46. For a late, trans-oceanic example of such a text, consider these lines:

> Beautiful dreamer, queen of my song,
> List while I woo thee with soft melody;
> Gone are the cares of life's busy throng,
> Beautiful dreamer, awake unto me!

Stephen Foster's "Beautiful Dreamer" is by genre a serenade, but could easily, as Czerny suggested above, be taken for a nocturne.

47. Ruth A. Solie, "Whose Life? The Gendered Self in Schumann's *Frauenliebe* Songs," in *Music and Text: Critical Inquiries*, ed. Steven Paul Scher (Cambridge, 1992), pp. 219–240.

48. Mary D. Garrard, "Artemisia and Susanna," in *Feminism and Art History*, ed. Broude and Garrard, pp. 146–171.

49. Todd, *Feminist Literary History*, p. 123.

50. The term "listen like men" is adapted from Jonathan Culler's "Reading as a Woman" in *On Deconstruction: Theory and Criticism after Structuralism* (Ithaca, N.Y., 1982), pp. 43–64. Culler derived his formulation from Peggy Kamuf's "Writing Like a Woman," in *Women and Language in Literature and Society*, ed. Sally McConnell-Ginet, Ruth Borker, and Nelly Furman (New York, 1980), pp. 284–299. The viewpoints of Kamuf and Culler have subsequently been criticized by a number of writers; for an interesting analysis of the dispute over "reading as a woman," and in particular its relationship to the question of essentialism, see Diana Fuss, "Reading Like a Feminist," in *Essentially Speaking: Feminism, Nature, and Difference* (New York, 1989), pp. 23–37.

51. On the "double-voiced discourse," see Susan Sniader Lanser and Evelyn

Torton Beck, "[Why] Are There No Great Women Critics? And What Difference Does it Make?" in *The Prism of Sex: Essays in the Sociology of Knowledge,* ed. Julia A. Sherman and Evelyn Torton Beck (Madison, Wisc., 1979), p. 86, and Elaine Showalter, "Feminist Criticism in the Wilderness," in *The New Feminist Criticism: Essays on Women, Literature, and Theory,* ed. Showalter (New York, 1985), pp. 263–264. Myra Jehlen describes much the same phenomenon in noting the frequency of "action despite dependence" in feminine creative spheres; see "Archimedes and the Paradox of Feminist Criticism," *Signs* 6 (1981): 581.

52. For Wieck, see in particular Clara and Robert Schumann, *Briefwechsel: Kritische Gesamtausgabe,* ed. Eva Weissweiler, 2 vols. to date (Frankfurt am Main, 1984–), and Beatrix Borchard, *Robert Schumann und Clara Wieck: Bedingungen künstlerischer Arbeit in der ersten Hälfte des 19. Jahrhunderts,* Ergebnisse der Frauenforschung, vol. 4 (Weinheim and Basle, 1985). For Mendelssohn, see *Letters of Fanny Hensel to Felix Mendelssohn,* ed. Marcia J. Citron (New York, 1987).

53. Borchard, *Robert Schumann und Clara Wieck,* p. 232.

54. Ibid., p. 292.

55. Although I will read the "double-voiced discourses" of the Wieck and Hensel nocturnes against models by Field and Chopin, I do not mean to imply that the relation of these men (or men in general) to this "feminine" genre was necessarily stable or unproblematic. But it exceeds the scope of this chapter to explore fully the male side of the equation here. I can only offer a few observations about Chopin's case (for a fuller investigation, see Chapter 3). While we have already seen how Chopin's nocturnes suffered critically in the late nineteenth century because of their affiliation with the feminine, in fact he had long before been marked as "feminine," "androgynous," or "hermaphroditic" by some of the metaphorical displacements of his contemporaries. Chopin's own understanding of the "feminine" nocturne unfolded in the context of these more general metaphorical substitutions, all complexly related but each also freighted with individual meanings. And that the metaphors continually evoke notions of androgyny, hermaphroditism, and femininity draws our attention to even more complicated contexts: Chopin's rather ill-defined sexual identity, and his relationships with women, above all with George Sand. Buffeted by all of these resonances, Chopin surely found writing nocturnes to be, at the very least, a psychically charged activity.

56. For a modern edition, see Clara Wieck-Schumann, *Ausgewählte Klavierwerke,* ed. Janina Klassen (Munich, 1987), pp. 27–30. Also available is a facsimile reprint of the original 1836 edition: Clara Wieck Schumann, *Selected Piano Music* (New York, 1979).

57. See Fanny Hensel, *Ausgewählte Klavierwerke*, ed. Fanny Kistner-Hensel (Munich, 1986), pp. 16–20.

58. Thus Czerny suggested that the character of the nocturne "must be calculated to create an impression of a soft, fanciful, gracefully romantic, or even passionate kind, but never of a harsh or strange." See *School of Practical Composition*, vol. 1, p. 97.

59. Schumann remarked in his review of Count von Wielhorsky's Nocturnes, op. 2, "in the first and last of the Notturnos are interwoven, after the example of some of Chopin's, agitated [*bewegtere*] middle sections, which already in Chopin are often weaker than his first inventions, here also delaying more than promoting continuity"; *Neue Zeitschrift für Musik*, 10 August 1838, pp. 56–57.

60. In a reversal of the patriarchal mode I have discussed here, Schumann's view of Chopin's middle sections may well reflect Wieck's practice in the genre. As we will see later in this chapter, her *Notturno* was very much on his mind around the time he drafted the review of Wielhorsky's Nocturnes.

61. Schumann, *Briefwechsel*, vol. 1, p. 90.

62. Ibid., p. 100.

63. Other changes include an added trill (note also the chromatic alteration that Schumann introduced into this figure, the upper note of which changes from c♯′ to c♮′), a simpler afterbeat following the trill (in place of Wieck's chromatic turn), and the simplification of Wieck's melody following the upward leap of an octave.

64. Schumann lopped off the first two measures of Wieck's Mazurka in G Major from the *Soirées musicales* to serve as the opening "Motto von C.W." in his *Davidsbündlertänze*, op. 6. Even in such a brief citation, Schumann could not restrain himself from revising his model: he altered Clara's third-beat dotted eighth – sixteenth note rhythms to eighth note – sixteenth rest – sixteenth note figures (in the second edition of 1850, he further shortened the first dyads by adding staccato dots to them); changed her downbeat accents to crescendos from the upbeat through the second beat; and converted the rhythm of her second beats from eighth note – eighth rest to a simple quarter note.

65. *Clara Schumann: The Artist and the Woman* (Ithaca, N. Y., 1985), p. 231. And we know that both Schumann and Wieck at some level shared pleasure in the published *Novellettes*. Robert: "Yesterday I also received my Novellettes; they have grown strong; four volumes of dear Clara [*Lieb-Clärchen*] . . . Bride, in the Novellettes you will come upon yourself in all possible registers and positions and other irresistible things. Yes, consider only me! I maintain: Novellettes could only be written by one who knows such

eyes as yours, who has touched such lips as yours. In short, one can no doubt produce something better, but scarcely something similar." Letter of 30 June 1839; Schumann, *Briefwechsel,* vol. 2, p. 608. And Clara: "I myself always find new beauties each time I replay one of his things (hence, e.g., this is now the case for me with the Novellettes). The Novellettes are an absolutely beautiful work. Intellect [*Geist*], soul [*Gemüth*], humor, the greatest tenderness. Everything is united in it, the finest characteristics are unlimited in it. One must know him as I do, and one will find his whole self in all his compositions." Diary entry of 29 August 1839, quoted in Borchard, *Robert Schumann und Clara Wieck,* p. 301.

66. Anna Burton, "Robert Schumann and Clara Wieck: A Creative Partnership," *Music & Letters* 69 (1988): 224.

67. Letters to Schumann of 22–23 April 1839 and 16 June 1839; Schumann, *Briefwechsel,* vol. 2, pp. 500, 577.

68. Wieck made only one substantive change to Schumann's theme: she omitted the repeat dots enclosing the passage between measures 9 and 24. One might argue that the initial statement of the theme in a variation genre demanded a greater fidelity to the source than would a quotation of a theme in works like the *Novellettes* or the *Davidsbündlertänze.* But this was not the case, as we may see from Schumann's own practice in his never-completed "Variations on a Nocturne of Chopin." Schumann altered the source (Chopin's Nocturne in G Minor, op. 15, no. 3) in several ways: he changed the melody, revoiced chords, reversed accompanimental figuration, and omitted a particularly dissonant measure (m. 19 in Chopin). For the text of Schumann's Variations, see Robert Schumann, *Variationen über ein Nocturne von Chopin (g-moll, op. 15 Nr. 3),* ed. Joachim Draheim (Wiesbaden, Leipzig, and Paris, 1992).

69. Carl Kossmaly's discussion of Schumann's *Arabeske* and *Blumenstück,* cited above, groups together in the same category Mendelssohn's "Songs without Words" and Field's nocturnes.

70. *The Letters of Fanny Hensel to Felix Mendelssohn,* pp. 222 and 521. I have modified somewhat Citron's translation.

71. That Hensel did not release this nocturne is in itself not unusual. Discouraged from publishing first by her father and then by her brother, and deeply conflicted herself (as suggests the letter cited in the previous note), she issued only a very small percentage of her entire output. (For a full discussion of this topic, see Marcia Citron, "Felix Mendelssohn's Influence on Fanny Mendelssohn Hensel as a Professional Composer," *Current Musicology* 37–38 [1984]: 9–17.) In no way would one want to consider all or even the majority of these unpublished works as "personal battles" with their respective generic traditions. But her *Notturno* does seem to embody a strikingly

divergent relationship to its generic tradition. And precisely because it was composed by a woman who felt constrained not to publish it, it was denied the possibility of participating in the subsequent tradition of its genre.

3. Small Fairy Voices

1. See, for example, Susan McClary, "Sexual Politics in Classical Music," in her *Feminine Endings: Music, Gender, and Sexuality* (Minneapolis, 1991), pp. 53–79; McClary, "Constructions of Subjectivity in Schubert's Music," in Philip Brett, Elizabeth Wood, and Gary Thomas, eds., *Queering the Pitch: The New Gay and Lesbian Musicology* (New York and London, 1994), pp. 205–233 (an earlier and briefer version of this essay appeared as "Schubert's Sexuality and His Music," *GLSG Newsletter* 2/1 [1992]: 8–14); and Robert Fink, "Desire, Repression, and Brahms's First Symphony," *repercussions* 2/1 (1993): 75–103.

2. I do not mean to foreclose the possibility that knowledge of a composer's sexual orientation can affect the reception of a musical work. But, as I explain below (see notes 56 and 57), I doubt that it would have been likely to do so before the latter part of the nineteenth century, when "sexuality" became a generally conceivable phenomenon in terms that resemble those of the late twentieth century.

3. Cited and translated in Jean-Jacques Eigeldinger, *Chopin: Pianist and Teacher as Seen by His Pupils,* trans. Naomi Shohet et al., ed. Roy Howat (Cambridge, 1986), p. 272 (hereafter cited as "Eigeldinger").

Liszt (or Carolyne von Sayn-Wittgenstein, who may have authored large portions of Liszt's biography of Chopin) also associated Chopin with Nodier when treating the composer's aversion to public performance: "Chopin knew that his talent—in style and imagination recalling Nodier, through purity of delivery, through familiarity with *La Fée aux miettes* and *Les Lutins d'Argail* [*sic*], through echoes of *Séraphines* and *Dianes* whispering their most confidential laments and most secret dreams—Chopin knew, we insist, that he had no effect upon the multitude and could not strike the masses." See Franz Liszt, *Frederic Chopin,* trans. Edward N. Waters (New York, 1963), p. 83.

4. Hallé used similar language when he recounted this scene in his autobiography (c. 1894–1895): "The same evening I heard him play, and was fascinated beyond expression. It seemed to me as if I had got into another world . . . I sat entranced, filled with wonderment, and if the room had suddenly been peopled with fairies, I should not have been astonished" (Eigeldinger, p. 271).

The angelic trope was later echoed in Balzac's letter of 28 May 1843 to Madame Hanska. Comparing Liszt and Chopin, Balzac wrote: "You should judge Listz [*sic*] only once you have had the opportunity to hear Chopin. The Hungarian is a demon; the Pole is an angel" (Eigeldinger, p. 285).

5. *La Presse,* 31 January and 25 February 1848, as cited in M. H. Girard, "Note sur Gautier et Chopin 'Le dernier concert,' " *La fortune de Frédéric Chopin* (Paris, 1994), pp. 56–57.

6. Cited and translated in William G. Attwood, *Fryderyk Chopin: Pianist from Warsaw* (New York, 1987), p. 244. The Marquis de Custine invoked similar language when he wrote Chopin to ask for tickets to the recital: "What, the sylph of the piano is to be heard, and I am informed about it by the public?", letter of February 1848 in Frédéric Chopin, *Correspondance de Frédéric Chopin,* ed. Bronislas Édouard Sydow, 3 vols. (Paris, 1953–1960), vol. 3, p. 321. This letter is mistakenly dated to "before 5 March 1838" in Fryderyk Chopin, *Korespondencja Fryderyka Chopina,* ed. Sydow, 2 vols. (Warsaw, 1955), vol. 1, p. 310.

Other instances of otherworldly metaphors provoked by Chopin's pianism include Ignaz Moscheles referring to Chopin's "delicate fingers" gliding "with elfin lightness" over the "harsh modulations" in his music (Eigeldinger, p. 272); Elizavieta Cheriemietieff calling forth angels and ethereal realms upon hearing Chopin play in private (Eigeldinger, pp. 162, 278); and Bohdan Zaleski hearing angels' voices in an elaborate improvisation by Chopin (Eigeldinger, pp. 283–284).

7. *Revue et Gazette musicale de Paris,* 21 October 1849, p. 334.

8. *The Illustrated London News,* 27 October 1849, as reproduced in Maria Mirska and Władysław Hordyński, eds., *Chopin na obczyźnie* (Cracow, 1965), p. 325. The views of this English critic show that the vision of Chopin as fairy or airy sprite was not held unilaterally: to invoke the mighty magus Prospero is to propose a quite different experience of Chopin's music than that explored in this chapter. But the prominence of the Ariel trope nonetheless seems clear: the critic still needed to draw on it even while proposing an alternative stylization.

9. *Journal des Débats,* 22 October 1849. The notion that Chopin's creations were most deeply felt by women was also sounded by Henri Blanchard in his article about Chopin's funeral: "This talent was especially understood, profoundly felt by women, not by those nice little human canaries [*serinettes*] who only aspire to make heard a brilliant fantasy in a salon in order to inspire those to marry them, and to say soon after, in speaking about music and the piano: 'Since my marriage, I have neglected all of that'; but by ladies, if not of high, then at least of good society, where one always recognized an aristocracy, that of talent. Mmes de Belgiojoso, de Peruzzi, etc. were the disciples, the admirers, the friends of the poor melancholic artist, of vaporous, fine, delicate inspiration. They loved to follow him when he lulled his intimate auditor with his capricious melodic arabesques over an unforeseen harmony,

strange, but distinguished, classic, pure, and nevertheless sickly, which seemed a swan song, a hymn of death"; "Obsèques de Frédéric Chopin," *Revue et Gazette musicale de Paris,* 4 November 1849, p. 348.

Two other obituaries are worth brief mention. Théophile Gautier, writing in *La Presse,* 22 October 1849, p. 1, began his memorial with a unique image: "The Novalis of the piano, Frédéric Chopin, is dead"; I suggest how Novalis might fit in with angels and fairies in the next section. And Auguste Luchet, in *La Réforme,* 5 November 1849, p. 2, used more familiar imagery: "They celebrated the funeral of that angel of the piano who is called F. Chopin."

10. *Les pianistes célèbres: silhouettes et médaillons,* 2d ed. (Tours, 1887), p. 11.

11. "Essay on the Works of Frederic Chopin," *Musical World,* as cited in Liszt, *Frederic Chopin,* p. 170.

12. Liszt, *Frederic Chopin,* p. 77. Liszt was not the only critic to associate the ballades with the supernatural trope. James Huneker subtitled his chapter on the ballades "Faëry Dramas"; most of the fairy imagery that he adduced derived from what he understood to be the poetic bases of the individual ballades, various poems by Mickiewicz. See *Chopin: The Man and His Music* (New York, 1900; reprint ed., New York, 1966), pp. 155–164. Nor was Liszt the last to evoke Queen Mab to help portray the effect of a piece by Chopin. Here is Frederick Niecks on the Berceuse, op. 57: "This melody is dissolved into all kinds of *fioriture, colorature,* and other trickeries, and they are of such fineness, subtlety, loveliness, and gracefulness, that one is reminded of Queen Mab"; *Frederick Chopin as a Man and Musician,* 2 vols. (London, 1902; reprint ed., New York, 1973), vol. 2, p. 267.

13. W. H. Hadow, *Studies in Modern Music: Second Series,* 5th ed. (London, 1904), p. 169. For drawing my attention to this and other examples of Victorian criticism of Chopin, I am indebted to Derek Carew, "Victorian Attitudes to Chopin," in *The Cambridge Companion to Chopin,* ed. Jim Samson (Cambridge, 1992), pp. 222–245.

14. H. R. Haweis, *Music and Morals* (New York, 1875), pp. 103–104. In the last sentence, Haweis quotes from Longfellow's "Evangeline" (I am grateful to Professor Jack Kolb of the University of California, Los Angeles, for identifying this quotation for me). The passage occurs near the very end of the poem, just after Evangeline has witnessed the death of Gabriel:

> All was ended now, the hope, and the fear, and the sorrow,
> All the aching of heart, the restless, unsatisfied longing,
> All the dull, deep pain, and constant anguish of patience!

The Poetical Works of Henry Wadsworth Longfellow (Boston, 1865), pp. 57–58.

15. Thomas Mann, *Doctor Faustus: The Life of the German Composer Adrian Leverkühn as Told by a Friend,* trans. H. T. Lowe-Porter (New York, 1948), p. 143. Leverkühn's pronouncement engages otherworldly themes both outside and within the novel. Looking externally, Shelley was often styled as an otherworldly spirit by his contemporaries. Indeed, he himself assumed the mantle of Ariel, in his "With a Guitar. To Jane." (For an interesting treatment of this poem in the context of a discussion of "transitivity" in both Shelley and Chopin, see Lawrence Kramer, *Music and Poetry: The Nineteenth Century and After* [Berkeley and Los Angeles, 1984], pp. 119, 121–123.) Within *Doctor Faustus,* Mann would return to the theme of supernatural sprites in the figure of the child Echo, Leverkühn's one true love, whose name resounds in the "Ariel's Songs" that he composes before the child dies.

16. Chopin, *Korespondencja,* ed. Sydow, vol. 1, p. 455. Custine's use of "Sylph" to describe Chopin may have originally derived from encounters with his playing and composing. Writing to Sophie Gay in June 1837 from his home in Saint-Gratien, Custine described the pleasures of hearing Chopin improvise: "I am still just being enchanted by the magician, by the sylph of Saint-Gratien. I had given him for themes the *ranz des vaches* and the *Marseillaise.* To tell you the use he made of this musical epic is impossible. One saw the shepherd people flee before the conquering people. It was sublime." See Marquis de Luppé's excellently documented biography, *Astolphe de Custine* (Monaco, 1957), p. 190.

17. Marie-Paule Rambeau draws frequent attention to the trope in the first two chapters of *Chopin dans la vie et l'oeuvre de George Sand* (Paris, 1985), pp. 35–135.

18. Letter dated end of May 1838, in George Sand, *Correspondance,* ed. Georges Lubin, 25 vols. (Paris, 1964–1991), vol. 4, pp. 428–439; references to angels occur on pp. 436–438.

This letter has simultaneously fascinated and disgusted many a commentator on Chopin. To note just one example, Édouard Ganche, in *Souffrances de Frédéric Chopin: Essai de médecine et de psychologie* (Paris, 1935), felt compelled to reprint the entire letter even while terming it, variously, "nauseating," "odious," and "abominable" (pp. 32–57; especially p. 32, p. 54, and p. 57). Indeed, he was particularly repelled by the angelic trope: "In this abominable letter and in her correspondence, George Sand shows the gist of her coarse nature. She designates Chopin by the most humiliating appellations: 'poor angel, the little one, this poor little being, our child, my little sufferer, my dear cadaver [*mon cher cadavre*], the old dodderer [*le père gâteux*] . . .' This is the ogress of a fairy tale who sees a sickly human creature, laughs at his sickliness that she will crush with her robustness, she knows, but which she envies. In this truthful story, Chopin was like a nightingale in the talons of an eagle. It happened, by a singular phenomenon, that the eagle became inoffensive and even protecting in listening to the song of the nightingale and in touching his weakness. Miracle of genius and of art" (pp. 57–58). Need one observe that this "fairy tale" tells us much more about Ganche than about Sand or Chopin? Indeed, two of his "humiliating appellations" resulted from his misunderstanding or misreading the Sand correspondence. If Sand ever referred to Chopin as *"mon cher cadavre,"* it surely was a jest shared by the composer. Sand joshed with her son Maurice in just this way, even using a pleasantry from the Berry dialect that Ganche might have misapprehended: "ne joue pas trop avec ton *ch'tit* et sec *calabre,"* where *"ch'tit"* and *"calabre"* mean "bad" and *"living* body or carcass" respectively (see letter of 11 November 1843 to Maurice Sand; *Correspondance,* vol. 6, pp. 274–275, and in particular Lubin's commentary on p. 275). Sand did at least once call Chopin a cadaver, but in an angry letter written to Emmanuel Arago in the midst of her rupture with the composer: "il y a neuf ans que pleine de vie, je suis liée à un cadavre" (letter of 18–26 July 1847; *Correspondance,* vol. 8, p. 48). This is hardly the same as calling him *"mon cher cadavre."* And Sand nowhere called Chopin *"le père gâteux."* What she actually wrote was *"le père Gatiau,"* a variant form of *"Père-Gâteau"* (meaning, roughly, "sugar daddy"), which refers to Chopin's generosity with gifts to the children (see letter of 6 June 1843 to Maurice Sand; *Correspondance,* vol. 6, p. 156, and especially Lubin's commentary).

19. Letter of 14 December 1838; Sand, *Correspondance,* vol. 4, p. 531. Sand used almost the identical words in writing to Marliani from Barcelona on 15 February 1839: "He is an angel of sweetness, of patience and of kindness. I care for him like my child and he loves me like his mother"; *Correspondance,* vol. 4, pp. 569–570.

20. Sand, *Correspondance,* vol. 4, p. 646.

21. See letters to Ferdinand François, 12 or 13 November 1843 (Sand, *Correspondance,* vol. 6, p. 915) and to Wojciech Grzymała, 18 November 1843 (*Correspondance,* vol. 6, p. 286). The sense of "poor angel" in the letter to Grzymała of late May 1838, cited above, is different: it is Sand's outcry in response to Chopin's prudishness, and to her questions "What wretched woman has left him with such impressions of physical love? He has thus had a mistress unworthy of him? Poor angel"; *Correspondance,* vol. 4, pp. 437–438. Arthur Hedley's translation of this letter (*Selected Correspondence of Fryderyk Chopin,* trans. and ed. Hedley [New York, 1963], p. 159) omits the second sentence quoted, as well as a number of other sentences and clauses, from this fascinating letter.

Sand also turned the angelic trope against the composer in a passage she penned in the manuscript of her *Histoire de ma vie,* but cancelled before publishing. In this passage, Sand portrayed Chopin as incapable of being satisfied with anyone outside his dream world; even a succession of angels could not withstand his demands. See George Sand, *Histoire de ma vie,* in *Oeuvres autobiographiques,* ed. Georges Lubin, 2 vols. (Paris, 1970–1971), vol. 2, p. 1303.

22. Still the most useful place to begin surveying the topic is A. J. L. Busst, "The Image of the Androgyne in the Nineteenth Century," in Ian Fletcher, ed., *Romantic Mythologies* (London, 1967), pp. 1–95. Also worth consulting are Fritz Giese, *Der Romantische Charakter I: Die Entwicklung des Androgynenproblems in der Frühromantik* (Langensalza, 1919); Mario Praz, *The Romantic Agony,* trans. Angus Davidson, 2d ed. (London, 1951), pp. 289–411; Carolyn G. Heilbrun, *Toward a Recognition of Androgyny* (New York, 1973); Sara Friedrichsmeyer, *The Androgyne in Early German Romanticism: Friedrich Schlegel, Novalis, and the Metaphysics of Love* (Bern, 1983); *L'Androgyne dans la littérature,* ed. Frédéric Monneyron (Paris, 1990); Diane Long Hoeveler, *Romantic Androgyny: The Women Within* (University Park, 1990); Camille Paglia, *Sexual Personae: Art and Decadence From Nefertiti to Emily Dickinson* (New York, 1991), 389–421; and Kari Weil, *Androgyny and the Denial of Difference* (Charlottesville and London, 1992). Jessica R. Feldman's *Gender on the Divide: The Dandy in Modernist Literature* (Ithaca and London, 1993), pp. 1–96, explores issues related to androgyny in the first part of the nineteenth century. A concise survey of "romantic androgyny" as it might have served Wagner's philosophical and musical needs is found in Jean-Jacques Nattiez, *Wagner Androgyne: A Study in Interpretation,* trans. Stewart Spencer (Princeton, 1993), pp. 111–127.

23. "The Image of the Androgyne," p. 38. See also Busst's general discussion of the "optimistic image of the androgyne," pp. 12–39, as well as Nattiez's treatment in *Wagner Androgyne,* pp. 111–127.

24. Charles Nodier, *Trilby; La fée aux miettes* (Paris, 1989), p. 45; H[enri] de Latouche, *Adieux: Poésies* (Paris, 1844), pp. 345–353. *Adieux* collects a number of poems actually written much earlier than its publication date. In a footnote to "Ariel exilé" (p. 345), Latouche acknowledges with thanks Nodier's citation of the role of his poem in the genesis of *Trilby.*

25. Paglia traces the chain of influences further back, arguing that Mignon of Goethe's *Wilhelm Meister* served as the prototype for the French Romantic androgyne. See *Sexual Personae,* p. 252.

26. The modern fortunes of *Gabriel* may be in for a change, for in recent years there have appeared both an excellent edition (Paris, 1988) by Janis Glasgow of the original French version (Paris, 1840) and an English translation of an 1867 printing of *Gabriel*—somewhat different from the original

version—by Gay Manifold (Westport, Conn., and London, 1992). Manifold also includes an appendix that outlines alterations Sand made when she revised the work into a play entitled *Julia* in the 1850s. I am grateful to Jean-Jacques Eigeldinger for bringing *Gabriel* to my attention.

27. See the speech of Gabriel's preceptor to the grandfather, which begins "since his earliest childhood . . . he has been imbued with the grandeur of the masculine role, and the abject condition of the feminine role in nature and in society"; *Gabriel*, pp. 52–53; *Gabriel*, trans. Manifold, p. 7.

28. *Gabriel*, p. 57; *Gabriel*, trans. Manifold, p. 10. In all of my citations from Manifold's translation, I have slightly modified the English translation to conform more precisely with the French original published by Glasgow.

29. *Gabriel*, p. 60; *Gabriel*, trans. Manifold, p. 12.

30. Act II, scenes 4–5; *Gabriel*, pp. 107–113; *Gabriel*, trans. Manifold, pp. 50–54.

31. *Gabriel*, p. 109; *Gabriel*, trans. Manifold, p. 51.

32. *Gabriel*, pp. 112–113; *Gabriel*, trans. Manifold, p. 53.

33. Later, after Astolphe has discovered Gabrielle's "true" sex and married her, his interpretation of her angelic form is further clarified. In a dialogue from Act III, scene 5 (in an earlier segment of which Gabrielle says "Look, Astolphe, you made me become a woman again, but I have not yet altogether given up being a man"), Astolphe tells Gabrielle "I know women, and you do not know them, you who are not half man and half woman as you think, but an angel in human form" (*Gabriel*, pp. 150–151; *Gabriel*, trans. Manifold, pp. 78–79; Manifold's text differs in many significant respects from that printed in the French original version). If Gabrielle is in Astolphe's mind a kind of angel, then he does not view angels as androgynous or hermaphroditic beings ("half man and half woman"). Rather, harking back to his earlier invocation of the trope, to be an angel would appear to involve some kind of cross-dressing.

34. Michel Poizat, *The Angel's Cry: Beyond the Pleasure Principle in Opera*, trans. Arthur Denner (Ithaca and London, 1992).

35. For an interesting discussion of themes of cross-dressing and mirror-gazing in a musical work, see Lawrence Kramer, "*Carnaval*, Cross-Dressing, and the Woman in the Mirror," in Ruth A. Solie, ed., *Musicology and Difference: Gender and Sexuality in Music Scholarship* (Berkeley, Los Angeles, and London, 1993), pp. 305–325. For all the acuity of its cultural analysis, however, this article remains wedded to the very techniques of formalist analysis it criticizes in the hands of other interpreters of *Carnaval*.

36. Compare, for example, the angelic imagery in Balzac's *Séraphîta*. Séraphîtüs-Séraphîta, an androgynous angel derived from the mystic doctrines of Swedenborg, does not so much represent sexual ambiguity as sexual alter-

nation (the character appears as male to Minna and female to Wilfrid) and synthesis (achieved through the loving union of Minna and Wilfrid). For a good discussion of angelic androgyny in Balzac, see Busst, "The Image of the Androgyne," pp. 78–85.

37. *Gender Trouble: Feminism and the Subversion of Identity* (New York and London, 1990).

38. Ibid., p. 140. The italics are Butler's.

39. Gautier and Sand differed in the goals of their explorations of the indeterminacy of gender. Gautier's interests lay more in the realm of aesthetics (as is clear from the famous preface to *Mademoiselle de Maupin*): the contingent identities in the novel are bound up with ideas of an aesthetics of impersonality, of *"l'art pour l'art."* Sand's target was contemporary political and social life: in order to challenge the accepted status of women in society, she focused on the artifice that upheld the gender system.

My understanding of *Mademoiselle de Maupin* is much indebted to Feldman's reading of it in *Gender on the Divide*, pp. 25–53.

40. "George Sand's Literary Transvestism: Pre-Texts and Contexts" (Ph.D. diss., Princeton University, 1988), especially pp. 199–235. See also Isabelle Hoog Naginski, *George Sand: Writing for Her Life* (New Brunswick and London, 1991), pp. 16–34, for a discussion of the topos of androgyny in Sand's life and work, and Kristina Wingård Vareille, *Socialité, sexualité, et les impasses de l'histoire: l'évolution de la thématique sandienne d'Indiana (1832) à Mauprat (1837)* (Uppsala, 1987), which examines androgyny in a number of Sand's works from the period before *Gabriel*.

41. There is an amusing reading of the mirrored, transgressive identities of gender of Chopin and Sand in a detail from Angela Carter's novel *The Passion of New Eve* (London, 1977), p. 132. Carter, describing the marriage between Eve (who underwent transsexual surgery to cease being the man Evelyn) and Tristessa (a male-to-female transvestite), clothes Tristessa in a bridal gown he had worn while acting in *Wuthering Heights,* and Eve in a costume originally meant for an actor depicting Chopin in the story of George Sand. For a discussion of this scene, see Marjorie Garber, *Vested Interests: Cross-Dressing and Cultural Anxiety* (New York, 1992), pp. 75–76.

And before leaving *Gabriel,* I should note that Sand's *roman dialogué* was not the first fictional work to portray an angelic Gabriel in sexual terms. In the pornographic poem *Parapilla* (published in 1776, attributed to Charles Borde, and based on an Italian *Novella dell'Angelo Gabrielo*), the Archangel Gabriel creates a magical flying phallus (a "winged penis"?) whose erotic exploits are traced across five cantos. For a *précis* of the plot, as well as some eighteenth-century engravings depicting Gabriel's *"outil"* in action, see the *Dictionnaire des oeuvres érotiques: Domaine français* (Paris, 1971), pp. 377–378.

42. Recall, however, that we have seen one instance of straightforward cross-gendering in connection with fairies, by the writer of the obituary of Chopin published in the *Revue et Gazette musicale de Paris*. This critic rejected the nickname "Ariel of the piano" for the deceased, and substituted in its place that of a female fairy, Queen Mab.

Moreover, the determinate sexual identities of these sprites were not always treated determinately in the world of opera. Both Johann Friedrich Reichardt and Johann Rudolf Zumsteeg, in their 1798 settings of Friedrich Wilhelm Gotter's operatic libretto, *Der Geisterinsel* (based on *The Tempest*), followed Gotter's instructions and assigned the part of Ariel to a woman.

43. I am indebted for this idea to Michel Poizat, who, in seeking to understand why the angel's voice is so often (and so mistakenly, in his opinion) thought to be only high, formulates a hypothesis around a perceived relationship between children and angels (even though Poizat ultimately rejects its application to the angel's voice); *The Angel's Cry*, pp. 128–131.

44. Michel Foucault, *The History of Sexuality, Volume I: An Introduction*, trans. Robert Hurley (New York, 1978), pp. 104, 153.

45. Busst notes that one of the principal "vices" associated with the pessimistic symbol of the androgyne is what he calls "cerebral lechery," a yearning that finds no object and no fulfillment in reality. Cerebral lechery most often may be detected in situations of total sexual abstinence; Busst offers an insightful reading of *Mademoiselle de Maupin* from this point of view. See "The Image of the Androgyne," pp. 42–44.

46. For remarkable testimony on the "fairy" as homosexual prostitute, see Earl Lind, *Autobiography of an Androgyne* (New York, 1918; reprint ed., New York, 1975), passim. And for a general account of the phenomenon of "fairies" in the early twentieth century, see George Chauncey, *Gay New York: Gender, Urban Culture, and the Making of the Gay Male World, 1890–1940* (New York, 1994).

47. Indeed, Balzac brought the two terms together when he described how the Finale of Beethoven's Fifth Symphony allowed one to "perceive beauties of an unknown kind, fairies of fantasy, these are the creatures who flutter with womanly beauty and the diaphanous wings of angels"; letter of 7–14 November 1837, in Balzac, *Lettres à Madame Hanska*, ed. Roger Pierrot, 2 vols. (Paris, 1990), vol. 1, p. 419. The adjective "womanly" can apply equally to men or women, and thus leaves open the sex of the fairies with angelic wings.

48. Letter of 20 July 1842; Sand, *Correspondance*, vol. 5, p. 375, note 1. Georges Lubin, the eminent editor of the *Correspondance*, also feels that *"Sans-sexe"* designates Chopin. Nonetheless, it has been suggested to me that Solange might have conceived *"Sans-sexe"* as a pun of sorts on *"Sand-sexe."* If punning were on Solange's mind (which I doubt), she cannot have meant

this *"San(s/d)-sexe"* to designate her mother, for after writing "Dis aussi à Sans-sexe de m'écrire," she continued directly *"il* ne m'a jamais adressé un mot depuis qu'il est à Nohant" (emphasis added). Solange did not refer to her mother as "il," and, in any case, the phrase would make no sense in reference to Sand, who had just written a letter to Solange. And I cannot accept that Solange intended some kind of complex mutation of meanings from the written *"Sans-sexe"* to the presumably read *"Sand-sexe."* Such word play, attractive to many of our postmodern sensibilities, seems highly unlikely at the hands of a thirteen-year-old girl writing in 1842.

A line from Chopin's letter to Julian Fontana of 7 March 1839, written during his recovery in Marseilles, may be relevant to Solange's remark: "I drink neither coffee nor wine—only milk; I keep myself warm and look like a young lady"; Chopin, *Korespondencja,* ed. Sydow, vol. 1, p. 337.

49. For evidence to this effect, see Sand's letter of 18–26 July 1847 to Emmanuel Arago; Arago's reply (in which he remarks that "for several years, [Chopin] was fascinated by her . . . I saw, saw, saw well that he had for her a profound sentiment that first resembled paternal affection, and that was transformed, perhaps unknown to him, when the child became a young girl, and the young girl a woman"); and a document from 1845 in Solange's hand with Chopin's name and initials repeated many times (suggesting, in Lubin's words, "a certain obsession" on Solange's part), all in Sand, *Correspondance,* vol. 8, pp. 46–50. For a perspicacious discussion of this evidence, see Rambeau, *Chopin dans la vie et l'oeuvre de George Sand,* pp. 104–107. Gastone Belotti denied strenuously that Solange did anything more than flirt with Chopin, but he failed to discuss any of the materials presented in Volume 8 of the Sand *Correspondance;* Belotti, *F. Chopin l'uomo,* 3 vols. (Milan-Rome, 1974), vol. 3, pp. 1183–1185.

50. Separate documents by George Sand and by Solange appear to comment—tangentially, at least—on matters surrounding the "sexless" Chopin. In the following passage from her *Histoire de ma vie,* Sand ostensibly describes her father: "He was as beautiful as a flower, chaste and soft like a young girl. He was sixteen, his health was still delicate, his soul exquisite. At that age a boy who is raised by a gentle mother is a special being in creation. He belongs to neither sex, so to speak; his thoughts are pure like an angel's; he does not have the pubertal coquetry, the restless curiosity, the irritable personality that often trouble the first coming into being of the woman. He loves his mother like the daughter never will and never can" (*Histoire de ma vie,* vol. 1, p. 76, as cited and translated in Dorelies Kraakman, "Reading Pornography Anew: A Critical History of Sexual Knowledge for Girls in French Erotic Fiction, 1750–1840," *Journal of the History of Sexuality* 4 [1994]: 528). But when we learn that Sand wrote these lines in 1847–48—

just when her relationship with Solange was at its most fractious and her ties with Chopin crumbling—it does not take much imagination to read into them echoes of Sand's attitudes toward these two. Surely, then, there is telling significance in the juxtaposition of the exquisitely chaste, angelic male figure who "belongs to neither sex," and the irascible daughter who engages in "pubertal coquetry" and does not love her mother.

Solange herself returned to idealized, angelic images of Chopin near the end of her life, in the course of a memoir of the composer that she penned in 1895: "The woman, the children (young Filtsch, who died so young!) brought a finer sense than masculine talents did to this celestial music, even when their fingers did not compare in strength and agility with the more practised and robust hands of the latter . . . Under the flexible and responsive fingers of Chopin's pale and frail hand the piano became the voice of an archangel, an orchestra, an army, a raging ocean, a creation of the universe, the end of the world . . . What suave grace, what angelical tenderness" (Eigeldinger, pp. 280–281).

51. Weil, *Androgyny and the Denial of Difference,* especially pp. 9–11. Not all commentators read difference into the relationship: Busst begins his otherwise excellent article by stoutly proclaiming the distinctions between the two terms "purely arbitrary" ("The Image of the Androgyne," p. 1).

52. Plato, *Symposium,* trans. Alexander Nehamas and Paul Woodruff (Indianapolis and Cambridge, 1989), p. 25.

53. For the notion of "absent presence," I am indebted to Weil, *Androgyny and the Denial of Difference,* p. 11.

54. The *"affaire Custine"* is amply documented in Luppé, *Custine,* pp. 96–101. See also Julien-Frédéric Tarn's monumental study, *Le Marquis de Custine* (Paris, 1985), pp. 68–70.

55. The two terms were often used synonymously in the early nineteenth century to refer to men who engaged in sexual relations with other men, though of course the latter term was at times reserved to describe men who pursued sexual relations with boys. On "sodomite" and "pederast" as synonyms, see Claude Courouve, *Vocabulaire de l'homosexualité masculine* (Paris, 1985), pp. 169–178; 191–198.

I do not however mean to assert a stable identity for these terms. "Sodomy" ("that utterly confused category," as Foucault termed it [*History of Sexuality,* p. 101]) encompasses in its multiple configurations a variety of sexual activity between members of the same sex, between males and females, as well as between humans and animals.

56. Much recent scholarship has addressed this issue. Most influential to my argument have been Foucault, *History of Sexuality;* Arnold I. Davidson, "Sex and the Emergence of Sexuality," *Critical Inquiry* 14 (1987): 16–48; Ed

Cohen, "Legislating the Norm: From Sodomy to Gross Indecency," *South Atlantic Quarterly* 88 (1989): 182–217; Robert A. Nye, "Sex Difference and Male Homosexuality in French Medical Discourse, 1830–1930," *Bulletin of the History of Medicine* 63 (1989): 32–51; David M. Halperin, "One Hundred Years of Homosexuality," in his *One Hundred Years of Homosexuality and Other Essays on Greek Love* (New York and London, 1990), pp. 15–40 and pp. 154–168; and Klaus Müller, *Aber in meinem Herzen sprach eine Stimme so laut: Homosexuelle Autobiographien und medizinische Pathographien im neunzehnten Jahrhundert* (Berlin, 1991). I have found Halperin's essay, which also appeared in an earlier version as "Is There a History of Sexuality?" *History and Theory* 28 (1989): 257–274, particularly cogent and helpful.

A number of writers firmly oppose the position I have espoused here, arguing strongly for something like a transhistorical concept of sexual identities. A collection of these writings may be found in Edward Stein, ed., *Forms of Desire: Sexual Orientation and the Social Constructionist Controversy* (New York, 1990; reprint ed., New York and London, 1992).

For an excellent survey of recent scholarship on sexuality, see Domna C. Stanton, "Introduction: The Subject of Sexuality," in Stanton, ed., *Discourses of Sexuality: From Aristotle to AIDS* (Ann Arbor, 1992), pp. 1–46.

57. The *Oxford English Dictionary* cites early nineteenth-century usages of "sexuality." But these construe the word as indicating "the quality of being sexual or having sex" in the biological sense. As such, it was typically applied to plants or insects; it did not yet refer to a manner of constituting human identity.

Not everyone would agree with my assertion that our modern conceptions of "homosexuality" and "sexuality" date from the later nineteenth century. The issue, particularly as it concerns homosexuality, has been debated intensely and complexly by historians of sexuality. Here I can only signal some of the more significant interventions. Foucault boldly announced that modern homosexuality began in 1870 (*History of Sexuality*, p. 43), a date—when generalized into something like the "second half of the nineteenth century"—that is also accepted by Davidson, "Sex and the Emergence of Sexuality," and Jeffrey Weeks, "Discourse, Desire and Sexual Deviance: Some Problems in a History of Homosexuality," in Weeks, *Against Nature: Essays on History, Sexuality and Identity* (London, 1991), pp. 10–45.

Others, most prominently among them Randolph Trumbach, have argued that the modern homosexual role may be dated to the beginning of the eighteenth century. Among his many articles, see "Sodomitical Subcultures, Sodomitical Roles, and the Gender Revolution of the Eighteenth Century: The Recent Historiography," in Robert Purks Maccubbin, ed., *'Tis Nature's Fault:*

Unauthorized Sexuality during the Enlightenment (Cambridge, 1985), pp. 109–121; "Gender and the Homosexual Role in Modern Western Culture," in *Homosexuality, Which Homosexuality?* (Amsterdam, 1989), pp. 149–169; "London's Sapphists: From Three Sexes to Four Genders in the Making of Modern Culture," in Julia Epstein and Kristina Straub, eds., *Body Guards: The Cultural Politics of Gender Ambiguity* (New York and London, 1991), pp. 112–141; and "Sex, Gender, and Sexual Identity in Modern Culture: Male Sodomy and Female Prostitution in Enlightenment London," in John C. Fout, ed., *Forbidden History: The State, Society, and the Regulation of Sexuality in Modern Europe* (Chicago and London, 1992), pp. 89–106. But as Eve Kosofsky Sedgwick properly notes, all of these arguments blithely assume that there is such a thing as *a* modern homosexual role that "we" are able to divine (they do so even as they articulate different versions of what they understand this role to be). This not only distills an oversimplified unity from a plurality of sexual roles but also incorrectly and dangerously presumes that "we" may reach a consensus about the "genuinely *un*known" (Sedgwick's italics); Sedgwick, *Epistemology of the Closet* (Berkeley and Los Angeles, 1990), pp. 44–48. To which I would only add that the same cautionary note needs to be sounded to those who would assert a singular, knowable "homosexual" or "sodomitical" role for any given culture of the past.

58. *History of Sexuality*, p. 43. See also Davidson's discussion of the rise of the "psychiatric style of reasoning" that begins around the mid-nineteenth century; "Sex and the Emergence of Sexuality," pp. 20–22.

59. This negative construction was obviously not the only one available. Klaus Müller, drawing on a corpus of autobiographical testimony, has begun the project of reconstructing the self-images of nineteenth-century male proponents of same-sex love; *Aber in meinem Herzen*, pp. 155–265. And Randolph Trumbach, in the studies cited above, has recovered some of the perspectives of sodomitical subcultures in eighteenth-century England.

60. The full title is *Histoire générale et particulière des anomalies de l'organisation chez l'homme et les animaux, ouvrage comprenant des recherches sur les caractères, la classification, l'influence physiologique et pathologique, les rapports généraux, les lois et les causes des monstruosités, des variétés et vices de conformation, ou Traité de Tératologie*, 3 vols. and atlas (Paris, 1832–1837).

For a good discussion of Geoffroy Saint-Hilaire in view of the cultural reception of sexual ambiguity, see Julia Epstein, "Either/Or—Neither/Both: Sexual Ambiguity and the Ideology of Gender," *Genders* 7 (1990): 99–142, and especially pp. 113–116.

61. Epstein, "Either/Or," p. 119.

62. *Histoire générale et particulière des anomalies*, vol. 2, p. 96. The sec-

ond, briefer commentary on the potentially deleterious effects that this form of hermaphroditism might have on the morals is found on p. 101.

63. Trumbach, "London's Sapphists," pp. 115–121, offers a number of examples of these usages from the seventeenth and eighteenth centuries. The latter kind of formulation remained common through the nineteenth century, as suggested by this discussion taken from Auguste-Ambroise Tardieu's *Étude médico-légal sur les attentats aux moeurs,* 4th ed. (Paris, 1862), p. 159: "Casper [Johann Ludwig Casper, author of important treatises on juridical medicine] also noted this particular taste for licentious images; one of the pederasts whose history he knew had accumulated copies of all the models of hermaphrodites in their seductive pose, and of numerous portraits of young boys."

64. Thus Ferdinand Hand claimed in 1841 that "the representation of sentiment in the notturno runs the danger of falling into the effeminate and languishing, which displeases stronger souls." Frederick Niecks, some half a century later, made a similar point: "These dulcet, effeminate compositions illustrate only one side of the master's character, and by no means the best or most interesting." For discussion and full bibliographical details, see Chapter 2.

65. Hadow, *Studies in Modern Music,* pp. 112–113, 155, 157.

66. Weininger added in a footnote: "His portrait also shows this clearly"; *Geschlecht und Charakter,* 8th ed. (Vienna and Leipzig, 1906), p. 82.

67. Adolf Weissmann, *The Problems of Modern Music,* trans. M. M. Bozman (London, 1925; reprint ed., Westport, Conn., 1979), p. 161. The German original, *Die Musik in der Weltkrise,* dates from 1922.

Here is Weissmann's earlier description of Debussy: "His big, stout body seemed to give promise of a strongly physical nature, but his tanned yet bloodless face, his domed forehead and deep-set eyes are a truer indication of his intellectual brilliance, of his scant masculinity, and of his struggle with an ever-present listlessness from which he nevertheless drew inspiration. He was essentially and naturally inactive . . . The morbid state of his nerves made him and his art egotistical"; ibid., pp. 152–153.

Weissmann's biography of Chopin (*Chopin* [Berlin, 1922]) abounds with discussions of the composer's feminine and effeminate nature. See in particular the chapter "Zur Psychologie des Musikers," pp. 82–104.

Nor does Weissmann exhaust the list of critics who imputed sodomitical meanings to Chopin's music. Derek Carew, in "Victorian Attitudes to Chopin," p. 227, cites a "German critic" from ca. 1909 who felt that a nocturne from op. 37 "bewitches and unmans" if we "tarry too long" in its "treacherous atmosphere." Finally, Edward J. Dent, in his introduction to the English translation of Weissmann's book, discusses Chopin's music and its relation to the quality that Weissmann terms *das Reizsame,* whose meaning is less "charm," according to Dent, but "itch or irritation." Dent continues: "Half a century ago there were musicians who stigmatised Chopin's music as morbid and decadent. We are not nowadays dangerously affected by the erotic element in Chopin, but we can see that from these beginnings there gradually developed that preoccupation with sexual passion which is to be observed in Wagner and in many later composers"; *The Problems of Modern Music,* p. xiii.

68. See Georges Canguilhem, *The Normal and the Pathological,* trans. Carolyn R. Fawcett (Dordrecht and Boston, 1978; reprint ed., New York, 1991), pp. 39–112. (The original French version dates from 1966.) Canguilhem notes that "semantically, the pathological is designated as departing from the normal not so much by *a-* or *dys-* as by *hyper-* and *hypo-*" (p. 42). There is a good summary and discussion of Canguilhem's thesis in Müller, *Aber in meinem Herzen,* pp. 40–46.

69. On the complex relationship between the concepts of "anomaly" and "pathological," with specific respect to Geoffroy Saint-Hilaire, see Canguilhem, *Normal and Pathological,* pp. 131–137.

70. On the "speaking body" in early nineteenth-century medico-legal tracts, see Müller, *Aber in meinem Herzen,* pp. 91–98.

71. J. Morel de Rubempré, discussing the "ills occasioned by onanism," includes "dorsal consumption" and "pulmonary phthisis"; see *Code de la génération universelle, ou les amours des fleurs, des animaux, et particulièrement de l'homme et de la femme, suivi de l'art de guérir l'impuissance ou faiblesse en amour, terminé par un traité de l'onanisme ou masturbation dans les deux sexes,* 2d ed. (Paris, 1833), p. 399. For a more general discussion of tuberculosis and masturbation, see Thomas Laqueur, *Making Sex: Body and Gender from the Greeks to Freud* (Cambridge, Mass., and London, 1990), pp. 227–230. On the perceived relationship between masturbation and sodomy, see George L. Mosse, *Nationalism and Sexuality: Middle-Class Morality and Sexual Norms in Modern Europe* (New York, 1985; reprint ed., Madison, 1985), pp. 11–12.

72. Marmontel, *Les pianistes célèbres,* p. 7. One might also include in this connection John Field's adage that Chopin was "a sickroom talent" and Auber's or Berlioz's epithet (it has been ascribed to both) that "he was dying all his life" (the French original is variously reported as "il se meurt toute sa vie" or "il se mourait toute sa vie"). The problem is that we have no firsthand evidence that either dictum was ever uttered. The supposed remark of Auber or Berlioz sounds suspiciously like a misconstrued reminiscence of a line from Berlioz's obituary of Chopin: "Alas! Chopin was lost to music for quite a long time" ("Hélas! Chopin était perdu pour la musique depuis assez long-

temps"). The obituary is reproduced in Mirska and Hordyński, eds., *Chopin na obczyźnie,* p. 325.

73. Examples include Ludwig Rellstab's feeling that the "debaucheries" *(Ausschweifungen)* and "trivial effeminacy" *(Weichlichkeit)* of the Concerto, op. 11, when juxtaposed against its finer qualities, could put one into a sick and miserable mood (review of op. 11, in *Iris im Gebiete der Tonkunst,* 6 June 1834, p. 90); August Kahlert's characterization of Chopin and Paganini as "pathological" *(krankhaft)* representatives of the new musical Romanticism ("Die Genrebilder in der modernen Musik," *Neue Zeitschrift für Musik,* 12 June 1835, p. 191); and two different British critics' perception of "sickliness" in the Scherzo, op. 20, and in the melodies of the Mazurkas, op. 41 (for the reference to "sickliness" and op. 20, see Jim Samson, *Chopin: The Four Ballades* [Cambridge, 1992], p. 5; for op. 41, see Frederick Niecks, *Frederick Chopin as a Man and Musician,* vol. 2, p. 279).

74. Something like these kinds of investigations has been undertaken in literary studies. For example, Weil discusses the possibility that Gautier's interest in fusing genres replicates his attempts to transgress boundaries of gender (*Androgyny and the Denial of Difference,* pp. 122–133).

75. For cogent analyses of the historiographical difficulties occasioned by formal description, see David Summers, " 'Form,' Nineteenth-Century Metaphysics, and the Problem of Art Historical Description," *Critical Inquiry* 15 (1989): 372–406, and Summers, "Form and Gender," *New Literary History* 24 (1993): 243–271.

76. *Music in Renaissance Magic: Toward a Historiography of Others* (Chicago, 1993), pp. 247–252.

4. Chopin's Last Style

1. Chopin was never prolific, but a tally of his publications reveals that his rate of production fell in this period from some five and a half opuses a year to just under three. I have touched on Chopin's decline in productivity twice before; first in a review of William G. Atwood, *The Lioness and the Little One: The Liaison of George Sand and Frédéric Chopin* (New York, 1980), in *19th-Century Music* 5 (1982): 244–247; second in "The Chopin Sources: Variants and Versions in Later Manuscripts and Printed Editions" (Ph.D. diss., University of Chicago, 1982), pp. 6–10.

2. Letter of 29 August 1842 to Pauline Viardot; in George Sand, *Correspondance,* ed. Georges Lubin, 25 vols. (Paris, 1964–1991), vol. 5 (1969), p. 765. In the second sentence, Sand refers to the planned visit to Nohant of Viardot.

3. Letter of 12 November 1844 to Eugène Delacroix; Sand, *Correspondance*, vol. 6 (1969), p. 691.

4. Letter of 21 August 1846 to Charles Poncy; Sand, *Correspondance*, vol. 7 (1970), p. 455.

5. Letter of 18–20 July 1845 to his family; Fryderyk Chopin, *Korespondencja z Rodziną*, ed. Krystyna Kobylańska (Warsaw, 1972), p. 140.

6. Letter of 8 July 1846 to Auguste Franchomme; Fryderyk Chopin, *Korespondencja Fryderyka Chopina*, ed. Bronislaw Edward Sydow, 2 vols. (Warsaw, 1955), vol. 2, p. 396. My text differs slightly from Sydow's in accordance with the autograph.

7. Letter of 30 October 1848 to Wojciech Grzymała, Chopin, *Korespondencja*, ed. Sydow, vol. 2, p. 285.

8. See letter to Julian Fontana assigned to early June 1841; Chopin, *Korespondencja*, ed. Sydow, vol. 2, pp. 20–21.

9. Chopin had, of course, mixed genres before his late period: we explored in Chapter 1 a paradigmatic example in the Nocturne in G Minor, op. 15, no. 3. Indeed, generic blends appear with some frequency among his earlier works (that is, those works coming before the Scherzo in B Minor, op. 20, roughly speaking). That the phenomenon then recedes somewhat in importance in the middle years of his creative output (encompassing, approximately, opp. 20 through 49) suggests that Chopin turned to the technique mostly in times of stylistic experimentation. In the early years, these experiments helped forge his personal artistic voice; in the later years, they aided his efforts to transform this voice.

10. Those who have commented on the issue with little or no documentation or discussion include Gerald Abraham, *Chopin's Musical Style* (Oxford, 1939), p. 111; Paul Hamburger, "Mazurkas, Waltzes, Polonaises," in *Frédéric Chopin: Profiles of the Man and the Musician,* ed. Alan Walker (London, 1966), p. 113; and Donald Jay Grout, *A History of Western Music,* 3rd ed., with Claude V. Palisca (New York, 1980), p. 579. Mieczysław Tomaszewski, "Uwagi o ewolucji stylu u Chopina," *Studia musicologica: aesthetica, theoretica, historica,* ed. Elżbieta Dziębowska, Zofia Helman, Danuta Idaszak, and Adam Neuer (Cracow, 1979), pp. 405–416, and especially pp. 414–415, treats only somewhat more amply the possibility of a final creative period commencing around 1845–1846.

11. Letter of 12–26 December, 1845; Chopin, *Korespondencja z Rodziną,* ed. Kobylańska, p. 151. Two exceptional pieces for which Chopin showed uncertainty as to the title are the Polonaise in F-sharp Minor, op. 44—I will discuss this example in the following section—and the Berceuse, op. 57, which he initially referred to as "les variantes" in a letter to the publisher

Maurice Schlesinger probably dating from December 1844 (Chopin, *Korespondencja,* ed. Sydow, vol. 2, p. 384).

12. One notable exception to this tendency appears to be the Polonaise in C-sharp Minor, op. 26, no. 1. The autograph *Stichvorlage* for this piece (New York, Pierpont Morgan Library) as well as the three first editions all read "Fine" at the conclusion of the Trio (the term *Trio* is mine, not Chopin's), which would indicate bipartite rather than ternary form. For a discussion of these sources, see Gastone Belotti, "Le Polacche dell'op. 26 nella concezione autografa di Chopin," in his *Saggi sull'arte e sull'opera di F. Chopin* (Bologna, 1977), pp. 349–367, and Belotti, "Le Polacche dell'op. 26 nel testo autentico di Chopin," *Saggi,* pp. 369–415. The first essay originally appeared in *Nuova Rivista Musicale Italiana* 7 (1974): 191–209; the second was printed in *Studi Musicali* 2 (1973): 267–313.

The manuscript evidence is somewhat equivocal. The word "Fine" is written at the end of a repeated passage in the Trio, one that Chopin indicated by marking off blank measures and entering in sequence, in each bar, numbers that refer back to the original statement of the passage. But Chopin often made mistakes in such numerical repeats. Since the resulting form would be unique to the genre, it seems still possible to me that Chopin's indication of "Fine" was simply a notational error, and that he actually intended the normal repeat of the Polonaise to follow the Trio.

13. Chopin, *Korespondencja,* ed. Sydow, vol. 2, pp. 341 and 32.

14. See Abraham, *Chopin's Musical Style,* p. 105. To speak of the "Tempo di Mazurka" as being an "interpolated Mazurka" is somewhat inaccurate, for the adjective implies a certain degree of autonomy for the section. The "Tempo di Mazurka" certainly shows many qualities of a mazurka, but no genuine mazurka displays the form of the passage in op. 44: in no way could the section be construed to act as a mazurka in its own right.

15. See Tadeusz Strumiłło, *Źródła i początki romantyzmu w muzyce polskiej. Studia i materiały,* Studia i materiały do dziejów muzyki polskiej, vol. 3 (Cracow, 1956), p. 112; and Józef M. Chomiński, *Fryderyk Chopin,* trans. Bolko Schweinitz (Leipzig, 1980), p. 129. Karol Hlawiczka, "Grundriss einer Geschichte der Polonaise bis zum Anfang des 19. Jahrhunderts," *Svensk tidskrift för musikforskning* 50 (1968): 51–124, and particularly pp. 75–84, discusses rhythmic relationships and borrowings among early polonaises and mazurkas.

16. Also unorthodox formally in op. 44 is the refrain made up of a sequential pair of cadences that sounds four times: twice in the opening section, once in the middle section, and once in the repetition of the opening section (mm. 27–34, 53–60, 103–110, and 286–293). Ordinarily the principal sections of a polonaise stand as discrete units, distinct from one another in tempo

and texture as well as in theme. The refrain probably contributed to Chopin's incertitude over the title as well, but for our purposes here this is less relevant.

17. On the general history of the free fantasy, see Peter Schleuning, *Die freie Fantasie: ein Beitrag zur Erforschung der klassischen Klaviermusik,* Göppinger Akademische Beiträge, no. 76 (Göppingen, 1973). On Polish fantasies composed before Chopin, see Alina Nowak-Romanowicz, "Polskie fantazje fortepianowe doby przedchopinowskiej," in *Studia musicologica: aesthetica, theoretica, historica,* pp. 349–358. Nowak-Romanowicz discusses among other works two fantasies that invoke elements of the polonaise, Franciszek Siekierski's *Polonaise quasi Fantasia* (1815) and Maria Szymanowska's *Fantaisie* (1819). Chopin thus did not invent this particular generic hybrid; rather, as is the case for so many other genres in which he wrote, the kind of musical structure he evolved for it is novel.

18. He used the title "Fantasy" one other time in his career, for the early Fantasy on Polish National Airs, op. 13, a potpourri based on three different tunes. The popular title for the work published posthumously as op. 66, the so-called Fantasy-Impromptu, likely does not derive from Chopin. The surviving autograph manuscript of the piece (dating from 1835) bears no title, but textual analysis of the manuscript copies suggests that Chopin probably sanctioned the use of only "Impromptu" in connection with the work. See Jan Ekier, "Das Impromptu Cis-moll von Frédéric Chopin," *Melos/Neue Zeitschrift für Musik* 4 (1978): 201–204.

19. Some prominent examples showing these characteristics are listed by Carl Czerny as models by "fine masters" for those who would attempt to improvise freely on several themes. See *A Systematic Introduction to Improvisation on the Pianoforte, Opus 200,* trans. and ed. Alice L. Mitchell (New York and London, 1983), p. 74. On pp. 75–85 Czerny printed an example of his own composition that also contains a long introduction and a slow central theme. His account of the improviser at work (p. 74) also characterizes aptly the interruptive qualities of many fantasy themes: "For here he can give free rein to his flights of fancy (albeit in rational form); and unexpected, interesting motives that are both arresting as well as useful frequently enter the fingers while playing."

20. I have borrowed this analogy from Leonard B. Meyer, who employs it to characterize what he views as the necessary compatibility between innovation and prevailing stylistic constraints. See "Innovation, Choice, and the History of Music," *Critical Inquiry* 9 (1983): 523.

21. Although the Polonaise-Fantasy has often been interpreted as a hybrid genre, it has—surprisingly—yet to be viewed simply as an alloy of the two genres in its title. Hugo Leichtentritt, *Analyse der Chopin'schen Klaviermusik,* 2 vols. (Berlin, 1921), vol. 1, pp. 110–121, described the work as a fantasy

with some elements of the polonaise laced in, with the whole shaped into a kind of sonata design. Lew Mazel (Lev Abramovich Mazel'), "O pewnych cechach kompozycji w swobodnych formach Chopina," in his *Studia chopinowskie,* trans. Jerzy Popiel (Cracow, 1965), pp. 251–258 (the article, originally in Russian, dates from 1960), saw a richer array of ingredients in the generic mixture. He summarized the work as a combination of complex ternary form with refrain-like and cyclic elements, these attributes arranged in such a way as to suggest at times a mixture of the polonaise, ballade, sonata, and theme and variations. Zofia Lissa, "Die Formenkreuzung bei Chopin," *The Book of the First International Musicological Congress Devoted to the Works of Frederick Chopin,* ed. Zofia Lissa (Warsaw, 1963), pp. 211–212, posited still more grafts. Her basic structure combined a synthesis of two sonata-allegro expositions with elements of a sonata cycle and theme and variation form, as well as references to the improvisation and the concerto. Eero Tarasti, "Pour une narratologie de Chopin," *International Review of the Aesthetics and Sociology of Music* 15 (1984): 53–75, although concerned primarily with probing the "concrete, psychological content" of op. 61 (p. 74), embraced Lissa's notion of generic mixture and proposed additional generic borrowings (including the mazurka and nocturne) of his own. Chomiński, *Fryderyk Chopin,* pp. 131–132, saw similarities between the Polonaise-Fantasy and Chopin's Ballades and F-Minor Fantasy, and identified the central slow section with the slow movement of a sonata. Generally, however, he retreated from the models of wholesale generic appropriation offered by Mazel and Lissa. While all of these writers responded to a significant aspect of Chopin's late style—generic borrowing—most advanced inordinately complex models that little touch the auditory experience of the work.

22. For an earlier example of this concept, applied on a broader scale, see the B-flat Minor/D-flat Major Scherzo, op. 31. Charles Rosen, *The Classical Style: Haydn, Mozart, Beethoven* (New York, 1971), p. 26, and William Kinderman, "Das 'Geheimnis der Form' in Wagner's 'Tristan und Isolde,' " *Archiv für Musikwissenschaft* 40 (1983): 182, both discuss this type of tonal pairing in Chopin. Gregory Michael Proctor, "Technical Bases of Nineteenth-Century Chromatic Tonality: A Study in Chromaticism" (Ph.D. diss., Princeton University, 1978), constructs a theoretical model for the changes in tonality that begin to occur around the second quarter of the nineteenth century.

23. That the slow middle section of the work (mm. 199–222) veers for the first time into B major does not precipitate large-scale harmonic tension with the tonic regions of F minor/A-flat major. Rather it engenders the sort of coloristic contrast characteristic of tonal parentheses.

24. The sketches for the Polonaise-Fantasy have been previously discussed and transcribed by Wojciech Nowik, "Proces twórczy Fryderyka Chopina w

świetle jego autografów muzycznych" (Ph.D. diss., University of Warsaw, 1978), pp. 231–270 (the transcriptions appear in an unpaginated appendix). My transcriptions differ in many particulars from Nowik's, and his commentary, written in the context of a study that probes the semiotic and psychological content of Chopin's autographs, explores other facets of the piece than those covered here. Nowik's dissertation nonetheless makes a valuable contribution, and has proven helpful in directing my own thoughts on Chopin's compositional process.

Jim Samson has twice investigated the sketches in interesting ways; see *The Music of Chopin* (London, 1985), pp. 203–211, and "The Composition-Draft of the Polonaise-Fantasy: The Issue of Tonality," in Samson, ed., *Chopin Studies* (Cambridge, 1988), pp. 41–58.

John Rink has examined the sketches as part of his significant inquiry into Schenker's theoretical notion of improvisation; see "Schenker and Improvisation," *Journal of Music Theory* 37 (1993): 1–54, and especially 26–41.

25. The following account of Chopin's general sketching habits greatly condenses material found in Chapter 2 of my dissertation, "The Chopin Sources," pp. 154–164. In that chapter I present full documentation for the assertions printed here.

26. To cite one example of many from Chopin's correspondence, the composer, after complaining to Julian Fontana of the delays in receiving his piano in Majorca, wrote: "In the meantime my manuscripts sleep, while I cannot sleep, only cough"; letter of 14 December 1838, in Chopin, *Korespondencja*, ed. Sydow, vol. 1, p. 332. George Sand's account appears in her *Oeuvres autobiographiques*, ed. Georges Lubin, 2 vols. (Paris, 1971); vol. 2: *Histoire de ma vie*, p. 446.

27. A notable exception to this rule is the sketch for the Berceuse, op. 57 (Warsaw, Chopin Society, M/2165), which arranges the music in columns of four-measure units in accordance with the repetitive structure of the piece. The drafts have been reproduced in facsimile in Alfred Cortot and Edouard Ganche, eds., *Trois manuscrits de Chopin* (Paris, 1932), and in Krystyna Kobylańska, *Rękopisy utworów Chopina. Katalog*, Documenta Chopiniana, no. 2, 2 vols. (Cracow, 1977), vol. 2, pp. 89–90.

28. Wojciech Nowik has discussed the abbreviations used in Chopin's sketches in "Autografy muzyczny jako podstawa badań źródłowych w Chopinologii," *Muzyka* 16 (1971): 65–84, and in "The Receptive-Informational Role of Chopin's Musical Autographs," *Studies in Chopin,* ed. Dariusz Żebrowski (Warsaw, 1973), pp. 77–89.

29. Details on the history of the main body of sketches may be found in Kobylańska, *Katalog,* vol. 1, p. 328, and, in a somewhat different version, in her *Frédéric Chopin: Thematisch-bibliographisches Werkverzeichnis,* trans.

Helmut Stolze, ed. Ernst Herttrich (Munich, 1979), p. 132. The sketches have been reproduced in Ferdinand Gajewski, ed., *The Work Sheets to Chopin's Violoncello Sonata: A Facsimile* (New York and London, 1988), pp. 2, 82–88. The shelfmark of the Warsaw leaf is M/1341.

30. Chopin therefore certainly did not begin work on the piece with the clear idea of anticipating its two principal tonalities with the two very first chords of the work (note also in Table 4.1 that he initially began the piece in C minor). On the other hand, it is tempting to think that one reason for his eventual decision to transpose the middle sections was his realization of the latent possibilities for large-scale harmonic implication contained in the opening of the piece.

31. If the insertions into the original layer were immediate, then this conclusion would not hold. But both the scarcity of such additions (the only other instance occurs on page 4, staff 10) and the lack of any polonaise rhythm in later original layers suggest that Chopin settled on the gesture relatively late in the genesis of the work, perhaps after he realized that the sketched piece already contained such fundamental elements of the polonaise genre as a lengthy introduction and a contrasting lyrical middle section.

32. Two of these *Stichvorlagen* are known to have survived, that used by Brandus for the French edition (in the private Parisian collection of the heirs of the Czech pianist Wilhelmine Clauss-Szarvady [1834–1907]), and that used by Breitkopf & Härtel for the German edition (Warsaw, Biblioteka Narodowa, Mus. 233). Jean-Jacques Eigeldinger has published a facsimile of the Brandus manuscript (Frédéric Chopin, *Deux Nocturnes op. 48; Polonaise-Fantaisie op. 61: Autographes en fac-similé* [Yverdon-les-Bains, Switzerland, 1986]), and has also discussed its contents in "Notes sur des autographes musicaux inconnus: Schumann, Brahms, Chopin, Franck, Fauré," *Revue de musicologie* 70 (1984): 107–117, and "Autographes de Chopin inconnus: Deux Nocturnes op. 48, Polonaise-Fantaisie op. 61," *Revue musicale de Suisse romande* 37 (1984): 154–171. In the latter article, Eigeldinger establishes that Chopin prepared the Brandus manuscript before the one for Breitkopf.

33. Nowik, "Proces twórczy," pp. 231–232, makes a similar point.

34. This section was sketched on pages 5, 4, and 3, in that order, as stated by Nowik, "Proces twórczy," pp. 248–250.

35. A more proximate cause for the curtailment of the theme to eight measures was likely the desire to simplify the shift into the B-flat major tonality at the beginning of the transition. Since the agitato transformation of the principal theme returns to the ascending whole-tone sequence of the original, the tonal goal of the last measures of the transformation is B-flat minor, as in the original. But whereas B-flat is only touched upon in the original statement, at the beginning of the transition it becomes a solid point of arrival.

36. Here our perception of the relationship between the melody that opens the transition (mm. 116–123) and the tune heard both within the slow section and at the juncture under discussion (mm. 182–189; 217–221) becomes crucial. Many analysts have claimed an affinity between the two themes (for the most explicit argument, see Hamburger, "Mazurkas, Waltzes, Polonaises," pp. 107–109). Were the melodies related, they would be distributed symmetrically about the middle section (one before it, one in the middle of it, and one after it) in the fashion of a refrain, and would presumably support, not deny, one's sense of ternary form in the piece. Except for similarities in rhythmic patterning, however, the themes differ sharply. The harmonic progressions are practically opposites, and all motivic similarities seem forced. Chopin cannot have conceived of the later theme as a transformation of the earlier; when he transforms a theme (as in the nocturnelike or agitato version of the principal theme discussed above), he maintains its intervallic shape while altering its function or character.

37. *Musical Form and Musical Performance* (New York, 1968), p. 84.

38. Anthony Newcomb has discussed just this kind of shift in formal implication in the music of Wagner and Schumann. See "The Birth of Music out of the Spirit of Drama: An Essay in Wagnerian Formal Analysis," *19th-Century Music* 5 (1981): 38–66; "Those Images That Yet Fresh Images Beget," *The Journal of Musicology* 2 (1983): 227–245; and "Once More 'Between Absolute and Program Music': Schumann's Second Symphony," *19th-Century Music* 7 (1984): 233–250.

39. Since 1958, the sketch has formed part of the collection of the Chopin Society in Warsaw. Its shelfmark is M/235.

40. The surviving copy in Franchomme's hand, written on one page, is evidently itself a copy of his earlier two-page manuscript; see the description of Franchomme's transcription given by Chopin's pupil Jane Stirling in a letter of 18 June 1852 to Ludwika Jędrzejewicz, in Hanna Wróblewska-Straus, "Listy Jane Wilhelminy Stirling do Ludwiki Jędrzejewiczowej," *Rocznik Chopinowski* 12 (1980): 147. The earlier Franchomme copy is now lost.

41. Both Maurice J. E. Brown, *Chopin: An Index of His Works in Chronological Order*, 2d rev. ed. (London, 1972), p. 174, and Kobylańska, *Werkverzeichnis*, p. 165, state that the separate issue of op. 68, no. 4 was released in 1852, three years before the rest of opp. 66–73. This date seems very unlikely on several accounts. First, the two issues, although printed from different plates, are nearly identical in musical content (the small differences are easily attributable to engraving practices); it would seem that Fontana was responsible for them both. But Fontana cannot have prepared an edition of the Mazurka in 1852; a letter of 12 December 1853 from Stirling to Jędrzejewicz states that at this date Fontana was still attempting to see Franchomme's copy of the piece (the letter is summarized in Mieczysław Karło-

wicz, *Niewydane dotychczas pamiątki po Chopinie* [Warsaw, 1904], p. 345, and in Edouard Ganche, *Dans le souvenir de Frédéric Chopin* [Paris, 1925], p. 146). In an undated letter to Jędrzejewicz that must follow the letter of 12 December, Fontana writes that he has on hand, among other works, seven mazurkas (he published eight in opp. 67 and 68), and asks if Jędrzejewicz has Franchomme's copy of the F-Minor Mazurka (Karłowicz, *Niewydane do tychczas*, pp. 371–372). Finally, the "Dernière pensée" edition contains two subheadings that securely point to a date no earlier than 1855. The first reads "Publié par J. FONTANA dans les Oeuvres posthumes, Livr. III. Op 68 No 8." The caption, therefore, mentions the 1855 complete publication. The second says "Beilage zur Berliner Musikzeitung 'Echo,' July. Jahrg.V." (The fifth *Jahrgang* of "Echo" was 1855.)

42. An edition of Hedley's reconstruction is published in John Vallier, ed., *Chopin: A Selection,* Oxford Keyboard Classics (Oxford, 1986), pp. 40–43; see also the commentary on p. 47. Bronarski's "La dernière Mazurka de Chopin" appeared in the *Schweizerische Musikzeitung/Revue Musicale Suisse 95* (1955): 380–387.

43. Fryderyk Chopin, *Mazurek f-moll ostatni,* ed. Jan Ekier (Cracow, 1965).

44. "Próba rekonstrukcja *Mazurka f-moll* op. 68 nr. 4 Fryderyka Chopina," *Rocznik Chopinowski* 8 (1969): 44–85; and "Chopins Mazurka F moll, op. 68, Nr. 4: 'Die letzte Inspiration des Meisters,' " *Archiv für Musikwissenschaft* 30 (1973): 109–127.

45. Fryderyk Chopin, *The Final Composition: Mazurka in F Minor Op. Posthumous (Fontana Op. 68, No. 4), A Completely New Realization,* ed. Ronald Smith (New York, 1975). My discussion of Smith's edition concerns only his treatment of form; I do not agree with some of the local details of his reconstruction.

A recent performing version of the sketch prepared by Milosz Magin (Fryderyk Chopin, *Mazurka en fa mineur: La dernière oeuvre de Chopin* [Paris, 1983]), evidently assembled without knowledge of Smith's effort, nevertheless presents a formal structure of the Mazurka identical to Smith's.

46. "Chopins Mazurka," p. 109.

47. Despite the heading "F mol[l] Maz[urka]" in Chopin's sketch, Franchomme faltered in identifying the genre on his copy; he first wrote "Valse," and then wrote over it "Mazurka."

48. Wróblewska-Straus, "Listy," p. 147.

49. The original is given in parallel French and German texts, with the text differing slightly in the separate "Dernière pensée" issue.

50. The Jędrzejewicz list, Warsaw, Chopin Society, M/301, bears the title "Kompozycyje niewydane" ("Compositions unpublished"); the notation

"Mazourki. dwa ostatnie" appears on the fourth page of the manuscript. For a facsimile of the list, see Kobylańska, *Katalog,* vol. 2, pp. 115–118.

51. See Kobylańska, *Werkverzeichnis,* p. xvii.

52. See Nowik, "Chopins Mazurka," pp. 110–111. Franchomme's proximity to Chopin in the summer of 1849 is confirmed by an entry in the composer's diary dated 28 July, cited in Fryderyk Chopin, *Selected Correspondence of Fryderyk Chopin,* trans. and ed. Arthur Hedley (New York, 1963), p. 368.

53. Chopin, *Korespondencja,* ed. Sydow, vol. 2, pp. 298, 305, and 457.

54. On Schubert's *Schwanengesang* and final sonatas, see Otto Erich Deutsch, *Franz Schubert: Neue Ausgabe sämtlicher Werke,* ser. 8, suppl. vol. 4, *Franz Schubert: Thematisches Verzeichnis seiner Werke in chronologischer Folge* (Kassel, 1978), pp. 617–618. On Beethoven's WoO 62, see Georg Kinsky, *Das Werk Beethovens: Thematisch-bibliographisches Verzeichnis seiner sämtlicher vollendeten Kompositionen,* ed. Hans Halm (Munich, 1955), pp. 508–509. A different spurious work was identified as Beethoven's "last composition" in England; see Anhang 15 in Kinsky, *Das Werk Beethovens,* p. 728. The British Library owns three Parisian publications claiming to be Bellini's "Dernière pensée": "A palpitar d'affanno," "Dans un moment," and "Adieux à ce monde." See *The Catalogue of Printed Music in the British Library to 1980,* ed. Laureen Baillie, vol. 4 (1981), pp. 370 and 375. On the inauthentic Weber work, see Friedrich Wilhelm Jähns, *Carl Maria von Weber in seinen Werken* (Berlin, 1871; reprint ed., Berlin-Lichterfelde, 1967), p. 446.

55. I have only scratched the surface of this genre of publication. With large works like the Mozart Requiem and with small pieces such as "Les derniers moments de Donizetti: Chant-élégie," by one A. G. Montuoro, publishers attempted to capitalize on the topos. One publisher, A. M. Schlesinger of Berlin (who also released Chopin's "last thought"), went so far as to make a small anthology of the "Dernières pensées" of Weber, Beethoven, and Bellini (see *The Catalogue of Printed Music in the British Library to 1980,* vol. 16 [1983], p. 229). The urge to mythologize the final days of an artist even affected the nineteenth-century view of Bach; see Christoph Wolff, "Johann Sebastian Bachs 'Sterbechoral': Kritische Fragen zu einem Mythos," *Studies in Renaissance and Baroque Music in Honor of Arthur Mendel,* ed. Robert L. Marshall (Kassel, 1974), pp. 283–297. And the phenomenon was not limited to composers. The first publication of Keats's "In After Time a Sage of Mickle Lore" was accompanied by an explanation that the poem was the author's last before his death (see John Keats, *Complete Poems,* ed. Jack Stillinger [Cambridge, Mass., 1982], pp. 484–485). Indeed, to judge from the many compositions invoking the "dying poet" (among others, a song by Mey-

erbeer and a piano piece by Gottschalk), the literary genre must have exerted a significant influence on the musical.

56. *Poems of Tennyson,* ed. Jerome H. Buckley (Boston, 1958), p. 13. Another poem to summon up the musical imagery of the swan song, and one of obvious significance in light of the above discussion, is Lamartine's "Le Poète mourant," published in 1823. See Alphonse de Lamartine, *Méditations,* ed. Fernand Letessier (Paris, 1968), pp. 153–157.

Finally, two more evocations of the *dernière pensée* or swan song are worth noting for their proximity to Chopin. George Sand's short story "Carl" evokes the topos several times, even including a musical example to illustrate the last musical thought of the title character. Sand published "Carl" serially in the *Revue et Gazette musicale de Paris:* 1 January 1843, pp. 1–3; 8 January 1843, pp. 9–11; and 15 January 1843, pp. 19–21. And Henri Blanchard's obituary for Chopin, cited in Chapter 3, links the swan song with a mode of reception experienced by some of Chopin's aristocratic female listeners: "They loved to follow him when he lulled his intimate auditor with his capricious melodic arabesques over an unforeseen harmony, strange, but distinguished, classic, pure, and nevertheless sickly, which seemed a swan song, a hymn of death"; "Obsèques de Frédéric Chopin," *Revue et Gazette musicale de Paris,* 4 November 1849, p. 348.

57. The fourteen-stave paper most commonly used by Chopin after the spring of 1845 shows a total span of 180–181.5 millimeters and stave lengths of 234–239 millimeters. For full documentation on the paper types of Chopin's later years, see Kallberg, "The Chopin Sources," pp. 371–389, and Kallberg, "O klasyfikacji rękopisów Chopina," *Rocznik Chopinowski* 17 (1985): 86–96. Table 4.2 differs somewhat from its analogue on pp. 381–382 of "The Chopin Sources," which does not differentiate between two separate types of paper. Chopin used a similar species, with a total span of 178–179 millimeters, but showing stave lengths of 228–231 millimeters, from roughly 1838 to 1841.

58. That Franchomme's copy of the Mazurka and two other posthumously copied leaves appear among this paper type does not alter the interpretation of the data. Franchomme and the other copyists presumably purchased their paper separately, and used it in different ways from Chopin.

59. See "Compatibility in Chopin's Multipartite Publications," *The Journal of Musicology* 2 (1983): 391–417.

60. A key word referring to op. 63 in a letter of 11 October 1846 from Chopin to his family has only recently been deciphered, and might shed light on the issues being discussed here. Chopin wrote, "I have 3 new mazurkas— I do not think with the old deficiencies, but one needs time to judge well. As one works, it seems good, otherwise one would not write anything. Only later reflection arrives—and discard or accept. Time is the best censorship and

patience the most perfect teacher." See Kobylańska, *Korespondencja z Rodziną,* p. 159. The newly legible word is "dziurami"—literally "holes" or "gaps," rendered here as "deficiencies." The autograph of the letter was acquired by the Chopin Society in Warsaw (shelfmark D/163), and my thanks are due to Hanna Wróblewska-Straus, Head of the Museum Department, who communicated to me the proper reading.

To what "old deficiencies" does Chopin refer? Could the composer have written the letter when the sketch was still part of op. 63? This speculation suggests two possible readings of the letter: either as an indication of Chopin's awareness of the novelty of style in the set, particularly in the experimental sketch, or as a sign that the "old" and "deficient" sketch had been replaced by the superior Mazurka eventually published as op. 63, no. 2.

61. Chopin rarely blurs structural boundaries in a mazurka, and when he does, it is usually for a special purpose. In the C-Minor Mazurka, op. 56, no. 3, Chopin shifts abruptly from the dominant of B-flat major to the dominant of B major in measures 57–66, and simultaneously sounds a new melody. But this new melody is deceptive, for the second section of the piece actually commences in B-flat major at measure 73. Here the false gesture establishes a tonal link with the first Mazurka of the set, a technique Chopin occasionally used to establish connections among the individual numbers of a publication. See Kallberg, "Compatibility," pp. 395–404.

62. See " 'Neo-romanticism' " in his *Between Romanticism and Modernism: Four Studies in the Music of the Later Nineteenth Century,* trans. Mary Whittall, California Studies in 19th Century Music, no. 1 (Berkeley and Los Angeles, 1980), pp. 16–17. The translation has also appeared in *19th-Century Music* 3 (1979): 97–105.

63. For a fascinating discussion of the issue of modernity in mid-nineteenth century art, see Linda Nochlin, *Realism* (New York, 1971), chap. 3.

5. Small "Forms"

1. The quotation comes from Arnold Whittall's interesting article on "Form" in *The New Grove Dictionary of Music and Musicians,* ed. Stanley Sadie (London, 1980), vol. 6, p. 709.

2. For all but Koch, I cite from the translations in Peter le Huray and James Day, eds., *Music and Aesthetics in the Eighteenth and Early-Nineteenth Centuries* (Cambridge, 1981): Kant, p. 219; Schelling, p. 280; Michaelis, p. 288; Nägeli, p. 398; Schilling, pp. 464–66; and Kahlert, pp. 561, 563. The Koch translation is my own; it derives from the 1981 Hildesheim reprint of the 1807 Leipzig original, p. 156.

3. Władysław Tatarkiewicz distinguishes at least five different meanings of *form* in the history of aesthetics; see "Form in the History of Aesthetics" in

Philip P. Wiener, ed., *The Dictionary of the History of Ideas,* 5 vols. (New York, 1973), vol. 2, p. 216.

For an exemplary analysis of the history of form in the first half of the nineteenth century, see Carl Dahlhaus, "Eduard Hanslick und der musikalische Formbegriff," *Die Musikforschung* 20 (1967): 145–153.

4. Cited and translated in *Music and Aesthetics,* p. 343.

5. The truly "essential" [*wesentlich*] concept for Koch was not *Form* but *Anlage,* or "plan," a mental construct in which the inner character and effect of the whole composition was revealed to the composer in a moment of inspiration. On Koch's "Anlage," see Dahlhaus, "Eduard Hanslick," pp. 150–151, and Nancy Kovaleff Baker, "The Aesthetic Theories of Heinrich Christoph Koch," *International Review of the Aesthetics and Sociology of Music* 8 (1977): 183–209.

6. The quotations come from *Music and Aesthetics,* p. 276. A further comment is necessary on Schelling's use of *form.* His discussion makes clear that, unlike the other aestheticians cited, he understood form in the platonic sense of "eternal and absolute archetype," a pure concept normally at some level of remove from the art work itself. ("Philosophy, like art, does not generally deal with tangible phenomena; it deals only with their forms or eternal essences" [ibid., p. 280].) The attraction of music for Schelling, though, lay precisely in the way in which it expressed, through rhythm and harmony, pure form of the platonic variety ("music brings before us in rhythm and harmony the form of the motions of physical bodies; it is, in other words, pure form liberated from any object or from matter" [ibid.]). As le Huray and Day observe, this claim closely anticipates Schopenhauer's famous assertion that listening to music brings us into contact not with an image of the will, but with the will itself (ibid., p. 275).

7. Something of this broadly aesthetic understanding of form still remains with us today: it is a common reflex for critics who define form to state that it embraces more than design or morphology. But ordinarily these other categories—pitch, duration, and so forth—are made to serve the understanding of morphology or design, rather than being allowed to stand as form independent of plan as could be the case in Chopin's day.

8. My thoughts on the relationship between form and genre were stimulated by Laurence Dreyfus's "Matters of Kind: Genre and Subgenre in Bach's Well-Tempered Clavier, Book I," a paper read at the 1986 Annual Meeting of the American Musicological Society. In this paper, Dreyfus attempts to make the case that form, rather than having acted as a synonym for genre before the mid-nineteenth century, instead was understood as a metaphor for it. As should be clear, my reading of the philosophical and musical evidence differs from Dreyfus's, who I think too restrictively equates form in its theoretical usages with shape.

9. Review of Chopin's Mazurkas, op. 17; *Gazette musicale de Paris,* 29 June 1834, p. 210.

10. *Allgemeine musikalische Zeitung,* 4 February 1846, col. 74.

11. See also Jim Samson, "Chopin and Genre," *Music Analysis* 8 (1989): 213–231.

12. Dreyfus, "Matters of Kind."

13. Discussions of structural form sometimes occurred in instrumental treatises. But normally these cropped up in connection with advice on how to improvise, a situation in which the instrumentalist essentially functioned as a composer.

Some interesting work has recently begun to explore the ramifications of the contexts in which eighteenth- and nineteenth-century discussions of structural form occurred. See Thomas S. Grey, "Richard Wagner and the Aesthetics of Musical Form in the Mid-19th Century," (Ph.D. diss., University of California, Berkeley, 1987); Mark Evan Bonds, *Wordless Rhetoric: Musical Form and the Metaphor of the Oration* (Cambridge, Mass., 1991)—but note also the important review of Bonds's book by Peter A. Hoyt in *Journal of Music Theory* 38 (1994)—Elaine R. Sisman, *Haydn and the Classical Variation* (Cambridge, Mass., 1993); and Ian Bent, ed. *Music Analysis in the Nineteenth Century. Volume One: Fugue, Form and Style* (Cambridge, 1994), pp. xi–xv (Bent's preface).

14. See the translation in Hector Berlioz, *Fantastic Symphony,* ed. Edward T. Cone (New York, 1971), pp. 220–248, and especially pp. 230–231.

15. Maurice Bourges, "Lettres à Mme la Baronne de *** sur quelques morceaux de piano moderne," *Revue et Gazette musicale de Paris,* 17 April 1842, p. 171. In the paragraph that follows the excerpt, Bourges discusses Chopin's Prelude, op. 45, hence the example in the last clause of the quotation.

16. It is possible that Chopin may have used some kind of formal analysis as a pedagogical tool. An anonymous Scottish pupil of his reported the following reminiscence in 1903: "My next lesson began with the Sonata [Beethoven, op. 26]. He called my attention to its structure, to the intentions of the composer throughout . . . From the Sonata he passed to his own compositions . . . He would sit patiently while I tried to thread my way through mazes of intricate and unaccustomed modulations, which I could never have understood had he not invariably played to me each composition—Nocturne, Prelude, Impromptu, whatever it was—letting me hear the framework (if I may so express it) around which these beautiful and strange harmonies were grouped." (I cite the translation found in Jean-Jacques Eigeldinger, *Chopin: Pianist and Teacher As Seen by His Pupils,* trans. Naomi Shohet et al., ed. Roy Howat [Cambridge, 1986], p. 59; the ellipses are mine.)

Two problems cloud the assessment of this reminiscence. First, it is not clear that her terms "structure" and "framework" refer to form in the structural sense under discussion here; they seem rather to concern explanations of unusual modulatory passages. And second, if she did mean to allude to morphological form, that her recollection was recorded more than a half-century after the fact raises the possibility that the Scottish lady was interpreting in a contemporary, early twentieth-century structural sense what had been a different meaning of form in her actual lessons with Chopin in 1846.

17. In "Criticism, Faith, and the *Idee:* A. B. Marx's Early Reception of Beethoven," *19th-Century Music* 13 (1990): 183–192, Scott Burnham persuasively argues that Marx's program was only to a limited degree motivated by contemporary philosophical thought such as Hegel's. But other unambiguously Hegelian music theorists like Krüger nonetheless took Marx to be one of their own. For this reason, in my view, it remains reasonable to number Marx among the Hegelians.

18. *Music and Aesthetics,* p. 535.

19. See Charles Rosen and Henri Zerner, *Romanticism and Realism: The Mythology of Nineteenth-Century Art* (New York, 1984), pp. 38–48.

20. *Neue Zeitschrift für Musik,* 12 June 1835, pp. 189–191.

21. Ibid., pp. 190–191.

22. From a review of the Nocturnes, op. 37, the Ballade, op. 38, and the Waltz, op. 42, *Neue Zeitschrift für Musik,* 2 November 1841, p. 141. My translation differs in several important respects from that offered by Paul Rosenfeld in Robert Schumann, *On Music and Musicians,* ed. Konrad Wolff (New York, 1946), pp. 142–143.

23. Indeed, he had already adumbrated his position in an earlier review of the Etudes, op. 25: "It is unfortunately true, however, that our friend writes little at present, and no works at all of greater compass. The distracting Paris may be partly to blame for this." *Neue Zeitschrift für Musik,* 22 December 1837, p. 200.

24. *Neue Zeitschrift für Musik,* 19 November 1839, p. 163.

25. *Revue et Gazette musicale de Paris,* 2 May 1841, p. 246. The "great contemporary poet" to whom Liszt referred was presumably Lamartine, whose "Les préludes" was published in 1823. Perhaps then it was also the Preludes that inspired the claim of another anonymous reviewer of the same concert that "to hear Chopin is to read a strophe of Lamartine" (*Le ménestrel,* 2 May 1841).

26. The reviewer for the *Allgemeine musikalische Zeitung,* 25 December 1839, col. 1040, partially shared Schumann's reaction, faulting numbers 1, 2, 5, 7, and 23 of op. 28 for being too short.

27. *Notes sur Chopin* (Paris, 1948), p. 32.

28. Carl Czerny, *A Systematic Introduction to Improvisation on the Pianoforte, Opus 200,* trans. and ed. Alice L. Mitchell (New York, 1983), p. 6.

29. Ibid., p. 17.

30. "Twenty-Four Preludes, op. 28: Genre, Structure, Significance," in Jim Samson, ed., *Chopin Studies* (Cambridge, 1988), p. 177.

31. Others who have argued along somewhat similar analytical lines— though with differing degrees of subtlety—for the musical unity of the set include Józef M. Chomiński, *Preludia Chopina* (Cracow, 1950), pp. 300– 333; Charles J. Smith, "On Hearing the Chopin Preludes as a Coherent Set," *In Theory Only* 1/5 (1975): 5–16; Judith Becker, "On Defining Sets of Pieces," *In Theory Only* 1/6 (1975): 17–19 (see also Charles J. Smith's reply to Becker, ibid., pp. 19–20); Lawrence Kramer, *Music and Poetry: the Nineteenth Century and After* (Berkeley and Los Angeles, 1984), pp. 99–103; and Anselm Gerhard, "Reflexionen über den Beginn in der Musik: Eine neue Deutung von Frédéric Chopins *Préludes* opus 28," *Deutsche Musik im Wegekreuz zwischen Polen und Frankreich,* ed. Christoph-Hellmut Mahling (in press).

In addition to the historical and formal arguments I will make later in this chapter, I would also fault on methodological grounds the positions of those who argue for unity on the basis of motivic repetition (this applies also to Kramer, who lobbies for a harmonic process as the determining feature that assures the coherence of the set). Briefly stated, the reductive methods used to draw the motives out of generally rather complex textures are highly suspect: critics identify pitches as being motivically significant only when they suit the analytical purpose at hand. The assumption of unity governs which notes are selected; in this circumstance, one could show any group of pieces to be "unified." And even if one grants that a motive recurs in several preludes, this scarcely ensures "unity." Rather the varied contexts of the motives can equally well accentuate the dissimilarity of the different preludes.

On these methodological points, see Leonard B. Meyer, *Explaining Music* (Berkeley and Los Angeles, 1973), pp. 59–79.

32. Not surprisingly, this practice apparently took hold around the turn of the century. James Huneker mentioned approvingly that the Russian pianist Arthur Friedheim played all of op. 28 through in concert (*Chopin: The Man and His Music* [New York, 1900; reprint ed., 1966], p. 131). And James Methuen-Campbell cites Cortot and Busoni as responsible for popularizing performances of the complete set (*Chopin Playing: From the Composer to the Present Day* [London, 1981], p. 23). Pianists apparently mirrored the actions of composers, who at this time seemed particularly concerned to articulate motivic connections across large expanses of music.

33. The key word, "individual," is curiously missing in the translations of both Paul Rosenfeld (in Schumann, *On Music and Musicians,* p. 138) and Edward Lowinsky (in Frédéric Chopin, *Preludes, Opus 28,* ed. Thomas Higgins [New York, 1973], p. 91).

34. Here too the most commonly cited English translation quite tellingly reveals recent attitudes. Thomas Higgins (Chopin, *Preludes,* pp. 91–92) renders Liszt's "ce ne sont pas seulement . . . des morceaux destinés à être joués en guise d'introduction à d'autres morceaux" as "they are not merely . . . introductions to other *morceaux.*" In addition to misguidedly paraphrasing the last portion of the quotation, Higgins's "merely" imputes an unduly negative connotation to Liszt's remarks: it is modern critics who would scorn the "merely" functional aspects of the prelude, not critics of Chopin's day.

35. Léon Escudier, in *La France musicale,* 2 May 1841, p. 155.

36. Friedrich Kalkbrenner, in his *Traité d'harmonie du pianiste: Principes rationnels de la modulation, pour apprendre à préluder et à improviser* (Paris, n.d.[1849]), p. 39, may have reinforced this perceptual model when he named Chopin (along with Mozart, Beethoven, Moscheles, Mendelssohn, and others) as the "most distinguished improvisers that have existed," in a context where "improvisation" also meant "preluding."

37. The program is reproduced in Maria Mirska and Władysław Hordyński, eds., *Chopin na obczyźnie* (Cracow, 1965), p. 302.

38. Chopin commenced his recital in Edinburgh on 4 October 1848 with the same "Andante et Impromptu," and a review in the *Edinburgh Evening Courant* of 7 October 1848 may further support the case for the "Andante" being op. 28, no. 8. The reviewer wrote: "The first piece was an 'Andante et Impromptu'; the opening movement being in three parts, with the theme standing out in alto relievo, as it were, from the maze of harmony with which it was surrounded" (I cite from the reprint of the review in William G. Atwood, *Fryderyk Chopin: Pianist from Warsaw* [New York, 1987], p. 256). The reviewer's description of the theme better fits the Prelude, where the theme sounds amidst a flurry of rapid fioriture, than the *Andante spianato,* where the theme constitutes the top voice in normal pianistic treble-dominated homophony. And the Prelude can be heard as "three-part," in the sense of statement-departure-return, whereas the *Andante spianato* is, properly speaking, not laid out in three-part form.

39. Although one might construe this listing to mean that each etude was preceded by a prelude, evidence from reviews of the recital and from elsewhere in the program—there is another mention of "Préludes"—indicates that Chopin twice played preludes in multiple groupings of some sort. Eigeldinger, *Chopin: Pianist and Teacher,* p. 293, suggests that Chopin offered a total of four preludes played in pairs.

40. I would recommend in particular Rose Rosengard Subotnik, "Romantic Music as Post-Kantian Critique: Classicism, Romanticism, and the Concept of the Semiotic Universe," in Kingsley Price, ed., *On Criticizing Music* (Baltimore, 1981), pp. 74–98; Kramer, *Music and Poetry,* pp. 91–124; Jim

Samson, *The Music of Chopin* (London, 1985), pp. 73–80 and 142–158; Lawrence Kramer, "Impossible Objects: Apparitions, Reclining Nudes, and Chopin's Prelude in A Minor," in his *Music as Cultural Practice 1800–1900* (Berkeley and Los Angeles, 1990), pp. 72–101; and Eigeldinger, "Twenty-Four Preludes, opus 28," pp. 167–179.

41. My discussion of closure is indebted in many respects to V. Kofi Agawu's excellent "Concepts of Closure and Chopin's Opus 28," *Music Theory Spectrum* 9 (1987): 1–17.

42. Ibid., p. 12.

43. Lawrence Kramer, in *Music and Poetry,* pp. 91–124, frames a discussion of these aesthetic issues as they manifest themselves in Chopin and Shelley in terms of his provocative concept of the "transit of identity."

6. Chopin in the Marketplace

1. In my Ph.D. dissertation, "The Chopin Sources: Variants and Versions in Later Manuscripts and Printed Editions," (University of Chicago, 1982), pp. 12–37, I examine comprehensively the development of copyright law in England, France, and the German-speaking states in the first half of the nineteenth century.

2. This statement is not entirely true when applied to France, for there was at least some legal precedent for still maintaining exclusive property rights when a work had been registered abroad first. In *Chaumerot v. C. Michaud,* the Cour de Cassation upheld on 30 January 1818 the copyright of a Frenchman who, having first published a work abroad, reprinted it in France, meeting the legal requirements for copyright in France before an unauthorized edition appeared. See the summary of the case printed in L. M. Devilleneuve and A. A. Carette, *Recueil général des lois et des arrêts,* 156 vols. (Paris, 1801–1964), ser. 1, vol. 5, pt. 1, pp. 415–416.

3. See the summary of *Cocks v. Purday* (2 Car. & K. 269 and 5 C. B. 860), a case over the infringement of copyright in "Der Elfin Walzer" by Joseph Labitsky, published in *The English Reports,* 176 vols. (Edinburgh, 1900–1930), vol. 175 (1930), pp. 111–112, and vol. 136 (1913), pp. 1118–1128 and 1177–1178.

That before 1848 considerable confusion surrounded the commonsensical system of simultaneous publication is demonstrated in a fascinating correspondence and series of editorials in the pages of *The Musical World* from March to December, 1841. The correspondents' debate is wide-ranging, touching on the status of music as a presumed "universal" language, on the ontological status of the musical work of art (in its forms both with and without words), on the kinds of gains or losses that the English public might enjoy or suffer under the system, on copyright litigation recently settled and currently under way, and so forth.

Remarkably, the debate even crossed over into a feud concerning Chopin, occasioned by the newspaper's negative review of his Mazurkas, op. 41 (28 October 1841, pp. 276–277). The reply by Chopin's English publisher Wessel (4 November 1841, pp. 293–294) initiated a series of letters from a number of correspondents, some defending Chopin, others denigrating him (only the original review and Wessel's first reply seem to have been noticed by Chopin scholars). One correspondent, though, noting that Wessel had mentioned having "purchase[d] the copyright" to Chopin's works, brought the two debates together (18 November 1841, p. 325). Portions of Wessel's reply are worth quoting here: "Sir,—Your correspondent has misinterpreted our meaning with regard to the copyright of the works of M. Chopin. Some years ago we purchased several of his compositions, which met with such success both at home and on the Continent, that we were induced to treat with him for *the whole of his future writings,* not one of which appeared abroad before they had become our property, though 'Beta' [one of the correspondents] would insinuate that they were published abroad previous to our becoming possessed of them, which is entirely erroneous. We were well aware that, in enforcing our claims to the proprietorship of these works, it would be necessary for them to appear in print *simultaneously at home and on the Continent,* to which technical legality we have circumstantially adhered" (25 November 1841, p. 343). To which another debater replied: "The *technical legality of 'printing simultaneously at home and on the Continent'* is new to me. Where is the expression (stated or implied) to be found?" (9 December 1841, p. 372). And, as we will see, Wessel hardly spoke the truth in claiming to have "circumstantially adhered" to this "technical legality."

4. I have twice reproduced these dates in tabular form; see "The Chopin Sources," pp. 42–44, and "Chopin in the Marketplace: Aspects of the Music Publishing Industry in the First Half of the Nineteenth Century," *Notes* 39 (1983): 537–538. Most of these dates have been incorporated into the individual entries for works in Józef M. Chomiński and Teresa Dalila Turło, *Katalog Dzieł Fryderyka Chopina / A Catalogue of the Works of Frederick Chopin* (Cracow and Warsaw, 1990), as well as in a synoptic table on pp. 42–44.

Some of these dates may conceal some simultaneous issues with England, for only the month was written across the title pages when editions were deposited for copyright purposes at the Paris Conservatoire.

5. Some of the differences in registration dates must also have arisen from lax business habits. From an unpublished letter of 15 November 1843 to Breitkopf & Härtel (excerpts printed in sale catalogue 172 [1972] of Hans

Schneider, where it is item number 33), we know that Chopin was attempting to set the date of publication for opp. 52–54 at about 15 December. The works were registered with the Dépôt légal on 14 December (indicating a small change in the original plans), but did not find their way into the Stationers' Hall ledgers until 1 March 1844. Chopin's English publisher Wessel, as we will see, was not terribly conscientious in running his shop, and for reasons unknown, perhaps because of delays in engraving the works, he must have allowed his date of publication to lag behind the others by two and a half months.

6. As when he wrote, in reference to dealings with his publishers, "I shit on all of that"; see letter of 25 April 1839 to Julian Fontana in Fryderyk Chopin, *Korespondencja Fryderyka Chopina,* ed. Bronisław Edward Sydow, 2 vols. (Warsaw, 1955), vol. 1, p. 347. Translations of this letter inevitably have opted for a coy rendition of the crucial word. In Fryderyk Chopin, *Selected Correspondence of Fryderyk Chopin,* ed. Arthur Hedley (New York, Toronto, and London, 1963), p. 176, Hedley prints the passage as "to hell with it all."

7. A notable exception is Jan Ekier, *Wstęp do Wydania Narodowego Dzieł Fryderyka Chopina. Część I: Zagadnienia Edytorskie* (Cracow, 1974).

8. See Simon Nowell-Smith, *International Copyright Law and the Publisher in the Reign of Queen Victoria* (Oxford, 1968), pp. 50–51. A useful discussion of the contractual options available to nineteenth-century authors is found in Robert L. Patten, *Charles Dickens and His Publishers* (Oxford, 1978), pp. 18–27.

9. The suggestion that plates were shipped abroad comes in the case summary of *Boosey v. Purday* (4 Ex. 145) in 1849. The trial concerned infringement of copyright in the sale of airs from Bellini's *La Sonnambula.* In the description of the facts of the case, one reads: "On the 9th of June, 1831, Ricordi assigned the opera, by deed, to the plaintiff, who had ten airs entered at the Stationers' Hall at 11 a.m. on the 10th of June, 1831, and copies were also deposited at the British Museum. These airs were exposed to sale on the same day, between twelve and one o'clock. They were printed from the foreign plates, the only additions thereto being the words 'Entered at Stationers' Hall' and 'London: Boosey & Co.' " See *English Reports,* vol. 154 (1915), p. 1160.

10. The history of Chopin's initial venture into the world of simultaneous publication is traced in Zofia Lissa, "Chopin im Lichte des Briefwechsels von Verlegern seiner Zeit gesehen," *Fontes Artis Musicae* 7 (1960): 46–57. Lissa based her discussion on letters found in Richard Linnemann, *Fr. Kistner 1823/ 1923: Ein Beitrag zur Geschichte des deutschen Musik-Verlages* (Leipzig, 1923), pp. 49–54.

11. See letter of 21 December 1832 from Farrenc to Kistner; Lissa, "Chopin im Lichte," pp. 51–52.

12. An excellent and detailed account of Schlesinger's career as a music publisher is Anik Devriès, "Un éditeur de musique 'à la tête ardente.' Maurice Schlesinger," *Fontes Artis Musicae* 27 (1980): 125–136. Schlesinger enjoys some renown among scholars of literature for having served as the model for Jacques Arnoux in Gustave Flaubert's *L'éducation sentimentale.*

13. From Farrenc's letter to Kistner of 17 April 1832; Lissa, "Chopin im Lichte," p. 49. The letter does not mention opus numbers, but identification of the works presents no difficulties.

14. See Lissa, "Chopin im Lichte," pp. 48–52.

15. The concerto deleted from the contract was Chopin's earliest, in F minor, and the concerto retained was his latest, in E minor, which Chopin had featured in his debut recitals in Paris. (On the E-Minor Concerto in Chopin's first Parisian recitals, see Jean-Jacques Eigeldinger, "Les premiers concerts de Chopin à Paris (1832–1838): Essai de mise au point," in *Music in Paris in the Eighteen-Thirties,* ed. Peter Bloom [Stuyvesant, N.Y., 1987], pp. 251–297.) Thus the two concertos came to be published in reverse chronological order not because the composer lost the parts on the way to Paris, as has often been postulated (see, for example, Gastone Belotti, *F. Chopin l'uomo,* 3 vols. [Milan and Rome, 1974], vol. 1, p. 221), but for sound business reasons: two concertos released at the same time would glut the market and harm each other's sales.

16. See letter of 2 November 1832; Lissa, "Chopin im Lichte," pp. 54–55.

17. See letter of 2 February 1833; ibid., p. 55. Later in this chapter I will examine the implications of the different modes of shipping Chopin's music to Germany.

18. In the case of op. 46, Chopin confirmed explicitly in a letter of 18 October 1841 to Fontana (Chopin, *Korespondencja,* ed. Sydow, vol. 2, p. 44) that he wished his friend's manuscript to be used by Schlesinger.

19. Excepted from this rule-of-thumb are cases where one French publisher purchased the assets of another and used the plates from the old firm in preparing the new edition. See, for example, the Rondo, op. 16, and the Mazurkas, op. 17, which were first issued by Pleyel, but then purchased by Schlesinger when the former went out of business in 1834.

20. See letters of 2 February and 16 April 1833; Lissa, "Chopin im Lichte," pp. 55–56.

21. See Thomas Higgins, "Tempo and Character in Chopin," *The Musical Quarterly* 59 (1973): 108–109.

22. Letter of 8 August 1839 to Fontana; Chopin, *Korespondencja,* ed. Sydow, vol. 1, p. 354.

23. Letter of 1 November 1841 to Fontana; ibid., vol. 2, p. 48.

24. Letter of 2 July 1852 from Fontana to Chopin's sister Ludwika Jędrzejewicz, as printed in Ekier, *Wstęp*, pp. 105–106.

25. Chopin, *Korespondencja*, ed. Sydow, vol. 2, p. 340.

26. Jan Ekier, *Fryderyk Chopin: Ballady. Kommentarze źródłowe* (Cracow, 1970), p. 31.

27. Bertrand Jaeger, in "Quelques nouveaux noms d'élèves de Chopin," *Revue de musicologie* 64 (1978): 83, and in "Les manuscrits de Chopin," *Schweizerische Musikzeitung/Revue musicale suisse* 119 (1979): 196, claims that the Scherbatoff exemplars of the Sonata, op. 35 and the Impromptu, op. 36 are printer's proofs. In fact, the exemplars are each early states of the first edition; Chopin altered each state shortly after publication. The autograph additions in the Scherbatoff exemplars only bring these exemplars into accordance with his later thoughts. (And he continued to make alterations in still later states of both these editions.) Deposit copies identical to the Scherbatoff exemplars in their unaltered condition are found in the Bibliothèque Nationale. Besides this bibliographical evidence, Jaeger's assumption falters on social grounds as well: surely the composer would not have presented a printer's proof as a gift to a countess.

28. The Breitkopf edition also prints the graces as quarter notes.

29. Chomiński and Turło, *Katalog*, p. 145, record the publication date in Leipzig as June 1840. The work was first advertised with a price on 1 July 1840; see the *Allgemeine musikalische Zeitung*, 1 July 1840, cols. 567–68. It is important to distinguish between those advertisements including the prices, indicating that a work was actually available, and those without, announcing intent to publish. Thus op. 37 first was advertised in the *AMZ*, along with opp. 35–41, on 5 February 1840, col. 119, but without a price.

30. A further argument against the state of the earlier exemplar reflecting only the order in which the engraver worked comes from the second Nocturne, where it is filled with phrase marks (although the later copy adds more) and the one pedal mark that exists in the French edition (as opposed to the heavily pedaled German edition) is shared by both the early and late exemplars.

31. The matter of the multiple states of the Troupenas edition of op. 37 is more complicated than I suspected when I first wrote this chapter. Krzysztof Grabowski, in his meticulously researched "L'oeuvre de Frédéric Chopin dans l'édition française" (Thèse de doctorat, University of Paris IV–Sorbonne, 1992), pp. 96–98, documents yet a third state of the Troupenas edition in the copy once owned by Chopin's student Camille Dubois-O'Meara. Additionally, Grabowksi demonstrates that all of the editions that Chopin issued with Troupenas (opp. 35–41, 43) exist in at least two states (pp. 93–101),

which suggests that particular difficulties must have attended the process of publication with Chopin. Perhaps this explains in part why Chopin never published anything again with Troupenas after the Tarantella, op. 43.

32. The Breitkopf & Härtel *Stichvorlage* of the Berceuse, op. 57 (Warsaw, Biblioteka Narodowa) is mainly in an unknown copyist's hand, and there is reason to believe that a manuscript for the Nocturne, op. 55, no. 1 (Cracow, Biblioteka Jagiellońska) in the same copyist's hand (both manuscripts contain entries by Chopin as well) was originally intended for use by a publisher.

Explicit testimony that the composer read his own proofs comes in a letter to Franchomme of 30 August 1846 concerning opp. 60–62: "Also ask Brandus to send me two proofs, of which I can keep one." Chopin, *Korespondencja,* ed. Sydow, vol. 2, p. 398.

33. Accurate versions of the French originals of these letters appear in my dissertation, "The Chopin Sources," pp. 62–63. The originals of the two letters are housed, respectively, in the Bibliothèque Nationale and in the Stiftelsen Musikkulturens Främjande, Stockholm.

34. Of course, the German firm knew full well that it was paying more than its French counterparts; see the letter from Heinrich Probst, Breitkopf's agent in Paris before Maho, dated 2 December 1839, excerpted later in this chapter.

35. See the list of works purchased from the assets of Pleyel in the *Gazette musicale de Paris,* 29 June 1834, p. 212. Schlesinger evidently purchased the manuscript of the Waltz, op. 18 as well. (See Anik Devriès and François Lesure, *Dictionnaire des éditeurs de musique français.* 2 vols. [Geneva, 1979], vol. 1, p. 128. The inclusion of the Preludes, op. 28 in the list of works sold to Schlesinger is surely an error, for the Preludes did not exist as an entity until 1838.) Pleyel may also have owned the rights to the Bolero, op. 19, for the entry for this work in the *Bibliographie de la France,* 1 November 1834, p. 204, lists Pleyel as the publisher. Presumably Pleyel would have sold the rights to Prillip, the actual publisher of the work.

36. Advertisement in the *Revue et Gazette musicale de Paris,* 15 November 1846, p. 368.

37. Grabowski, "L'oeuvre de Frédéric Chopin dans l'édition française," pp. 102–103.

38. Chopin had issued works with Haslinger and Mechetti of Vienna prior to his first contact with Leipzig, but the Viennese works were not issued simultaneously abroad.

39. Farrenc to Kistner, 17 April 1832; Lissa, "Chopin im Lichte," p. 49.

40. A manuscript for the Ballade, op. 23 once existed, but now is evidently lost. See the letter of 1 February 1878 from Breitkopf to Chopin's sister, Isabel Barcińska, printed in Krystyna Kobylańska, *Rękopisy Utworów Chopin. Katalog,* 2 vols. (Cracow, 1977), vol. 1, p. 126. A full manuscript score for the

Concerto, op. 21 (Warsaw, Biblioteka Narodowa) was also once in the Breit-kopf archives, but it is a strange manuscript indeed, for it lacks all the telltale engraver's marks that would identify it as a *Stichvorlage*. But why else would it have been in the archive? Kobylańska's assertion, *Katalog*, vol. 1, p. 117, that the manuscript served as a *Stichvorlage* for the Schlesinger edition is plainly wrong, and results from a misreading of the information on the title page. Perhaps the manuscript, which bears signs of use, was rented out to conductors for performance. Final judgment must await a detailed study of the manuscript.

41. Wilhelm Hitzig, " 'Pariser Briefe'. Ein Beitrag zur Arbeit des deutschen Musikverlags aus den Jahren 1833–1840," *Der Bär: Jahrbuch von Breitkopf & Härtel 1929/30* (Leipzig, 1930), pp. 27–73. A translation of and commentary on this correspondence has recently appeared in *Breitkopf und Härtel in Paris: The Letters of their Agent Heinrich Probst between 1833 and 1840*, ed. and trans. Hans Lenneberg (Stuyvesant, N.Y., 1990); Lenneberg also reproduces the original German versions of the letters. Some of Lenneberg's translations improve on my original efforts, and I have at times modified these accordingly. Probst writes in a wonderfully casual, non-literary German, and I have made every effort to preserve this style in the translations.

Hans-Martin Plesske, "Das Leipziger Musikverlagswesen und seine Bezie-hungen zu einigen namhaften Komponisten: ein Beitrag zur Geschichte des Musikalienhandels im 19. und zu Beginn des 20. Jahrhunderts" (Ph.D. diss., University of Leipzig, 1974), pp. 162–167, treats briefly Chopin's relations with his German publishers, and includes some citations from the Probst-Breitkopf correspondence.

42. Hitzig, "Briefe," p. 33.

43. Ibid.

44. Ibid., p. 34. Hitzig claims that the letter was written by Härtel to Probst, and, confusingly, gives three dates for the letter (Leipzig, 11 and 29 November 1833, and Paris, 21 November 1833). But the contents of the letter, which refer to recent events in Paris (among which was the latest Berlioz concert), point clearly to Probst as the author.

45. Ibid., p. 35.

46. Ibid., p. 36.

47. Ibid., pp. 37–38. *"Le Pianiste"* refers to a journal devoted to pianists, piano music, and pianos that published for two short years in 1834–1835.

48. Ibid., p. 40. In the last sentence, Probst actually wrote "Kistner," but he clearly meant to say "Peters."

49. Ibid.

50. Ibid., p. 41.

51. Letter of 22 December 1830 to Chopin's family, and letters of [1834]

and 11 April 1835 from Nicholas to Fryderyk; Fryderyk Chopin, *Korespondencja Fryderyka Chopina z Rodziną,* ed. Krystyna Kobylańska (Warsaw, 1972), pp. 67, 96, 104.

52. Hitzig, "Briefe," pp. 41–42.

53. Ibid., p. 42.

54. Ibid., p. 43.

55. Lissa, "Chopin im Lichte," pp. 46–47, alludes briefly to these receipts; Ekier misinterprets the receipt of 9 January 1836 (for op. 23) in *Ballady,* p. 12; and a few have been included in publications of Chopin's correspondence. I have published them in the appendix to "Chopin in the Marketplace," pp. 819–824. No mention of them is found in Oskar von Hase, *Breitkopf & Härtel, 5.* Auflage, 2 vols. (Wiesbaden, 1968), vol. 2, pt. 1, pp. 139–142 (the section on Chopin).

56. A similar problem exists when Chopin in letters used the word *manuscrit.* See Ekier, *Wstęp,* pp. 95–96.

57. Hitzig, "Briefe," p. 44.

58. Ibid., p. 45.

59. Ibid.

60. Ibid., p. 46. The Nocturnes, op. 32, were published by Schlesinger in Berlin.

61. Ibid., p. 48.

62. Ibid., p. 52.

63. Ibid., p. 53.

64. Ibid.

65. Ibid., p. 55.

66. Ibid.

67. Ibid., p. 56.

68. I know of one other instance when Chopin sent proofs to Germany after 1835. For the first and only time in his career, Chopin arranged to publish one of his works with the Parisian firm of Pacini, and it was likely this unique circumstance along with a rapidly approaching deadline that induced Chopin to recommend the following procedure to Breitkopf: "As Mr. Pacini is publishing the 30th of the month a *Waltz* by me in *Les-cent-et-un,* I think I am doing the right thing in sending you a proof. I hope that the publication will not suffer difficulties—the price remaining in proportion to our last arrangements"; letter of 18 June 1840, Chopin, *Korespondencja,* ed. Sydow, vol. 2, p. 333.

69. Hitzig, "Briefe," p. 57.

70. Ibid., p. 59.

71. Ibid., p. 65.

72. See Chopin's letter of 30 June 1835 to Breitkopf, printed in facsimile in Maria Mirska and Władysław Hordyński, eds., *Chopin na obczyźnie* (Cracow, 1965), p. 174, and published in Gastone Belotti, "Il problema delle date dei Preludi di Chopin," *Rivista Italiana di Musicologica* 5 (1970): 165. This article is also reprinted in his *Saggi sull'arte e sull'opera di F. Chopin* (Bologna, 1977), pp. 191–247; Chopin's letter appears on p. 197.

73. See Félicien Mallefille, "A M. F. Chopin, sur sa Ballade Polonaise," *Revue et Gazette musicale de Paris*, 9 September 1838, pp. 362–364.

74. Hitzig, "Briefe," p. 65.

75. Ibid., p. 67.

76. Ibid., p. 66.

77. Ibid., p. 67.

78. Ibid., pp. 68–69. Lenneberg's translation unaccountably stops after the sentence "No, he said, 3500 francs or nothing"; *Breitkopf und Härtel in Paris*, p. 69.

79. Heller recounted to Niecks that Breitkopf & Härtel wrote to their Paris agent (Probst) that they would continue to publish Chopin's works even though, given his by no means large sales, he charged too much. (See Frederick Niecks, *Frederick Chopin as a Man and Musician*, 2 vols. [London, 1902; reprint ed., New York, 1973], vol. 2, pp. 116–117). But the fact that Breitkopf continued to pay these prices argues against low sales.

80. Hitzig, "Briefe," p. 70.

81. Chopin, *Korespondencja*, ed. Sydow, vol. 1, p. 454.

82. Hitzig, "Briefe," p. 71.

83. Ibid., p. 72.

84. Chopin did however see proofs of his early Sonata in C Minor that the Viennese publisher Haslinger sent him with the hope that the composer would correct them and approve their publication. See letter of August 1845 to his family, in Chopin, *Korespondencja z Rodziną*, ed. Kobylańska, p. 147.

85. One such instance occurs in the manuscript for the Mazurka, op. 30, no. 2 (Warsaw, Biblioteka Narodowa), where, among other places, editorial accidentals are found in the right hand in measure 5, beat 3, measure 22, beat 1, and measure 39, beat 1 (in the grace note).

Perhaps the most famous emendation by a Breitkopf "editor" was to add repeat dots to the double bar that marks the beginning of the "Doppio movimento" of the first movement of the Sonata in B-flat Minor, op. 35. These dots appear in no other source, and are quite wrong: Chopin intended the repeat of the exposition to commence with the opening "Grave."

86. A copy of the earlier state is housed in the Joseph Regenstein Library of the University of Chicago. A facsimile of the later state appears in Jan

Bogdan Drath, comp. and ed., *Waltzes of Fryderyk Chopin: Sources. Volume I: Waltzes Published During Chopin's Lifetime* (Kingsville, 1979), pp. 120–127.

87. See the discussion of "Vertrieb" in von Hase, *Breitkopf & Härtel,* vol. 1, pp. 193–202. The figures cited in these pages are for a period roughly ten to fifteen years before the peak of Chopin's career; if anything, Breitkopf's size and scope only increased in the 1830s and 1840s.

88. See, for example, Nicholas Chopin to Fryderyk, 13 April 1833, in Chopin, *Korespondencja z Rodziną,* ed. Kobylańska, p. 88.

89. Italian editions of Chopin's music are treated in Gastone Belotti, "La fortuna in Italia dell'opera di Chopin durante la vita del compositore," *Saggi sull'arte e sull'opera di F. Chopin,* pp. 410–451.

90. See the set of receipts for the three Etudes published in François-Joseph Fétis and Ignaz Moscheles, *Méthode de Méthodes de piano* (Paris, 1840). Two are published in Chopin, *Korespondencja,* ed. Sydow, vol. 1, p. 453 (19 November 1839) and vol. 1, p. 454 (1 December 1839). The latter prints incorrectly "Cinq cents francs" for the proper "Deux cents francs." The third receipt, dated 6 December 1839, is mentioned in Thomas Higgins, "Whose Chopin?" *19th-Century Music* 5 (1981): 69. Belotti, "La fortuna in Italia," pp. 435–451, finds several instances of Italian editions appearing to derive from French editions, among them the Lucca print of the Preludes, op. 28 and the Pasquale Artaria edition of the Waltz, op. 18. He adds, though, that it is often difficult to ascertain precisely which edition served as the basis, because the Italian edition often contains additional "editorial" emendations not found in either the French or German editions.

91. Maurice J. E. Brown, "Chopin and his English Publisher," *Music & Letters* 39 (1958): 363–371; Brown, *Chopin: An Index of His Works in Chronological Order,* 2d ed. (London, 1972).

92. See Arthur Hedley, "Some Observations on the Autograph Sources of Chopin's Works," *The Book of the First International Musicological Congress Devoted to the Works of Frederick Chopin, Warszawa 16th–22nd February 1960,* ed. Zofia Lissa (Warsaw, 1963), p. 476.

93. These documents were conserved as a group in the Ashdown archives in London when I worked with them in 1979; in recent years some of them have appeared piecemeal for sale in auction catalogues. The loss of integrity of this remarkable collection is unfortunate.

94. Letter of November 1832; see Chopin, *Korespondencja z Rodziną,* ed. Kobylańska, p. 215.

95. The other is an undated note to Novello, published in Dieter Zimmerschied, "Die Kammermusik Johann Nepomuk Hummels" (Innaugural-Dissertation, Johannes Gutenberg-Universität, Mainz, 1966), p. 521.

96. The letter is printed in its entirety and in the original German in Kallberg, "The Chopin Sources," pp. 114–115. It tumbled out of a ledger of copyright assignments in the Wessel archives while I was visiting the Ashdown offices.

97. See Dieter Zimmerschied, *Thematisches Verzeichnis der Werke von Johann Nepomuk Hummel* (Hofheim am Taunus, 1971), p. 188.

98. Chopin, *Korespondencja,* ed. Sydow, vol. 2, pp. 21–23.

99. Ibid., p. 361.

100. Letters of 9 October 1845 and 30 August 1846 to Léo, and 13 September 1846 to Franchomme; see ibid., pp. 391, 398, 401.

101. Ibid., p. 401.

102. See Brown, "Chopin and his English Publishers," p. 369.

103. All the contracts are reproduced in Appendix B of Kallberg, "The Chopin Sources."

104. On the London trip, see Belotti, *F. Chopin l'uomo,* vol. 1, pp. 590–593.

105. Letter of 23 April 1840; Chopin, *Korespondencja,* ed. Sydow, vol. 2, p. 8.

106. Ekier, *Ballady,* pp. 27, 30–31.

107. Jan Ekier, in the notes to his edition of the Impromptus, also concludes that the English and French editions were engraved from separate manuscript *Stichvorlagen*; see Frédéric Chopin, *Impromptus,* ed. Ekier (Vienna, 1977), pp. xvii–xviii.

108. The original French version of the receipt appears in Kallberg, "The Chopin Sources," pp. 128–129.

109. See the letter of 18 September 1841 to Fontana; Chopin, *Korespondencja,* ed. Sydow, vol. 2, p. 37. Examples of the offending titles include "Murmures de la Seine" (Nocturnes, op. 9), "Le Banquet infernal" (Scherzo, op. 20), "Les Plaintives" (Nocturnes, op. 27), "Les Soupirs" (Nocturnes, op. 37), and "La Gracieuse" (Ballade, op. 38).

110. Chopin, *Korespondencja,* ed. Sydow, vol. 1, p. 357.

111. The letter is published in the original French in Hanna Wróblewska-Straus, " 'Za miesiąc z Paryża więcej Wam napiszę,' " *Ruch Muzyczny,* 17 December 1978, p. 17. Wróblewska-Straus maintains that the letter "doubtless" refers to op. 41 and the "Trois nouvelles Etudes." However, the Wessel contracts prove that Chopin could only be writing about opp. 41 and 42—see the contract of III.40. In any case, the Etudes should not have entered into the question, for they were published not by Wessel, but by Chappell.

112. See letters of 18 September 1841 to Fontana and 5 October 1841 to Schlesinger; Chopin, *Korespondencja,* ed. Sydow, vol. 2, pp. 37, 342.

113. Chopin, *Korespondencja,* ed. Sydow, vol. 2, p. 41.

114. From a letter of 9 October 1841; ibid., p. 42.

115. Ibid., p. 45.

116. Letter of 3 December 1841; ibid., p. 343.

117. It is interesting to note that op. 50 was included in this contract, even though it could not have been ready for publication in January 1842. The other six works, opp. 44–49, were registered in Stationers' Hall just six days after the signing of the contract, or on 20 January 1842, whereas op. 50 was not entered until 21 July 1842 (and not until 14 September 1842 in the Dépôt légal).

118. The letter forms part of the collection of Moscheles correspondence in the Bibliothèque Nationale. The complete original (in German) appears in Kallberg, "The Chopin Sources," pp. 133–135.

119. For evidence relating to opp. 46, 48, and 49, see the critical commentaries attached to Frédéric Chopin, *Nocturnes,* ed. Jan Ekier (Vienna, 1980), pp. xl–xli; and Frédéric Chopin, *Klavierstücke,* ed. Ernst Herttrich (Munich, 1978), "Kritischer Bericht," pp. 2–4.

120. Ekier, *Ballady,* p. 54. The variants appear in measures 35 and 97. Ekier cites as other Wessel variants the printing of grace notes with two flags rather than the slashed single flag in Schlesinger. But all Wessel editions print the grace notes thus; here we have an example of house policy rather than of textual variance.

121. Chopin, *Klavierstücke,* "Kritischer Bericht," pp. 2–3.

122. Grabowski, "L'oeuvre de Frédéric Chopin dans l'édition française," p. 89. Grabowski looks closely at the multiple states of the French editions of opp. 44, 46–49, on pp. 88–92.

7. The Chopin "Problem"

1. See Jerome J. McGann, *A Critique of Modern Textual Criticism* (Chicago, 1983), pp. 40–44. For a reply to some of the issues raised in McGann's provocative book, see G. Thomas Tanselle, "Historicism and Critical Editing," *Studies in Bibliography* 39 (1986): 1–46, especially 19–27.

2. McGann amply discusses this point in *A Critique of Modern Textual Criticism,* pp. 51–94.

3. On 30 August 1846, Chopin wrote to Auguste Franchomme concerning the Nocturnes (as well as the Barcarolle and Polonaise-Fantasy): "Also ask Brandus to send me two proofs, so that I can keep one." See Fryderyk Chopin, *Korespondencja Fryderyka Chopina,* ed. Bronisław Edward Sydow, 2 vols. (Warsaw, 1955), vol. 2, p. 398.

4. See Chopin's letters of 30 August 1846 to Franchomme and to Auguste Léo in Chopin, *Korespondencja,* ed. Sydow, vol. 2, p. 396–398, as well as

that of the same date to Wojciech Grzymała, in Hanna Wróblewska-Straus, " 'Kochany Delacroix list Ci ode mnie duży zawiezie,' " *Ruch Muzyczny* XXIV, 13 (1980): 16–18.

5. Basing the primary text of an edition on the French autograph is clearly problematic, since this solution sanctions a version Chopin expressly rejected for publication. The variant readings that are found in this autograph might more appropriately be signaled in a critical commentary.

6. I have discussed some of the musical ramifications of Chopin's revision in the Nocturne in B Major in "The Chopin Sources: Variants and Versions in Later Manuscripts and Printed Editions" (Ph.D. diss., University of Chicago, 1982), pp. 248–275 and 309–310.

7. Some basic information about the chronological and genetic relationships among these autographs is clear. The sketch was completed by late spring 1847, the Brandus *Stichvorlage* by June 1847. The Caraman autograph dates from early July 1847. Less is known about the other two autographs, but it is safe to assume that they were given as gifts before the work was published, hence before late 1847 or early 1848. As to genetic relationships, textual analysis suggests that the sketch served as the basis at different times for each of the remaining autographs. I document these assertions in "The Chopin Sources," pp. 275–301.

8. Example 7.2 is derived from Silvain Guignard's excellent work, *Frédéric Chopins Walzer: eine text- und stilkritische Studie*, Collection d'études musicologiques/Sammlung musikwissenschaftlicher Abhandlungen, vol. 70 (Baden-Baden, 1986), pp. 230–239.

9. The Waltz in F Minor, op. 70, no. 2, was one of Chopin's favorite gifts: he presented autographs of it to acquaintances at least five times.

10. A pristinely clear reproduction of the altered pages of the Stirling edition appears in Frédéric Chopin, *Oeuvres pour piano: Fac-similé de l'exemplaire de Jane W. Stirling avec annotations et corrections de l'auteur (Ancienne collection Edouard Ganche)*, introduction by Jean-Michel Nectoux, preface by Jean-Jacques Eigeldinger (Paris, 1982), pp. 34–35.

There can be little doubt that Chopin himself made the changes. The B-major chord added to the downbeat of measure 54 is clearly in his hand. Moreover, the x's placed in Stirling's score at the end of measure 35 and the beginning of measure 54, which informed her which measures should be joined in the revision, correspond to signs of connection that Chopin frequently used in his sketches.

11. For a discussion of this concept, see Georg von Dadelsen, "Die 'Fassung letzter Hand' in der Musik," *Acta Musicologica* 33 (1961): 1–14.

12. Chopin, *Oeuvres pour piano*, pp. 195–196.

13. For some editors, the matter is further complicated when the passage

recurs in measures 34–36; some sources offer different readings in the two passages. But alternate phrasing and rhythmic variations of otherwise identical passages are a hallmark of Chopin's style: the later passage cannot ordinarily be used as evidence in determining the reading of the earlier one.

14. My own critical judgment, as readers may tell from my arguments in Chapter 4 (and I explored the issue at much greater length throughout my dissertation, "The Chopin Sources") is that musicians would not find as much that is musically effective in Chopin's early, "private" readings as they would in, say, Schubert's or Schumann's. The cases are really very different: with Schubert and Schumann, a significant span of time typically elapsed between successive versions of works (the versions of Schubert's *Der Jüngling am Bache* date from 1812, 1815, and 1819, and more than a decade passed between Schumann's first, radical versions of many of his early piano works and the more conventional revisions he authored shortly before mental debilitation ended his career). With Chopin, differing versions more often appeared within a single, circumscribed period of time; indeed, as I have already described, they frequently appeared "simultaneously," or one after another in manuscripts prepared over the course of a few weeks. Consequently he was less likely to ignore or betray an original conception, as scholars have argued for Schubert and Schumann. For Schubert, see Richard Kramer, *Distant Cycles: Schubert and the Conceiving of Song* (Chicago, 1994), pp. 37–46; for Schumann, see the chapter "Schumann: Triumph and Failure of the Romantic Ideal," in Charles Rosen, *The Romantic Generation* (Cambridge, Mass., 1995), pp. 646–710, as well as the liner notes to Rosen's splendid recording of Schumann's "Revolutionary Masterpieces" (Nonesuch 79062). Rosen also explored many of these issues of revision and editorial method as they apply to early nineteenth-century literature; see "Romantic Originals," *New York Review of Books,* 17 December 1987, pp. 22–31.

15. Two recent studies argue persuasively for a historically informed understanding of the ontology of the musical work. See Lydia Goehr, *The Imaginary Museum of Musical Works: An Essay in the Philosophy of Music* (Oxford, 1992), and Leo Treitler, "History and the Ontology of the Musical Work," *Journal of Aesthetics and Art Criticism* 51 (1993): 483–497. Treitler develops many of his points from examples that I presented in the earlier published version of this chapter.

Credits

The essays in this volume originally appeared as follows:

1. "The Rhetoric of Genre: Chopin's Nocturne in G Minor," *19th-Century Music* 11 (1988).
2. "The Harmony of the Tea Table: Gender and Ideology in the Piano Nocturne," *Representations* 39 (Summer 1992).
3. "Small Fairy Voices: Sex, History, and Meaning in Chopin," in John Rink and Jim Samson, eds., *Chopin Studies 2* (Cambridge, 1994).
4. "Chopin's Last Style," *Journal of the American Musicological Society* 38 (1985).
5. "Small 'Forms': In Defence of the Prelude," in Jim Samson, ed., *The Cambridge Companion to Chopin* (Cambridge, 1992).
6. "Chopin in the Marketplace: Aspects of the International Music Publishing Industry in the First Half of the Nineteenth Century," *Notes: The Quarterly Journal of the Music Library Association* 39 (March 1983 and June 1983).
7. "Are Variants a Problem? 'Composer's Intentions' in Editing Chopin," *Chopin Studies 3* (1990).

I am grateful to the editors and publishers of all of these publications for extending permission to reprint.

For permission to reproduce illustrations I wish to thank the following:
The Collection of Robert Owen Lehman, on deposit in The Pierpont Morgan Library (Figure 1.1).
Historisches Museum Basel (Figure 2.1).
Staatsbibliothek Preussischer Kulturbesitz (Figure 2.2).
Towarzystwo imienia Fryderyka Chopina (Figures 4.1 and 4.2).
Verlag Valentin Koerner and Sylvain Guignard (Example 7.2).

Index

Aesthetic categories: and sexual difference, 41–42
Agawu, Kofi, 156
Alpers, Svetlana, 39
Androgyny, 70–79
Angels: and sexual ambiguity, 77
Arago, Emmanuel, 256n49
Ashdown, Edwin, 200, 203
Auber, D. F. E., 261–262n72
Autonomy: aesthetics of, 30–31

Bach, Johann Sebastian: English Suite in D Minor, 6
Balzac, Honoré de, 72, 247–248n4, 255n47
   La Fille aux yeux d'or, 72
   Sarrasine, 72
   Séraphîta, 71, 72, 79, 253–254n36
Beethoven, Ludwig van, 123
   Symphony no. 5 in C Minor, op. 67, 255n47
   Symphony no. 9 in D Minor, op. 125, 8
Bellini, Vincenzo, 124
Belotti, Gastone, 264n12
Berlioz, Hector, 24–25, 63–64, 261–262n72
Blanchard, Henri, 36, 38, 248–249n9, 272n56
Blumröder, Christoph von, 32–33
Bourges, Maurice, 34, 142
Brandus, G., 218, 220–221. *See also* Chopin, Fryderyk: and French Publishers
Breitkopf & Härtel, 170–173, 210, 218, 220, 280–281n5, 284n32; Cho-

pin's receipts with, 185–189; "editorial" emendations by, 198. *See also* Chopin, Fryderyk: and German publishers
Bronarski, Ludwik, 120
Brown, Maurice J. E., 200, 269n41
Burnham, Scott, 276n17
Burton, Anna, 246n66
Busst, A. J. L., 71
Butler, Judith, 75

Cage, John: *4'33"*, 9
Canguilhem, Georges, 261n68
Caraman, Juliette von, 221
Carter, Angela, 254n41
Chaulieu, Charles, 147–148; Prelude in D-flat Major, 148
Cheriemietieff, Elizavieta, 248n6
Chopin, Fryderyk: "last style" of, 9, 89–134; and Polish romantic nationalism, 21–29, 194; and Polish national opera, 28; and pathology, 40, 70, 83–85, 121–123, 190; and manliness, 42–43; and otherworldly metaphors, 62–70; sexual meanings in, 62–86; as "Ariel," 62, 65–67, 147, 157; and androgyny, 71, 78; as angel, 72, 76; as "*Sans-sexe*," 78, 79; and hermaphroditism, 79–80; and Debussy, 83; and effeminacy, 84; rate of production, 89–90; counterpoint in, 90; compositional process of, 99–100, 101, 104–105, 216, 218–228; and *dernière pensée*, 120, 124, 127;

Other books in the *Convergences* series: